FORTE

FORTE

The Autobiography of
Charles Forte

PAN BOOKS

First published 1986 by Sidgwick and Jackson

This edition published 1997 by Pan Books
an imprint of Macmillan Publishers Ltd
25 Eccleston Place, London SW1W 9NF
and Basingstoke

Associated companies throughout the world

ISBN 0 330 35041 2

1 3 5 7 9 8 6 4 2

A CIP catalogue record for this book is available from
the British Library.

Typeset by SetSystems Ltd, Saffron Walden, Essex
Printed and bound in Great Britain by
Mackays of Chatham plc, Chatham, Kent

To Irene

Acknowledgements

I am grateful for the assistance of Brian Connell, Toby Roxburgh and Jean Chalmers. I am especially grateful to William Armstrong of Macmillan General Books without whose editorial help and encouragement this book would not have been published.

Contents

Foreword to the First Edition
by Lord Thorneycroft

IMAGINARY TALES RELATING to an industrial dynasty seem to capture the fascinated attention of the public. This book is about a real one. Charles Forte, who wrote it, has created a dynasty in his own lifetime every bit as dramatic and exciting as anything to be found in fiction or shown on television.

The story – told in his own simple and direct phrases will, I believe, attract the interest of thousands of men and women who ponder how it can be possible in this day and age to carve out a pathway to success.

The account he gives of the building of a great company carries us forward from the young man counting potential customers outside the proposed site of his first milk bar in London, through periods of risk and uncertainty, to the chairmanship of one of the greatest hotel and catering complexes in the world.

In some ways Charles Forte must have changed on his way up but in essentials not, perhaps, a lot. The close attention to detail, the knowledge of every aspect of his trade, the determination to find some way of getting the capital to start and expand his business, the courage to stake all he had in order to achieve his ends, his courage, his ability to recruit, influence and lead those associated with him, his gift of friendship and, perhaps above all, his faith in himself.

It is a thrilling story as he fights his way forward. There were moments when he had little else to support him other than his own self-confidence, but he succeeded and each success brought even wider horizons. There came a moment when it looked as though all that he had worked for and created might be taken from him, but he triumphed here too. There are some other desperate moments, but even then he always finds room for laughter.

Surrounded by a loyal and loving family and staunch and faithful associates, he is handing the reins of power increasingly to his son Rocco who, even before he had assumed the role of chief executive, had already made a notable contribution to the firm.

It is a story of a triumph written by a man who does not flinch from examining the causes of failure as well as those of success. If any man wants to know how to win he should read this book.

Peter Thorneycroft
1986

CHAPTER ONE

The Clan

IT SURPRISES PEOPLE when I say that I feel as much Scottish as I do English or Italian. Scotland is where I first became aware of the world, first experienced the pleasures and pains of life. It is with my arrival there that my continuous stream of memory begins.

William Wallace, the Scottish patriot, was my first childhood hero and I can still remember the excitement I felt at the age of eighteen when I went into the Great Hall at Westminster to see the spot he stood on when condemned to death.

Scotland was also where I made my first proposal of marriage – at the age of ten. It was to the prettiest girl in the class, who was called Mary Stephenson. Her reply, when it came, was blunt.

'My mother says I cannot marry you because you're an Italian.'

'Can't marry an Italian?' I queried. 'I've got a castle in Italy. You tell your mother that.'

I am glad to say that Mary Stephenson later acquired a most satisfactory husband – not me. In 1983 I heard from her again. She was living in a retirement home near Stirling and I sent her some flowers. Writing to thank me, she said that my success had not surprised her: 'You always were good at sums.'

While I regard myself as Scottish-Italian, I also appreciate Dr Johnson's dictum: 'The noblest prospect which a Scotchman ever sees is the high road that leads him to England.'

But my first journey was from Italy to Scotland. I have a vivid memory of arriving with my mother at Edinburgh station in 1913. To me it seemed a building of overwhelming majesty. I remember a maelstrom of noise and activity; the violent hissing of escaping steam, the huge glistening engines, the clatter and crashing of rolling stock, and more people packed together in one place than I had ever seen before.

Neither my mother nor I could speak a word of English. We stood nervously on the platform waiting for my father and were very relieved to see him making his way through the crowds. He took charge of us and we left Edinburgh to begin our new life in the lovely small Scottish town of Alloa.

This journey to Scotland was the result not only of our family circumstances but part of a chain of events going back many years.

My birthplace was Monforte (or, as it used to be known, Mortale). For about five hundred years the Fortes have lived in this remote mountain village which is huddled on a rocky promontory over 2,000 feet above sea level, south of Rome and north of Naples, overlooking the picturesque Valle di Comino.

Up till the nineteenth century the Fortes dominated the locality. All the land around the village belonged to them. On these mountain pastures grazed cattle, sheep, goats, and hundreds of horses destined eventually for the Neapolitan army.

I was born in the middle of a violent thunderstorm at four o'clock on a November morning in 1908 and showed every sign of leaving this world before the morning was out. My parents' first child had already died at birth. Moreover my mother was not particularly strong and was by no means as robust as many of the other village girls. Understandably the family was extremely anxious about her second *accouchement.*

As soon as I was born it was clear that I was having difficulty in breathing, probably due to pneumonia, which was a recognized killer of babies in mountain villages. Today's sophisticated medical treatment – oxygen tents and the like – had not reached us and nature was left to take its course. Infant mortality was accepted as the will of God and the village priest was on hand to comfort the bereaved families.

As it became clear that I was getting worse, all the known conventional remedies having failed, in desperation the family doctor applied leeches. Appalling as it sounds to use this mediaeval remedy on a new-born baby, in my case it seems to have worked. Apparently the moment the leeches began to swell with my blood my condition improved and soon I was yelling lustily. I have good reason to be thankful to the leeches.

You reach Monforte by driving south from Rome towards Naples on the autostrada. After a hundred kilometres or so there looms up on your left the impressive bulk of Monte Cassino with the great restored monastery dominating the peak. Here you turn further inland, into the Valle di Comino. Very soon the evidence of industrial society is left behind as you wind through small, quiet villages. They are modestly prosperous, as farming provides a subsistence. The countryside is unexpectedly green. Because of the occasional heavy rainfall, you will not find here the parched landscape familiar to other Mediterranean countries and some other parts of Italy.

The first town of any consequence is Atina about thirty-two kilometres inland. This old Roman settlement is perched on the flank of a hill with a lovely fourteenth-century church in a beautiful market square.

Follow the rocky river valley for a few more kilometres and you start a gentle climb up the bending road to Casalattico, which boasts a mayor and a parish council; then on up through a series of hairpin bends to the top of the hill, which is crowned by the tiny scattered village of Monforte, in its turn dominated by the peaks of the pre-Apennines.

Recently, in a reference book for Monte Cassino, I found 'Casalattico at the feet of Murturu', which in the dialect of those days meant Mortale, a name deriving from its role as a place of execution. The date was 1009. That is the oldest reference that I have found personally to the village. The signposts say Monforte these days, whether as a compliment to the most extended family in the region or because the old name has a slightly sinister connotation, I am not sure.

Although it stands at 2,500 feet, Monforte does not seem windswept or isolated because the immediately surrounding peaks are somewhat higher; and off to the north-east, closing the horizon, are the much higher mountain tops of the Abruzzi. It is spectacularly beautiful. The hills are densely covered right up to the top with a mixture of mountain oaks, beech and pine, through which tracks have been cut for cart and animal. The air is fresh and the pervading green wonderfully restful.

Village is almost too grand a description for what is a hamlet of some forty houses haphazardly scattered. There is a small open square in the centre called La Soda. The children still play ball there, just as I did when I was a child. It is asphalted over now with a children's playground with slides and swings to one side. Next to it are a couple of concrete courts on which the inhabitants play *bocce*, the Italian equivalent of the French game of *boule* (the Italian version is played with a wooden rather than a metal ball). There are seven or eight rough wooden benches round the square where people sit and gossip but there is no bar or obvious central place of resort, not even a shop. The inhabitants have to go a kilometre or so back down the hill to Casalattico to make their modest purchases.

Most of the houses are traditionally constructed from the rather beautiful local stone quarried from the surrounding hills. The garden walls are made in the same way. Some of the newer houses are plastered on the outside and painted white; nearly all have green shutters and tiled roofs. All the houses have kitchen gardens, some of which are quite large. Most have vines trained on stakes and lateral wires so that they end up looking like a row of crosses. There are some, but not a great many, olive trees, and patches of vegetables, which are keenly cultivated, and interspersed with ornamental trees, oleanders, magnolias, rose bushes and acacias.

Few of the people still living there now are near or distant relatives of mine. But it is still the ancestral home of the Forte family whose members, scattered all over Britain, Ireland and America, own much, if not all, of the land around, right down into the valley.

My father's house, where I was born, is just off La Soda to the south-west. I have had it completely restored in recent years, repainting the granite portico over the entrance, installing heavy oak doors and shutters and a new spiral staircase inside. Like most of the houses, it has wrought iron railings and gates and more wrought iron on the balconies and over the windows. I keep it up as a holiday home for any member of my family who wishes to use it.

Along another path on the other side of the square is a house belonging to my late uncle, my mother's brother. A little further down is a charming villa with a courtyard, belonging to my favourite cousin, Pace. Her late husband, Armando, used to run the local wine co-operative. The wine is thin and undistinguished, of no great commercial value. It does not travel, but is nevertheless very drinkable and in that environment preferable to the richer Italian wines of other regions.

To complete the contrast between the drowsy present and the busy past, when the Forte clan played the most important part in the local economy, and before so many of its members dispersed to other countries, I have to take you along what must be called the main streets in the hamlet. They run to the north and both are characteristically named after heroes of the *Risorgimento*.

The via Garibaldi is just about the width of a car as it dodges between the houses. On the left is my brother's new house, the Casa Rocco, and after about a hundred yards you turn to the left, up the even narrower via Cavour, which leads into another tiny square, in fact the central square of the village. On one side is a small church dedicated to Sant' Antonio di Padova, the patron saint of Monforte. The church, which has a pedimented façade, faces the largest house in the square, also by far the largest in the village, which was built centuries ago by one of my ancestors. He also built the church.

The house, known as Il Portone, has a handsome iron fanlight above the stone porch and a large stone pigeon-loft on the roof. It is built of grey local stone, the same stone as the house which I live in when I go back there and which my father built in 1900. You must not imagine a majestic old house, but when Il Portone was built it was very imposing for a time when many people still lived in huts with straw roofs. But we are all a little proud of the place because it symbolizes a certain continuing affluence, which goes back many years.

In the old days, before the telephone, carrier pigeons were kept there to maintain communications with Rome and Naples. It is in a sad and tumbledown condition now and there is almost nothing I can do about it because in these parts the Code Napoleon still governs all inheritance. Every child gets an equal share of the

parents' estate, with the result that Il Portone is now owned by
thirty or forty people, and it would be extremely complicated
getting so many people to agree on how to restore it. Very recently,
however, it was declared a National Monument and the Italian
Government is making money available for its restoration. It
certainly needs it.

I give the village what help I can although the requests are few
and the amounts no more than a few thousand pounds. For many
years I have also enjoyed contributing, as my father did before me,
to the celebrations surrounding the feast day of Sant' Antonio di
Padova on 13 June. I have a great affinity for Monforte and always
feel at home when I go back there but the contrast with the village
at the beginning of the century is striking.

When I say the Fortes form a clan, the parallel with Scotland is an
interesting one. There were numerous families all with the surname Forte, although in many cases the relationship was quite
distant. Our origins have been lost with the passage of time,
records have been burned or mislaid and nobody quite knows
which part of Italy we first came from.

One theory has it that the family originated in a village on the
borders between the Papal States and the State of Naples and, to
escape from the constant guerrilla warfare, made for these remote
valleys and hills. It could well be. We have certainly long been an
important family in the area and must have been of some
consequence because there is a record of Ferdinand II of Naples
attending the wedding of a Forte daughter.

The Fortes enjoyed the status of what the Scots would call
'bonnet lairds', not grand hereditary lairds in the true sense but
nevertheless owning substantial tracts of land and employing
outside labourers, even though they worked alongside them.

Down in the valley, which tends to flood in the spring, there are
stretches of rich alluvial fields called locally 'the land under the
water'. On this the Fortes produced wheat, corn, and barley. Up
in the hills they burned wood and made charcoal, and in my
young days there were still over a thousand sheep grazing up
there. The clan also bred and sold horses, not thoroughbreds but
sturdy cart and wagon horses. At one time they had a contract to

supply these horses to the Neapolitan army, based 140 kilometres away. Then there were the pigs. Every smallholding had a pig-pen. However, when the Fortes took all their pigs to the market in Atina every other pig-owner stayed away or the price would fall!

The Fortes worked hard. When they relaxed, which was not often, they went out rough shooting, played *bocce*, enjoyed the occasional wedding, but they still worked side by side with, and were practically indistinguishable from, their day labourers. It was a matter of the greatest pride that they were never themselves employed by anyone except by another Forte in a free exchange of labour. I do not want to make my ancestors sound grander than they were. Although they owned the land they lived on, they worked hard with their hands and led the most frugal existence.

I can remember as a lad being taken off for the day in a cart accompanying a team of threshing horses. Agriculture may still have been primitive but it was picturesque. The wheat was laid out in serried ranks and the grain separated from the chaff by two teams of four horses tramping round and round on the wheat. The horses were then unpaired and two or three men, or even more according to the amount of grain, finished the job by pitch-forking the wheat and chaff into the air, the breeze separating the two; a scene that had probably not changed since Roman or even earlier times. It was skilled work by man and horse and the Fortes possessed both the horses and the skill. Once they had threshed their own grain they hired the teams out to the surrounding villages.

But this idyllic existence was doomed. The family had suffered a crippling financial blow in the 1870s, a time of great unrest in Italy. The emergence of the modern kingdom of Italy was accompanied by revolution, civil war and brigandage.

The Fortes were an obvious target for any group of rascals looking for ransom money. The victim they had apparently chosen was Michelangelo Antonio Forte, my grandfather on my mother's side. The brigands made a mistake, however. They captured, and carried off, another member of the family called Constantino Forte, who was my mother's great uncle.

They demanded a huge ransom. I don't know the exact amount but it took two sturdy mules to carry the coins. Now this was before

the days of a monetary economy, when goods were customarily
exchanged in the form of barter. To raise a sum of money like
that was a major problem.

The ransom note was cruelly frank: 'If you don't pay, we cut off
your son's ear. The second time we ask, we cut off his nose.' And
they meant it. The brigands' tactics were in fact not unlike those
of the kidnappers of the late Paul Getty's grandson, Paul Getty III,
who was brutally abducted in Rome in 1973 and lost an ear when
his parents ignored their demands.

Luigi Forte called the family together. There was never a
minute's hesitation – the money had to be found and the only way
to do it was to realize the family's assets. Without complaint they
sold everything they possessed. The women gave their meagre
jewellery, the men their sheep and horses, finally mortgaging their
land.

Nevertheless most of the money had to be borrowed from the
very rich Visocchi family, who owned most of Atina and were
friends of Luigi. The balance was provided by the family as best
they could, and thus it was that Constantino was rescued. The
experience was to leave such a lasting effect on him that he had a
bad heart for the rest of his life. However, the Fortes are a hardy
lot and, in spite of his reputedly weak heart, Constantino lived to
within a few months of his hundredth birthday!

The feud with the kidnappers lasted for some time and was only
finally eradicated when my grandfather Antonio eventually cleared
the area of the *briganti* by leading a small force of the long-
suffering locals against them.

Whatever the fate of the brigands, the whole family was still
saddled with this enormous debt. However many sheep, horses
and pigs they kept, however much grain, chickens and cheese they
produced, some part of it had to be used to pay off the debt. As
the years went by the family started to disperse as the men were
forced to seek their fortunes in other lands and remit some of the
money home.

One such was my own father, Rocco, who made his way to
America and was given a job in a factory in Pittsburgh. Within a
relatively short space of time he had become a foreman, which,
for an Italian from an agricultural community with a poor com-

mand of the language, was indeed a remarkable achievement. He did not, however, settle down in the States, where the life did not suit him, but returned to Monforte with a useful nest-egg which contributed to his own position and the support of his relatives.

He built himself a house, which I still own, and in 1905 married his distant cousin Maria Luigia. Their parents' names meant that both bride and bridegroom were surnamed Forte, although I would not attempt to draw the genealogical tree, which could cover pages. My father's mother was a Frattarelli from Pastena, a town some eighty or ninety kilometres from Monforte, chiefly remarkable for the immense age to which most of the inhabitants lived. My grandmother was a perfect example: she lived to be a few weeks off a hundred. Her great ambition had been to reach a hundred because then it would have been customary for the bishop to officiate at her funeral. But the bishop overlooked the small lapse of a few weeks, and officiated anyway.

One day she pulled her plain gold wedding ring off her finger. 'I have been keeping this for you,' she said. I have always felt honoured that she chose me out of many grandchildren.

My maternal grandmother had the splendid name of Porzia Maria Cafolla, and came from a well-known family in the area.

I was the eldest of four children. My brother Giulio was eighteen months younger than me, Anna, the only girl, was four years younger, and Michael was five years younger. I believe that Giulio was the most intelligent of the four of us. He was taller than my father, but not a tall man – medium-sized perhaps. Most of the time we agreed on things; when we did not I must say he was forceful in making his views known. He was killed in a car crash and this was terribly upsetting for me and it was a tragic moment for the whole family. In a strange way he was like my son Rocco, but with a quieter, more analytical attitude to things. He was exceptional and I think if he had lived we would have been either great rivals or great partners.

My father was hard-working and intelligent, already with a wider view of the world than most members of the Forte family, and when he returned from America he tried to settle back into the existence that he had left. We lived comfortably enough but he was a man of ambition and even the beauty of the surroundings could not tie him to the place. He could see his children being destined for the same sort of pastoral and slow-moving life in what was doubtless a backwater, and this unfulfilled existence, offering little future for his family, didn't suit him.

The channel to further adventure was provided by my father's second or third cousin, Pacifico Forte, who had also broken away from the family and started to make a career for himself in Scotland. Pacifico had always been a bit of a maverick and stood out from the rest of the family. For years he was entrusted with the task of supervising the taking of the horses, cows, sheep, goats and pigs to market in Atina. He had a natural air of authority, was a good organizer and always managed to get his motley flocks to the market on time.

On one of these occasions, or so the family legend has it, Pacifico met a Scotsman, said to be a grocer, but a grocer with style, a rich man who did not have one grocery shop, but many. We speculate as to whether it may have been Sir Thomas Lipton on some unexpected foray. Whatever his identity he was a grand Signor and he took to this young man, who may have done him a favour of some kind or been helpful. The fact remains that he said to Pacifico, probably in a friendly and non-committal fashion: 'If you ever come to Scotland, come to see me and I will help you.'

Pacifico took this literally and one day set off from Monforte on foot with just enough money in his pocket to pay for emergencies. His departure was much regretted. He was a useful man in the community and the family was sorry to see him go. He walked across Italy and France, taking odd jobs, mainly on farms, on the way, eventually reaching Calais. He had enough money to pay for the passage and for the train journey to Edinburgh, where he went to see his unidentified and probably startled benefactor. It was thus that he managed to set himself up in business.

He opened up in a tiny hole in the wall in Kincardine on Forth, selling lemonade, chocolates and cigarettes. He worked hard and with great integrity. Soon he had an ice-cream shop in Dundee. All the time he kept in constant communication with Monforte and gradually persuaded half a dozen of the family to come and help in his enterprises. My uncle Alfonso made his way there to join him and the next to heed the call was my father, in 1911.

By this time the Forte 'empire' in Scotland included two more small shops, one at Loanhead near Edinburgh and another at Biggar, both of which were being run by my uncle. In the course of the year my father learned the ropes at Loanhead and was left in charge of the shop. Here, in the most basic way, he discovered the principles and practice of business: how to pay rent, settle bills, operate a tiny bank account, serve customers and make a profit. He quite soon justified his half share.

It was a small shop: I remember it still from my very early childhood. At the back there was a billiard-room with two tables, which brought in a flow of customers. The front room was an Italian café, and in another room the ice cream was made. The whole mixture was prepared and frozen there; and as my father was keen, busy and kept everything spotlessly clean, he enjoyed an immediate success. But soon the shop at Loanhead was too small for him. He bought an establishment in Alloa and called it the Savoy Café. He imported a soda fountain from the United States and a coffee machine from Italy and it was not long before the Savoy Café became the focal point for the local inhabitants and the fashionable place to go.

About three years later, my mother received a letter in Monforte from my father, saying that at last he felt his future was sufficiently assured to have us join him and resume the home life that he had missed. And that letter and the many years of family history I have recounted explain why Mother and I were standing that day at Edinburgh station.

CHAPTER TWO

An Unconventional Education

ALLOA IS SITUATED on the north bank of the River Forth, in Clackmannan, about thirty miles upstream from Edinburgh. In my boyhood days I suppose it had a population of about twelve thousand. It was a thriving town, making yarn, glass, pottery, brass and ironwork, and exporting coal, although the docks dried out at low water. It was also the home of the famous Alloa ale. It had half a dozen handsome public buildings and the rolling countryside was only a bus ride out of town.

The Savoy Café was on Mill Street, the main shopping street. It was large, seating fifty to sixty people, and next door to the La Scala Cinema, which brought in a thriving custom in the evening. My father ran it and my mother helped in between her domestic tasks. There were also two or three assistants, working all hours of the day, serving ice cream, cakes and sandwiches. At teatime the café was always full. It was kept spotless, the service was willing and friendly, and indeed for many years the Savoy remained the most popular place for shoppers, housewives and their families to go.

My parents had taken a convenient flat on the opposite side of the street, above a newsagent's and a fruiterer's. It was large and comfortable with three bedrooms, which meant that I had one of my own, a kitchen, sitting-room, and a dining-room which we seldom used. We even had one and a half bathrooms, one with a proper tub and the other, in the washroom, with an enormous sink, in which I usually washed.

The family had begun to move up into middle-class society. I say 'move up' because although in Monforte we had a certain status as landed proprietors, the land was worth little and we might have seemed a primitive lot, with little money and a rudimentary mountain style of dress. In Scotland we entered the lowest rung of middle-class society, as shopkeepers, café proprietors, and ice cream merchants. But soon my father had become friendly with Stanton, the largest grocer in the town, Cairns, the ironmonger, Dow, the butcher, and many other members of the Alloa community.

On one occasion we mixed in even more exalted circles. I remember with my father calling upon the Earl of Mar and Kellie at his country seat just outside the town. My father had been asked to advise the Earl on his vines. We had a cup of tea with him in what seemed to me an enormous room, and I can still remember standing in the hot-house with the two men engaged in earnest conversation with my father pruning one of the vines, to show how it was done.

Winters at Alloa were cold but our flat was cosy. Heating was by coal fire and there was the usual grate in the kitchen, where we used to eat. The dining-room was used only for special occasions, to entertain visitors, who were mainly relations from other parts of Scotland. My mother was houseproud and an excellent cook, so we were warm and comfortable and certainly very well fed. By the standards of those hard times I was a very lucky little boy. There was always a bottle of wine on the table and from quite a young age I would be allowed a glass mixed with water in the continental fashion. The wine and other Italian delicacies were delivered to us by Valvona, the Italian grocer in Glasgow. We had a lady who came in to help with the housework and the general atmosphere of well-being and rural propriety, which my parents had brought with them from Monforte, was always maintained.

By this time, after my year in Loanhead, I was beginning to speak English, but with a marked Scottish accent – which I still partly retain despite my sixty years in the South. At home we spoke Italian, my father and mother with an edge of the Abruzzese dialect. I was sent to a kindergarten, which was run by a Miss Fiddler. How my father ever got me into this élite establishment I shall never know, because there was the inevitable undercurrent of the snobbery of those times in our small town. However, my father may only have been an Italian immigrant with a café, but he had a quiet, persuasive way with him and a natural dignity which must have had its effect. Anyway, I was accepted and attended the school for nearly eighteen months.

Children can be unkind to one another and particularly to one who does not speak the language very well or whom they regard as different. But at Miss Fiddler's I had very little trouble of this sort, perhaps because everyone was amused by me. The one incident that sticks out in my mind was when three or four of us were standing up in front of Miss Fiddler, reciting, and I needed to blow my nose.

'Haven't you got a handkerchief?' Miss Fiddler asked.

'Yes, Miss Fiddler.'

'Well, where is it?'

'It is in my breeks.'

Everybody burst out laughing. Nobody said 'breeks' at school. They were made to say trousers, certainly a more genteel expression than breeks, even though this is a perfectly good Scottish word. But I stood corrected. Miss Fiddler kept in touch for quite a long time after I left the school. She died only fifteen years ago.

I then went to the junior section of Alloa Academy. In the early stages I was teased rather more by the other boys. The nickname for an Italian was 'tally wally' and they used to taunt me with this. Inevitably I got into several fights. I was not a big fellow, any more than I am now, but I was strong for my age and, when I was forced to, I was always able to look after myself. I soon came to be accepted, however, because I was friendly and good at games. I played cricket but preferred soccer and rugby. At rugby I was a useful scrum-half and I went on with the game for several years as a young man, playing regularly for Weymouth after my parents had moved to the South of England.

I cannot claim to have been much of a scholar, although I managed to scrape through the exams. In the early stages my father gave me some help with my homework, but there came a point when he could do so no longer. He was quite a well-read man, although largely self-taught, as his only education had consisted of three or four years' walking down the hill to the very rudimentary school at Casalattico.

The triumph of these early school years came when I was in the fifth grade at the Academy. I had written an essay which the teacher, Miss Hunter, had singled out to show to all the staff and the headmaster as an example of how someone of foreign origin could write an outstanding composition. She even wrote a note to my father and mother, and they of course were delighted and it remained a topic of conversation for days, the source of as much pride as if I had obtained a university degree.

Looking back I suppose I must have been a rather spoilt little boy. I had been the most fractious member of the family back in Monforte and I think my parents brought me over to Scotland to keep a closer eye on me. In Alloa I lived a more disciplined life – going to school and receiving parental supervision must have had their effect. I do not recall causing any real trouble at home, although occasionally I was obstreperous. My father only thrashed me once – and with good reason. I had been showing off to several kids by hanging over a deep well – if I had fallen down it this story would have been abruptly terminated.

I was better off than most of the boys. My father was not ungenerous with pocket money and my finances were helped by my mother's brother, Alfonso, who would often slip me half a sovereign, despite my father's protests. Alfonso was a dandy, perfectly dressed, shoes always shining, and possessed of a series of girl friends. He taught me to drive and I remember him telling me: 'Now you want to get there quickly, don't you? Well, drive slowly!' He also taught me to play golf and I recall how before a game he would pull the sleeves of his pullover up and standing on the tee say: 'Right, Charles, now we are ready for the fry.' He meant the 'fray'. I met him once when I was on holiday in Monforte and asked him what he was doing. He told me: 'I was just looking around to see if somebody would give me a reason to laugh.' On another occasion my brother Michael was getting married, and Anna was busy trying to find someone to sing in the church. Alfonso told me: 'Anna is looking for someone to sing. If only she was looking for somebody to cry, I could fill that role very well indeed. My God, how I could cry!'

Even at that age I was interested in the business that was being

— • —

conducted around me and was conscious of the hard work it demanded. I was not, however, made to participate, except for running minor errands here and there.

One day when I had on my school blazer, of which I was exceptionally proud, my father told me to take a box to the station.

'How do I do that?' I asked.

'There is a barrow,' he said. 'Take it up to the station and do it now.'

I found myself clattering this undignified conveyance up the cobbled High Street of Alloa to the station, which was about ten minutes away, with my school-friends cycling past, shouting: 'There's Charlie. Look at Charlie!' Did my father do this on purpose to take me down a peg?

I have very few recollections of any incident relating to the First World War. I do remember the arrival of the Black Watch in Alloa though: the streets filled with those glamorous kilted soldiers. I also remember listening to Lloyd George. I was about ten at the time and he must have been campaigning in the so-called 'khaki election' of 1919. He stood on a box in a doorway at the corner of the main street in Alloa, haranguing a crowd of about a hundred people, including me. I vividly recall this strange-looking man with long hair waving his hands about excitedly. None of his words, however, lodged in my mind.

At the age of twelve I went to St Joseph's College, Dumfries, then a private Catholic school. My parents took me there more or less by force. They obviously, and quite rightly, thought I was getting too independent and spoilt. Fond as we were of each other, I had reached a stage where I was growing away from them. They were essentially Italian villagers living in Scotland; I had become in effect Scottish, with a different, perhaps more liberal, outlook. I also found them over-protective. I had to beg them once to let me go camping in the hills with my schoolfellows. They were reluctant, thinking it unsafe and dangerous to my health. Anyway, they had made up their minds to send me to boarding school. My father was typical of the ambitious parent lacking a formal education: he was determined that I should get a much better academic start than he had had, and that meant the best available school.

St Joseph's College was a very good school, run by the Marist fathers, and well equipped with excellent playing fields. I was miserable from the first day I went there. I got into a fight nearly every day and was caned for it the following morning, three times on each hand – which hurt. One of the problems was that I simply could not eat the food. It was perfectly good school food, if you like that sort of thing, and there was plenty of it. But I had been spoilt by my mother's cooking. The full bowls of badly-cooked porridge for breakfast were a poor substitute for the bacon and eggs, and indeed the porridge, I had at home. Within a week I had written to my father saying: 'Unless you come and fetch me I am going to run away.' I suppose this was an early revelation of my character. I have always had very definite ideas of what I want to do, and am not swayed by what other people want from me.

A few days later my father arrived, dressed in a new tweed suit, trying to look like an English country squire, something he did not quite manage to achieve. He was, however, a good-looking man, with sterling manners. As soon as I saw him I fell on his chest, demanding: 'Take me away. I don't want to stay here.'

'Wait a minute,' he said. 'But why?' He was confused and disappointed and he tried his best to persuade me to stay but I knew he understood my feelings.

I was insistent. 'No, I want to come home with you now.'

So off we went to see the headmaster, a small, wizened, amenable man. The course of the interview was not quite as expected.

'Oh, Mr Forte,' he said, 'I am glad to see you. Charles is getting on very well.' And then turning to me, he went on: 'You like it here, don't you?'

I summoned up courage: 'No, I don't, sir.'

'It is all right,' my father interrupted hastily. 'He's a bit home-sick.'

'But I thought you were happy here,' said the headmaster.

'Of course he is happy here,' said my father, whose English was beginning to break under the strain. 'But I think I will take him home for a few days.'

'Well, if you want to do that, by all means,' said the headmaster reluctantly, 'but I don't advise it. Now that he is here he should get used to it.'

He was quite right, of course, and for all I know the entire course of my life would have been different had I settled down and studied. I would probably have gone on to university and taken up some entirely different career. But I believe that Fate ordains many things.

My father could see that I was not to be persuaded. He was a very determined man himself and once he had made up his mind to accept my point of view he did not waver. But being tactful he said: 'Good. I think he will return. I will persuade him. He has told me he doesn't like it and he can't settle down, but I think he will come back.'

'Well I hope he does,' replied the headmaster as we left.

I have never told this story before – out of respect for the Marist fathers and all the good that they have done for education. Throughout my life when people have said: 'Oh, you went to the Dumfries College, didn't you?' I have always given an unqualified 'Yes'.

Clearly I was now the cause of a family crisis. The remedy they devised was to send me back to Italy. 'I am going to take you on holiday,' my father said placatingly. His intention was to send me to school there. Even on the long train journey home I caused my father anxiety. He woke up to find me pouring with blood. The heavy mahogany cover of the washbasin had banged down on my nose, breaking it, and today my nose still has the slight look of a boxer's.

Eventually we reached Monforte, where I was reunited with my two brothers and my sister, while my father took counsel with a close family friend, Padre Edmondo, a Franciscan from Rome. The Padre was an archaeologist, busy restoring the famous catacombs under the church of San Pancrazio, in the ancient part of the city. He recommended that my brothers and I be sent to the Collegio Scheppers in Rome, run by the Fratelli di Misericordia.

It was one of the finest boarding schools in Italy. Pupils were taught there through the elementary stage and afterwards attended the famous Mamiani school for their lessons, while still boarding at the Collegio. I had already completed the elementary stage of my education at Alloa, so I was able to get through the four-year course at the Collegio in eighteen months as all I had to do was to improve my Italian. At thirteen and a half I passed on to the Mamiani, where I stayed for a further three years.

The Mamiani was excellent and the Collegio Scheppers was very comfortable. My father had certainly been well advised. I have always been grateful to him for sending me there. It was an expensive school and must have cost him a great deal. I certainly couldn't run away from there.

Before he left for Alloa my father tried to steer my interests in the right direction. In Scotland my main interest had been sport, which he did not consider important. (I did persuade him to take me to a football match once but that was an exception.) He had an inbred passion for music and opera and took me to see one of his favourite operas: *Cavalleria Rusticana*. Thinking the title meant 'Rustic Cavalry', I accepted with alacrity, keenly anticipating a circus act with horses charging about the stage. However, *cavalleria* in Italian also means politeness or courtesy, which is the true meaning of the title, and I was to be disappointed.

Things did not start off too well at my new school. These were sophisticated boys, the sons of professional people and gentry. They wore light clothes and shorts and looked most elegant. My best friend was Carlo Crivelli Visconti, a descendant of one of the most famous families in Italy, but once again, I was surrounded by a crowd of boys to whom I was foreign. I was doubly strange to them. Not only was I an *Inglese* but I was also a *ciociaro*, which can roughly be described as a country bumpkin, because they knew I came from a tiny village up in the hills. I certainly looked different in my unfashionable English shorts and thick brogues. On top of all this, the little Italian that I knew was almost unintelligible.

But luckily it did not lead to bloodshed – or to the cane – as it had in Scotland. Even though when the older boys wanted a laugh they would say, 'Go and dress *al inglese*,' and I would put on my 'funny' clothes, the teasing soon became perfectly good-humoured. I had only one proper fight all the time I was there. It was with a bigger fellow, a year older than I was, who tended to throw his weight about. I have always reacted pugnaciously to aggressiveness and I stood up to him. We had a terrific fight which ended with me underneath him on the floor. He was, however, much more friendly from then on.

Normally five years were spent in the *gimnasio*, followed by three in the *liceo*. I managed to struggle through into the fifth year of the *gimnasio* by the time I was seventeen, which was quite a feat, even though I was a year or so older than the others.

Rome can be freezing cold in the winter and the school was in a vast building with no central heating. We slept in two large dormitories, with about sixty boys in each. Early in the morning we were woken, not by a bell, but by a monk who used to walk up and down slowly clapping his hands until we gradually came to life.

The headmaster, Father de Angelis, was a humane man. He never formally caned, but occasionally gave one a clout, an experience I distinctly remember when I was discovered forging the signature of one of the teachers, Fratello Faustine, on our report card. In fact, I had been concocting glowing accounts of my friends' behaviour, and I was found out only by the headmaster noticing that we were all behaving too perfectly.

What to me made my stay at the Mamiani worthwhile was the football. I had begun to play quite well and was captain of the school team in my last year. On one occasion I was picked for the Rome boys' team to play against Turin in the local stadium. We also used to play against a side of English Fathers (most of whom were Irish) and succeeded in holding our own. I knew a few minor English swear words which I shouted with a Scottish accent, egged on by some of the young Fathers.

Rome, I adored. Then it was a charming city with no more than eight hundred thousand inhabitants, very little traffic, and lovely restaurants to which my mother, a real gourmet, introduced me. I was also entranced by the Gregorian choir in St Peter's and I became fascinated by architecture and architects, particularly Borromeo, who built many of the finest Roman buildings and churches.

This was the time of Mussolini's rise to power. I have a vivid memory of seeing him marching, erect and alone, down the street to the Quirinale to pay his respects to Victor Emmanuel III, a stocky, muscular man in a frock coat, wearing a top hat too small for his bulging forehead. In front of him was an escort, behind him was an escort, flanking him were *carabinieri*, with the crowd pressing hard on the escorts' heels.

I returned to Alloa only for the summer holidays. During the Easter holidays, and for nearly all of the Christmas holidays, I stayed in Monforte with my mother's sister, Aunt Civita, and her husband, Uncle Camillo. They were marvellously kind to me. I had a room of my own in their house and was terribly spoilt. For those three years they acted as loving parents and I became very fond of them.

During the holidays I led a bracing open-air life, often walking in the hills with two or three friends and their dogs. This was where I first learned to shoot. It was very rough shooting, and hard going, certainly not the type of shooting that I am now used to. Almost everyone in the village owned a shotgun and several hung behind the door in my father's house. We went after hares and wild pigeons, occasionally partridges, and from time to time we would down a larger bird called a *cotornice*. A brace of birds or a hare meant a good day's shooting.

My Scottish holidays were very different from my Italian ones but just as enjoyable. In Scotland I played tennis and football and went fishing on the loch. I was equally at home in both places but in Monforte I was treated as somehow special – as a member of the family, who also possessed the aura of an education at a good Roman school and experience in the world outside.

By the time I was seventeen I had decided what I wanted to do – to follow in my father's footsteps. I could visualize no other career. My unorthodox education had made it impossible for me to consider university, even if I had been able to get in. Nor was I cut out for the academic life. At that age I wanted to be a successful businessman and I knew that I had the Forte ambition. Helpful though the Fortes were to each other, and appreciative of each other's talents and successes, there was a competitive edge to their dealings, as in most families. I had already made up my mind that I would be the most successful Forte of all.

My father had prospered while I was away at school. In five years his business had expanded from the Savoy Café in Mill Street to others in Alva and Kincardine on Forth, and to a second shop in Alloa, where he had also started a wholesale chocolate and cigarette business, which was doing well. Rather more important for me in the future was his partnership with two of his cousins in an enterprise in Weston-super-Mare in Somerset – the first of a string of cafés and ice cream parlours which members of the family opened up all around the English coast.

I was expecting a certain amount of resistance to my plans because my father had always laid such store by my getting a proper education and starting life with better qualifications than he had. When I returned to Scotland, I found him in a good mood and very glad to have me back.

'Don't you want to continue with your studies?' he asked me.

'No, how can I?' I said. 'I have been a couple of years behind everybody else and I don't like the thought of trying to get into university. I want to do some work. I want to do something.'

'Well, what do you want to do?'

'I want to come into the business. What can I do?'

'Would you like to go to Weston-super-Mare and work with your Uncle Dominic?' he asked.

This was Dominic Forte, who was not really an uncle but a second cousin of my father's and yet another member of the clan who had made his way to Britain. He had gone into partnership with his brother, Antony and my father, to open the café at Weston-super-Mare. I was delighted by the idea. My father discussed it with Dominic and it was settled.

My father did insist, however, that I stay for six months in Scotland to study book-keeping and accountancy. One of his accountants gave me private lessons and I learnt how to draw up a balance sheet and keep proper financial records. I stayed in the Alloa flat, which was even more luxurious than I had remembered, and my father moved me by easy stages into his affairs. I even went along with him to see the bank manager to negotiate an overdraft. My languages came in useful on this occasion. I had kept up my English and it was much better than his, so as an interpreter I was able to explain the intricacies of our affairs.

The café at Weston-super-Mare was large and imposing, in an excellent position right on the sea-front. The two floors, furnished with hefty Lloyd Loom armchairs, could seat over a hundred people and the shopfront was faced with marble. The establishment was called 'The Ice Cream Parlour'. It was really an American soda fountain with a kitchenette, where they made sandwiches and prepared snacks, and there was an *espresso* machine for the coffee.

The spaciousness and elegance of the establishment were a revelation to me. 'The Ice Cream Parlour' became very popular: indeed people still talk to me about it. The original premises were bombed and destroyed in the Second World War but my company still has a presence in Weston-super-Mare, a hotel called The Grand Atlantic, probably the most prominent hotel in the area.

Uncle Dominic was an extraordinary character. Of medium height with reddish-blond hair, he had a face dominated by a large jaw. He looked dreamy, with somewhat bulbous eyes behind thick spectacles. His eyesight was bad because he was always reading, mostly at night in artificial light. He was a vegetarian and a physical fitness fanatic. One of his feats was to walk up and down the stairs on his hands – he was as agile as a cat. He had also a cat-like fetish for cleanliness and took three or four baths a day. He would ask me if I had had a bath, and when I answered 'Yes', he would say, 'Well, have another one.' He was immensely tough. When he was in Scotland he got into a quarrel with the miners' boxing champion of Midlothian, whom he insisted on challenging to a fight. Although he was knocked down sixteen times he kept getting up. Eventually the miner refused to continue with the slaughter, although Uncle Dominic was prepared to fight to the end.

One of the first things he did was to give me a complete set of Gibbon's *Decline and Fall of the Roman Empire*, which he made me read right through so that he could ask me questions about it. He was an exceptionally well-read man, with a great store of disconnected knowledge which he delighted in producing at a moment's notice. His aura of eccentricity was added to by the broad Scottish accent in which he volubly communicated his thoughts, philosophies and learning. On one memorable occasion we had some visitors from London and for some reason the conversation turned to astronomy. Uncle Dominic joined us and I introduced him. At first glance he had no particular sparkle and a stranger might have thought him somewhat dull, until he started talking. He rapidly launched into a lecture on astronomy lasting for about an hour, sparkling with light years, the diameter of planets and stars, and much more. His audience was spell-bound.

If my time by the seaside sounds like a rest cure, it was not. Uncle Dominic made me work from about eight in the morning until two the following morning, but he worked with everyone else. However sleepy I was feeling, he would get me and his nephew Bertie out of bed at dawn and we would run along the front to the local baths, where we used to do ten or twelve lengths up and down. We would then jog back to the café to a very good breakfast prepared by the housekeeper, before opening up. At three o'clock he would say: 'You go and have your lunch, come back at five.' Sometimes it would be at one, to come back at three. Later on in the evening he would occasionally send me upstairs to have a rest and read Gibbon. It improved my English remarkably and I can answer questions about Roman history to this day.

Uncle Dominic remained a bachelor. I suppose nobody wanted to marry someone quite so eccentric, although he did try on one or two occasions. But his eccentricity was no barrier to his business success, and he became quite a wealthy man.

My sojourn with Uncle Dominic resulted in a new role for me: as a match-maker. Also working with Dominic was an older cousin of mine, called Vincent. One day a girl came into the shop, aged about seventeen, looking for a job. She was nicely spoken, I liked her, so I gave her a post as a counter-assistant. I then left to join my father in Bournemouth.

Vincent rapidly fell in love with the girl, who was called Lilian, but when he came to visit me in Bournemouth, I could see that he was very downcast: he told me about his family's opposition to Lilian.

'What's the matter with you?' I said. (At twenty-three I had become the great philosopher.) 'What's the bloody matter with you? You don't know what to do? You're in love with that girl?'

'Yes!'

'You like her? She's a good girl and she's a nice girl?'

'Yes!'

'Then *marry* her!'

Vincent was always led by me. He was a gentle soul, very intelligent. 'But she's English.'

'And you are Scottish – you were born in Greenock, Scotland.'

So I travelled to Weston-super-Mare, and found Lilian there, very despondent. I gave her the same kind of inspiring talk. The result was an engagement and a very happy marriage – but I was the only one who turned up to the wedding! I am glad to say that this romance had a happy ending. Vincent's father, George, became devoted to her. Eventually when George made his will, he instructed the solicitor to provide two-thirds to his sons and one-third to his daughter, Lilian. The solicitor said: 'Mr Forte, surely you mean your daughter-in-law, not your daughter?' George told him forcibly to use the word 'daughter'.

Vincent died some years ago, a rich and happy man. I still correspond with Lilian. The last letter she wrote me in 1985 began: 'As long as there are postmen, life will have a zest . . . .'

I spent a year and a half with Uncle Dominic and parted from him with mutual regret. But my father had by now decided to leave Alloa for good, entrusting the establishments in Scotland to relatives. He chose Bournemouth as his first base in the south, opening a large café there, in the main shopping street, the first of many, and he sent for me to join him. Eventually he was to sell up his Scottish activities and concentrate entirely on the south. This was just the start. (There are still Forte cafés in Bournemouth, founded a few years later by my Uncle George and his family, all of which are now part of Trusthouse Forte.)

Work with my father was exciting. I had only been with him in Bournemouth for about a year when he took over a large café in Weymouth for another Forte relative. Again, it was a substantial establishment, at 1 Frederick Place. He had it redecorated and re-equipped. On an excellent site, it was successful from the start. It is still there, but not part of my present company.

We all worked extremely hard. This sort of Italian family enterprise with everyone in it together has a very special quality. Why did we succeed? Because we were anxious to please our customers, to serve good-quality food and products, and to keep the premises spotlessly clean. We shared the work, never kept to set hours and remained a closely-knit affectionate family unit, both at work and at home. While the younger members of the family had an active outside social life, we were our parents' social life as well as their family, and even at that age we realized their dependence on us.

In the café I was a member of the team. I was not an employee, paid a salary, but a junior partner, sharing in all the discussions about what to purchase and what to sell, helping with the administration and the account books. I did not have to help clean the place up in the morning – that was done by members of the staff – but whatever was necessary during the day, I did. I would give a hand to wash up an accumulated basket of dirty dishes or wipe out the glasses and stack them on the shelves again, see customers to their places and help to wait at table, or just stand there as the manager to make sure that everyone was being looked after.

My financial arrangements I can only describe as loose but adequate. My father paid for everything I wanted. If I needed a new suit I was told to go and get one. If I needed cash, I was allowed to draw what was necessary but my requirements were modest.

It might be romantic to pretend that my life has been a rags to riches story, but it would not be true. I have always been reasonably well dressed and well shod. I still have shoes that I had made at Lobb's forty-six years ago when I paid six guineas for them. I came from the best kind of family background, with loving parents; I had a good job and work that I liked doing. My people were honest, decent and hard-working. I was very fortunate.

By the time I was twenty-two, I was due for promotion. Father was still expanding his business. He went into partnership with a nephew by marriage, son of an elder sister of my mother's, whose name was also Charles Forte. He was nearly twenty years older than I was and a very skilful man with long experience in the catering business. They opened up two establishments in Brighton, of which by far the more important was the Venetian Lounge. I moved along the coast with my cousin, Charles, to become its manager.

The premises were large, long and T-shaped but had become rather run-down. I replanned the décor, rearranged the seating –

always in consultation with my father and Cousin Charles – and it very soon became a success. I cleaned it up, stopped the rowdies coming in, and installed an orchestra for afternoon tea; many people still remember the Venetian Lounge as one of the most popular places in Brighton.

This was the first venture for which I took primary responsibility and I learnt a great deal from it. I followed the rules applied here again and again, and they always worked. These were: excellent service, an inspired and well-paid staff, pleasant décor, good value and quality, and giving one's undivided attention to the business in hand.

My cousin and I had a flat with a housekeeper and lived perfectly comfortably. Although I had to give up my rugby I continued to swim and also took up golf, which I still enjoy. In the evenings I went out dancing and acquired my first girlfriend.

Then my parents moved to Brighton and bought a house there; I went to live with them, even more comfortably. I could have made this the height of my ambition, living out my days in modest provincial ease. But I knew the business, at least at this level, and I was still in my early twenties, active and ambitious.

CHAPTER THREE

Into Business

ONE AFTERNOON IN 1934 I was taking a short break in the office of the Venetian Lounge, leafing through a copy of the London *Evening Standard*, when my eye was caught by an item in the Diary column. It said that an Australian, the Hon. Hugh D. Macintosh, had opened a milk bar in Fleet Street. Milk in Fleet Street! I had no idea what a milk bar was but it sounded interesting, so I took a day off and went up to London to have a look at it. Compared with our elaborately furnished cafés it seemed remarkably bare, quite small, with a large serving counter, the minimum number of stools, chairs and tables, and only two or three assistants.

It was certainly an original approach to catering, and one which appealed to me. I also noticed that it was very busy. I went to the counter and ordered a milk shake. In Brighton we served something not dissimilar in a conical glass with milk, ice cream, strawberry syrup, shaken up in an electric mixer. The result was much thicker than Macintosh's milk shakes, which were mainly milk with only a little ice cream and fruit syrup, and of course richer. The flavours he offered were chocolate, strawberry and vanilla. You could also order plain ice cream and milk in glasses, but no sundaes and no other food. The service was quick, and the turnover fast. My first impression was confirmed: this milk bar was a very good idea.

Back in Brighton I told my father about it, 'Only selling milk?' he said. 'You can't make any money just with milk.'

'Quite a lot of people have made money with milk,' I told him.

We had a lively discussion. My father remained unconvinced. But I felt sure that I was right and wanted to follow it up, so I wrote to Hugh Macintosh. I explained that I was twenty-six with excellent experience in the soda fountain and ice-cream parlour business, that I had visited his milk bar in Fleet Street and had been very impressed. I also made several suggestions for improving the business, which included adding sandwiches and other light food to the existing menu.

Then a degree of poetic licence crept in. I mentioned that I had a couple of thousand pounds available and would like to go into partnership with him, either in his present milk bar or in a second one. I stressed how hard-working I was and asked for an appointment. The sum of money I suggested investing, £2,000, was a slight flight of fancy. I suppose I had about £400 saved up at the time but I assumed that I could raise the rest from my father or other members of the family.

Macintosh wrote back asking to see me. I travelled up to London again, but the first attempted meeting was a mixture of farce and near disaster. His office was across the road from the milk bar, a very modest place. Going up some rickety stairs I was confronted by an elderly lady, who must have been at least sixty, and appeared to be his secretary.

'My name is Charles Forte and I have come to see Mr Macintosh,' I said importantly.

Something between a scream and a bellow came from the closed door behind her.

'I am very sorry, but Mr Macintosh is not feeling well today and he won't be able to see you,' she said.

'But I have an appointment with him.'

'Yes, I know. We had no way of telephoning you. You did not give us your telephone number.'

'Oh yes I did, it's on the letterheading.' I had written on official Forte paper from Brighton to enhance the general impression.

'Oh I see. Well, I didn't realize that,' she apologized. 'I could have 'phoned you.'

'Yes you could. I have come all the way from Brighton and have wasted a day. I am very disappointed. When can I see Mr Macintosh?'

'I am very sorry,' she said. 'I will make another appointment.'

'Can we make it now?'

'No, I had better speak to him and I will let you know.'

I went over to the milk bar to have another milk shake and a look around, then made my way back to Brighton, as disappointed as any eager young man would be. A few days later I received a letter from Macintosh himself in his own handwriting. 'I am sorry I could not see you. I did not feel well,' he wrote. (I suspect that he had probably had too much to drink.) However, he suggested another meeting, so up I went to London again.

He was an agreeable man and we had a friendly chat. I blew my own trumpet vigorously (as Mark Twain said: 'If you don't blow your own trumpet, nobody will blow it for you.'). I told him again how hard-working I was, that I knew the business backwards, that if he would put me in over the road as managing director I would really make the place pay – with sandwiches, ice cream sundaes, pastries, and a coffee machine – in fact thus adding my own experience to his.

He did not seem enthusiastic: 'Serving a variety of foods is not the purpose of a milk bar,' he said. 'You have got to expand it as it is. That is how it is done in Australia.'

'When people are there, instead of spending fourpence on a milk shake, they will spend a shilling on a milk shake and a sandwich,' I replied. 'I will do the practical side. You could become chairman. You have more experience than I have in advertising and finance. You could concentrate on that side of the business. We would make a very good combination. I'm offering to put in £2,000 and to go fifty-fifty. If we need more money after that, we can raise it together.'

'Let me think about it,' he said non-committally. 'I will let you know.'

A few days later – I must say he was perfectly punctilious in his correspondence – he wrote back: 'Dear Mr Forte, I have thought the matter over and I have come to the conclusion that I do not think the proposition you put to me is of interest.' That was that. Later he told me: 'How could I go into partnership with someone who wanted a salary of £500 a year? That was more than I was taking out of the business.'

By now I had the bit between my teeth but the next stage took quite a while. I had several long conversations with my father, who tried to dissuade me from going to London, saying I would do much better staying where I was. However, he could see that I was determined to try my luck and eventually promised to put up a few hundred pounds and give his guarantee for another thousand or so.

Thus armed I began to haunt the streets of London. I was not looking for a little coffee shop or restaurant site in a back street – I wanted somewhere in the centre of things or nothing. I walked the length of Piccadilly and Shaftesbury Avenue, round Leicester Square, but could see nothing available. Week after week I went up, a day or two at a time. Then one day, in Upper Regent Street, where the polytechnic is, next door to Boosey & Hawkes, the music publishers, I found an empty shop.

I looked up and down the street. There was a Lyons tea shop opposite. Further down there was a branch of the ABC (the Aerated Bread Company), a prosperous catering company. That seemed a good sign. I visited the site again usually staying at the Cumberland Hotel, little dreaming that one day my company would own it. On my trips I would soak up the bohemian atmosphere of the Café Royal in Regent Street. I was fascinated with the place and had even less idea that one day we would own that as well.

Mornings, afternoons, and evenings, I would stand on the pavement outside the empty shop with a recording counter. I checked the number of people walking by. I counted the numbers in the queues at the nearby bus stop; I counted the students and teachers coming in and out of the polytechnic; and became increasingly convinced that this was the site for me.

The building was called Marcol House. Through the intervention of Basil and Howard Samuel, two young and enterprising property agents, I was able to arrange an interview with the administrator of the property. Basil and Howard were intrigued by me. They were even younger than I was, but had already established a considerable real-estate business. I was truly impressed by them, and they remained life-long friends.

The administrator was a pleasant, quite elderly man. I went straight to the point: 'You have an empty shop downstairs to let. I would like to take a lease.'

'What is your business?'

'I want to open a milk bar.'

'*What* is a milk bar?'

I explained that there was one in Fleet Street which he could go and see but that I wanted to set up something rather more elaborate with a good shopfront. We had a longish conversation in which I told him who I was and what I had done, and I must have made a favourable impression in spite of his reservations.

'I don't think my people will consider letting it as a milk bar,' he demurred. 'They would have something more in the line of a recognized business in mind, a bank in particular.'

'But this is a good business, it is necessary, it is wanted, it is something useful,' I insisted. 'I would like you to think about it.'

'Very well,' he said, 'come and see me again.'

'When?'

'Well, let us say in two days' time.'

'Good, thank you, I will,' I replied.

Samuel helped me organize all the routine business of references and after another interview with the landlord they let me have the shop on a twenty-one-year lease at a rent of £1,000 a year. It sounds modest enough, but remember this was over fifty years ago. To me it was a small fortune. Moreover, the property company was taking no chances with me. Theirs was a valuable and prominent site and I was unknown. At first they insisted the rent should be guaranteed.

'I know my father will guarantee it,' I said.

They also wanted a bank reference but instead they accepted a further guarantee from my cousin Charles Forte, whose generous action was typical of our family solidarity.

At this stage I had perhaps £500 or £600 of my own money but I was going to need between £3,000 and £4,000 to set the place up and open it. The shopfront alone was going to cost in the region of £700 to £800.

Nobly, if reluctantly, my father put up £1,000 in cash, maintaining that the whole thing was a gamble. I then went along to see a firm of catering equipment manufacturers, Gardner & Gulland. Tom Gardner, the senior partner, was an outgoing man with imagination and without his help my first enterprise could never have succeeded. I asked him if he would let me have the necessary equipment on credit. He knew of Hugh Macintosh's milk bar and so was not averse to the idea. Yes, he would give me credit, but he told me that I was still dangerously short of money. I accepted his advice and began to look around for some more.

My family had an acquaintance with a pleasant young man called Peter Burton, whose father had been in the textile business and had left him fairly well off. He came in for £1,000 and a job. I also met a man named Roy Marsh on the Milk Marketing Board. He put in a couple of hundred pounds of his own and brought in a friend of his, Harry Roberts, as another investor. It was still not quite enough so I went back to Tom Gardner. There is nothing to equal the effrontery of a young man with a set ambition.

'Look, Tom,' I said brazenly, 'why don't you take a share as well?'

It was the turning-point. 'All right, I will,' came the answer.

'How much?'

He made up the balance of necessary capital and I was left with a sixty per cent share of the business. So it was that I opened the Meadow Milk Bar.

To all outward appearances it was a success right from the start. It was a busy part of London and people certainly flocked in for their milk shakes. It should have been a resounding commercial success, but before the first year was out I found that I was not making a profit. Something was wrong. Either my expenses were too high or my income was too low. The margins were not right. Was I charging too little or was I spending too much?

I now learnt a lesson that I shall never forget. I realized that until I could find the right balance between income on the one hand, and the cost of raw materials, wages, rent, rates, and other overheads on the other, the sums would not add up. In fact, there and then I worked out the essential ratios which would guarantee the profits. In making these calculations I saw I had the choice between cutting down on the operation or expanding. I came to the conclusion that I had to increase the income without a proportionate rise in overheads. Not only would I have to enlarge the premises at some cost, but at the same time I realized that I would have to reduce wages, which meant reducing the number of staff.

At that time I employed twenty-six people. I calculated that I would have to dismiss three of them. This was one of the most difficult decisions I have ever had to make. I worked every day with these people. They were hand-picked by me, capable, decent, and hard-working. Jobs were not easy to come by in the 1930s, and now I was faced with telling three of them to go. It needed a lot of courage, but it had to be done. If I had not done this, I doubt whether I would have ended up employing over sixty thousand people.

But how was I to enlarge the premises? Fate took a hand. A week or so after my decision the shop next door, a corner shop, became vacant. Again I went to see the agent.

'I want to expand into the property next door which is now vacant.'

'Quite impossible, that is a corner shop. I admire what you are doing. Indeed, I like what you are doing, but you are taking on too much with the extra shop.'

'Not at all. I will take it on and make a success of it.'

I tried to explain that we had a healthy turnover and bright prospects. After a further enthusiastic barrage of facts and figures from me, the agent said he would consider the situation, and a few days later he told me I could have the shop. I even managed to persuade the landlord to knock down the intervening wall at their own expense, so expanding the premises up to the corner, in return, of course, for an increase in rent. I still needed some more money, however. I went to see another relative, Celeste Forte, of Exmouth. The meeting was very brief. I said: 'Celeste, I need some money.' He asked what it was for; I told him and said I needed about £700. He looked at me quietly and without a word opened up the drawer of his desk, took out a cheque book, wrote out a cheque for £700, and handed it to me.

'When do you want it back?' I asked.

'As soon as you can.'

'Two years?'

'That will do.' No fuss at all.

It taught me something: it is not only what you give but how you give. I have been grateful to him for the rest of my life.

I was over the crisis. From then on business improved, the bar became better known, and we at last started to make some money. These days we would say that our 'negative cash flow' was changed to a 'positive cash flow' – expressions that would not have meant anything to me at the time.

So the business was now well and truly launched. I began to look for another site. Again Basil and Howard Samuel came in at the right moment with premises at the top of Charing Cross Road, just off Oxford Street. I checked the site every day for a week, morning and evening, walking up and down outside it, observing the number of potential customers passing the door, exactly as I had done with the Regent Street branch. I also checked the through-put at weekends. Eventually I was satisfied. Conrad Hilton, the founder of the world-famous hotel chain, once said that the three most important things in the hotel business are 'Site, site, site.' In catering this is even more true, although I have ventured to change Conrad's dictum to: 'Site, site, management.'

I was quoted a rent for the lease of about £500 a year, exclusive of rates, on the Charing Cross Road site. I made some simple calculations to see whether I could achieve the ratios that were working for me in Regent Street. I then presented the whole project to my bank, which was Lloyds at that time, and asked for £2,500. The loan was agreed, subject to proper guarantees. Mine alone was not sufficient and my cousin Charles came in again to save the day. I had also gained the support of Tom Gardner, who willingly agreed to provide the equipment on the same extended terms as for Regent Street. I now owned my second milk bar.

I installed a manageress at the Regent Street branch and was pleased and somewhat surprised to discover that she ran it just as profitably as I had. The lady's name was Rose Cicconi, a London-born girl of Italian origin. (She stayed with the firm throughout her working life, eventually taking charge of personnel, together with another long-serving employee, Miss McDowell.) A further lesson was to be learnt here: expansion was possible providing I could delegate to the right people.

I now concentrated on the Charing Cross Road milk bar, which flourished from the start. I found that I was now making a profit on both establishments of nearly £3,000 a year, which, I suppose, one would have to multiply by twenty times to compare with values of today.

About this time, my bank manager introduced me to another client named James Knapp-Fisher, who came from a well-to-do family and was the son of Sir Edward Knapp-Fisher, Custodian of Westminster Abbey. Jimmy Knapp-Fisher was looking for an investment and had obviously been told that milk bars were the coming thing. He gave me lunch at Gennaro's in Frith Street and we got on well together. He was tall, genial, whimsical and talkative. He had a friend named George Martelli, a retired naval officer and a journalist, with substantial private means. They each put up £2,000 for my third milk bar at 141 Oxford Street, a corner site which immediately attracted custom. This £4,000 together with another credit arrangement with Gardner & Gulland made the enterprise possible.

Things were really moving now and I was determined to keep pace with public interest and demand. I opened a fourth milk bar in Brighton, in premises which my father very cleverly spotted near the station. This time I am glad to say that I needed no further financial assistance on the part of my family.

I had another relative called Carlo Forte (not the Charles who had guaranteed my overdraft). He had a modest café in Worthing and was extremely pleasant and hard-working, if not the greatest businessman. His café had only a seasonal trade, was not on the best of sites, and was understandably not prospering. I had on one or two occasions given him some urgent financial help in meeting pressing creditors. One day he introduced me to a friend of his named Eric Hartwell. Eric was not much more than twenty at the time and I took to him immediately. He had designed and printed a selection of decorative menus and display cards, which he was selling to restaurants and bars in the Brighton area. He was also a part-time traveller selling electrical goods and had been discussing with Carlo the installation of a large commercial refrigerator.

Shortly after this meeting Carlo told me that Eric was thinking of investing £1,000 in the Worthing café. I suggested to Carlo that this would be unwise and made a counter-proposal: I would give them both a job in a new milk bar I was about to start up, subject to Eric investing his £1,000 in it. It was, in fact, my fifth and most important milk bar, in Leicester Square.

I had been offered this site, next door to the Empire Cinema, by an up and coming property agent, Joe Levy. The rent was reasonable and the ratios seemed to work. We put everything we had into it, including Tom Gardner's best equipment, Eric's money and a bit more of my own. At a total cost of £7,000 we opened the most splendiferous milk bar in London. We spent £1,000 on the shopfront alone and had the floor beautifully tiled. Again, I pledged myself personally to the hilt – it seemed that all my borrowings and also the new lease required my personal guarantee. By now this type of business had gained acceptance, and I did not have to bring in further guarantors.

We splashed out on a gala opening, graced by Sabu the Elephant Boy, whose film was running next door. He was as little averse to publicity as we were – he arrived on an elephant! One of the guests at the party was none other than Hugh D. Macintosh. One of his Black & White Milk Bars was just around the corner off Leicester Square, only a few hundred yards from us. At the party I made one of my first public speeches and described Hugh as a neighbour. He replied, congratulating me on my milk bar, and ended up by saying: 'Yes, we are close neighbours now, too close maybe.' But there was so much custom in the area that both businesses were profitable. None the less I have always been careful not to open too closely to my near competitors.

Eric Hartwell had made it perfectly clear that if he put up £1,000 he wanted to become a partner in the business, and a working partner. In those days he was a tall, thin, stringy youth, anxious to get on, active, very definite in his views, someone who did not tolerate fools easily, very disciplined and most hard-working – just the sort of man I needed, but not a conventional character by any means; in fact, I have never met anyone quite like him. He has been a staunch colleague, living through every set-back and success and recently retired from his position as chief

executive, a rich and successful man. From the very start I had the
greatest confidence in him and he was always intensely loyal to me
and the business.

We very soon had occasion to demonstrate the mutual confidence we had built up. Perhaps I had expanded too fast for the
relatively slim resources I controlled. Although we were making
profits, all the cash we had generated was going into investment
and the repaying of loans. I was carrying a substantial load of debt,
had guaranteed the Leicester Square lease, and suddenly found
myself desperately in need of ready cash.

I went to the bank, who asked for further guarantees. I
volunteered my own guarantee. They accepted this but then asked:
'What other collateral or guarantees can you give us?' I had no
suitable collateral, but I promised to find some more guarantors.

I spoke to Jimmy Knapp-Fisher, George Martelli and Eric
Hartwell. Between them they provided the guarantees that,
together with mine, were necessary to raise a loan from Lloyds
Bank for about £2,000. This saw us through the crisis, which only
lasted a few months. We breathed freely once again so I have every
cause to be grateful to these three, and I am glad that I have been
able to repay them all for the confidence they showed in me then.

My business had been built up in less than five years, but I have
not yet mentioned the help I received from my sister Anna and my
brother Michael. Anna joined me in Regent Street and then
Michael when we started the second milk bar in Charing Cross
Road.

At this time my father decided to retire. He sold all his business
interests and in 1938 he and my mother moved to the outskirts of
London, buying a house in Surrey where I saw my father and
mother nearly every day. We continued to be very close to each
other and he was glad to see my business prospering.

CHAPTER FOUR

Interned, Mobbed, and Married

WHEN WAR BROKE out in 1939 our business remained more or less unaffected at first. In fact, if anything, our affairs improved. The phoney war period lasted until late the following spring and despite the black-out and the sound of air-raid sirens the Blitz did not come until the autumn. London was still full of people and those going into uniform seemed to make a point of spending part of their leave in the capital if they possibly could. My staff had very strict instructions to exclude rowdies and troublemakers and the milk bars always remained safe for families to visit. I visited each one every evening and at most times of the day, to make sure that everything was going smoothly and that they were kept clean and efficient. We must have gained the reputation of having well-run establishments. Many other premises were forced to close when the pubs closed, but we were allowed to stay open until midnight. The Black & White chain, which Hugh Macintosh had built up to fourteen establishments, was not so favoured. They were required to close at ten o'clock at night.

Almost as soon as war broke out Eric Hartwell left for the army. The colonel of the territorial unit in Worthing was a friend of his and Eric wanted to join that particular regiment. I did try to dissuade him, which, I admit, was selfish. 'Why don't you wait until you are called up, for God's sake?' I said to him. 'There is no need for you to rush off.' However, he was not to be deterred.

His investment in the business remained intact and I paid his salary throughout the war. Peter Burton, who had been one of the original investors, was still working with me. He had very bad eyesight and wore thick glasses, and so it was not until much later that he was called up. My sister Anna and brother Michael continued to help in the business, too.

We had by this time taken over a building in Percy Street on the edge of Bloomsbury. It comprised little more than a large warehouse with a basement, with four or five tiny offices upstairs. This became the headquarters of all my enterprises and Michael, Anna, Peter Burton and I had our offices there. In the basement we carried out simple manufacturing operations. We made our own soups for the milk bars, and very good they were too, much better than anything available in tins. We cut sandwiches there and baked our cakes. We made our own ice cream.

Percy Street served as the distribution centre for all our outlets, cutting our costs considerably. We employed about thirty people there, mainly catering staff. It kept the whole operation under a central administration and, modest as it was in scale, provided (with its cost, quantity, and quality control) a microcosm of the methods of organization we would operate on a large scale twenty or thirty years later.

There was one cloud on the horizon. My father had never taken out naturalization papers so we all still had Italian nationality. At the time of Munich, sensing that in due course Mussolini would fight on Hitler's side, I applied for naturalization. At some point the Home Office stopped all naturalization proceedings. I made strenuous efforts to push my case but I had no influential friends to help me. (In fact it was not until six months after the war was over that the papers did actually come through.)

Italy had not yet entered the war but I found my position increasingly worrying, especially as there was hardly anyone who could help me. Jimmy Knapp-Fisher was working in intelligence and had, in effect, disappeared from the London scene. George Martelli was also away, back with the navy as a war correspondent for the *Daily Telegraph*. I had to do something and went to see an acquaintance called Benjamin Hale, the marketing officer for the Milk Marketing Board. He did what he could and came with me to the Home Office, where we saw an official who dutifully made a note of my case, but of course nothing happened. I even wondered if I could join one of the services as a catering adviser or officer.

Not surprisingly nothing came of these rather erratic badly thought-out initiatives.

In June 1940 Italy came into the war on Germany's side and the fate I dreaded came knocking at the door. It took the form of a pleasant plain clothes police officer named Wood, whom I had got to know. I think I met him at a party and he would sometimes drop in at the office or one of the shops for a cup of coffee.

'Charles,' he said, 'I'm afraid you are on the list. I am going to have to take you in to be interned.'

No other member of the family was affected – my parents, my brother, my sister and all my cousins remained at liberty. Perhaps I had drawn too much attention to myself by pressing for naturalization.

Unpleasant and, indeed, depressing as the process was, at least it was carried out in a civilized fashion. Wood allowed me to get a taxi with him back to my Hallam Street flat, where I packed a few essentials before being taken to Savile Row police station. The police sergeant in charge was again pleasant if dispassionate. I was asked to empty my pockets.

'Have you ever been in a police cell?' Wood asked me.

'No.'

'Well, for a little while you will be in a police cell here.'

'A police cell?' I was stunned.

'Yes,' the sergeant intervened. 'You won't be there long. You'll be all right.'

From there I was taken first to Kempton Park. There were hundreds of us and we slept rough before being shipped to the Isle of Man. I could not sleep in the crowded saloon so I went on deck and curled up on a coil of rope to doze. I was tired, worried, miserable, and I did not have a penny in my pocket to buy myself food or drink on board, though I noticed that some of the other internees had. All my money had been left at the police station.

On landing we were marched with our suitcases to a boarding house on the front. The whole sea front had been taken over and there were well over three thousand Italians from all over the British Isles in what was known as the Palace Camp, surrounded by barbed wire. Although we were never pushed around or ill-treated in any way, we were still prisoners. I was not only miserable but angry, unreasonably I suppose. Angry with myself because I had had plenty of time to become naturalized. Ten years had passed since I was twenty-one, but I had done nothing until it was too late. I was also angry with the authorities, and bitter. I could hardly sleep for worry. I was worried about being an internee. I was worried about being cut off from my mother and father at a time when they needed me most. And I was worried about the business. I became even more anxious when the bombing started. Fortunately the business had so far remained untouched. It was a British company with British partners and was therefore not affected by the wartime legislation concerning enemy property.

The worst part of the initial period was sitting around with nothing to do but play cards and talk. This did not last long, however. As I spoke better English than most, the camp commandant, Captain Myers, asked me to become the liaison between the internees and the camp command. I was given an office and an assistant and soon became very busy. One of my jobs was to write petitions to the Home Office on the internees' behalf, to vet their applications and help them write their letters. Of course everybody was petitioning the Home Office – including me. I stated my own case very forcibly, but after a few weeks I gave up any hope of being released.

I acquired a degree of minor importance in the camp and was allowed in and out of the palisade to walk across to the commandant's office without an escort. It gave me a certain sense of freedom and dignity. To an extent the work reconciled me to the miserable circumstances I was in. I began to feel less bitter and more philosophical. Perhaps after all I was comparatively fortunate: in the Western Desert, in the air, and on the sea thousands of men were suffering and dying. I made myself accept that internment was my part in the war.

One day Captain Myers said to me: 'There are some fascists in there, aren't there, Forte?'

'Where?'

'In the camp. Who are they?'

'Look, Captain Myers,' I said, 'first of all there aren't any fascists. They are all people like me. They have no interest in politics and if they had, do you want to treat me as a spy or as a man who is helping you to do this work? You don't think I would tell you, do you?'

'I don't know.'

I looked him straight in the eye. 'Well, I know.'

He gave me an odd look, whether of approval or disapproval I do not know. I was convinced the conversation would lose me my job – the only thing that made the camp bearable. Presumably he wanted someone at his beck and call who would tell him what was going on. That was not my responsibility, which was to act as an intermediary between him and the internees.

I did my work meticulously and was fully occupied. When Captain Myers asked me how I thought the war was going, I remained completely non-committal. He must have known what my true feelings were, although I never discussed them. I did not want to pander or toady. Although close members of my family were still living in Italy, I knew perfectly well whom I wanted to win the war.

I had been completely anti-fascist since I was a teenager in Rome and saw a relative being slapped in the face at a railway station by a militia officer. I myself was standing at the corner of the street on one occasion when a squad of fascists came marching through carrying their flag. At the Scheppers we wore a school uniform with a semi-military cap and, as the fascist flag went past, it simply did not occur to me to raise my hat to it as others were doing. Before I realized what was happening, I got two or three sharp taps on the peak from a stick while my assailant shouted to me to take my hat off. I did so quickly enough but the incident rankled.

I had been on the Isle of Man for about three months when the Home Office set up a tribunal to consider the flood of petitions it had received. The tribunal's composition was predictable enough. The chairman was a K.C. named Sullivan. There was a socialist, a conservative, a trade unionist and someone representing a Jewish organization, about eight people in all.

For some reason, either because the Home Office felt they had been a little hasty in my case or because the enigmatic Captain Myers had unexpectedly put in a good word on my behalf, I was the very first internee to be called before the committee at their first session. It was not an enjoyable experience. They had a big window behind them while I sat with the light in my eyes. The questions came thick and fast. What about my Forte cousin in Stirling who was the secretary of the local fascist party? I told them he was not my cousin, although he was certainly related to me. In any case, I said, I have a much closer relative who has just been shot down in a Spitfire.

'You say you are anti-fascist.'

'Yes, I always have been.'

'Who do you want to win the war?'

'I won't answer that question,' I said.

'Well, how have you shown your anti-fascism? Have you written against the fascists?'

'No, I am not a writer.'

'Have you spoken against them?'

'Yes, very often in private but not in public. I am not a public speaker.'

Anyone with any sense of dignity would have behaved in the same way. Although most of the questions were reasonable and the people on the tribunal were polite, I found some of their questions offensive. Finally I stood up: 'Look, I have had enough of these questions, this is no longer a tribunal, this is the third degree and I am walking out.'

Sullivan looked concerned and most of the tribunal seemed taken aback by my outburst. I got up and walked to the door where a young soldier from a Scottish regiment who was on guard with a rifle stopped me.

'Let him through,' said the chairman, and the lad stood aside. Back in my boarding house all the other internees crowded round me. 'What was it like?' 'How did you get on?' By this time my sense of outrage had evaporated.

'I'm in here for the duration I suppose,' I replied ruefully. My acute misery returned.

Three days later one of the internees came rushing up to me: 'You're free, you're free. There's a message at the commandant's office for you. I think it's your release.' I was flabbergasted; I had been told that the verdict took about three weeks to come through.

The internee was right. There was a telegram on Captain Myer's desk instructing him to release me. But I suppose the people on the tribunal had sensed that, although I was certainly an alien, I was absolutely harmless. They appreciated where my true sentiments lay.

In no time I was back in London to the delight and joy of my family. They had braved the Blitz and somehow Michael and Anna had kept the business going splendidly. The milk bars were continuing to function – but only just. I found considerable financial problems awaiting me, but fortunately at just the right moment for us a moratorium on rents was declared.

Looking out of my office in Grosvenor House today at the tranquil beauty of Hyde Park, it is hard to visualize the conditions in London forty years ago. The inhabitants of the capital were in great danger and distress. The Allies were fighting back in North Africa, but the invasion of Europe was still two years away and in the meantime the remaining population simply had to stick it out.

All our premises were damaged by the bombing, although none was completely destroyed or put out of business. A land-mine on a parachute dropped near Leicester Square and blew our beautiful shopfront through to the back. Power cuts were frequent and we had to serve people by candlelight. There were queues of mothers with children and on my visits I would often serve behind the counter myself, giving a hand to see that they all got something to eat and drink. To me this was more than just a business. I felt that our catering establishments were our contribution to the war effort and I was anxious to serve as many people as I could with at least a modicum of food and drink. Sometimes we could hardly stand because we were so tired, but we kept going.

We simply could not cope with the rush at certain times of day and an order for four milk shakes – lemon, peach, strawberry and raspberry – would be passed on by me as: 'Four strawberry milk shakes.' My sister was once driven to lecturing me on practising what I preached.

Supplies were really quite good. We would put in our requisition to the Ministry of Food, listing what we had consumed, and the replenishments were almost automatic. We only went short from time to time. Butter was the chief problem and we never had enough. The book clerk at Percy Street who entered the supplies was a young man named Allen, who later went into the marines. One day I saw one of our cooks making up some sandwiches with some lovely-looking yellow butter. I went upstairs to Allen and said: 'Where does that butter come from? I don't recognize it as part of our normal stock.'

'Oh, it's very good butter, Mr Forte,' he said. 'I get it from a fellow who comes up with a van. He drops it off and I pay him sixpence a pound and off he goes.'

'Sixpence a pound?' I shouted. The controlled price of butter was then about one and sixpence. 'You bloody fool, that must be stolen butter you're buying. No one can buy butter at sixpence a pound.'

'Oh!' he said, bemused. 'I hadn't thought of that.'

'Stop buying it immediately,' I ordered him.

The incident really scared me. If you broke wartime rules you went to gaol and your name would be splashed all over the papers as a black market dealer. I was acutely conscious of the fact that I was of foreign origin and could well have an accusing finger pointed at me. The entire business could be ruined if I became involved in a scandal of this sort – and I would be in a police cell for a second time.

These laudable sentiments did not, however, protect me from another extremely unpleasant incident. A presentable young fellow came to see me in Percy Street. He was very polite, nicely turned out, and said that he and his partner had acquired a substantial quantity of sugar syrup. Would I like to buy any of it? Now this was one commodity of which we were short, so I said yes, but also explained that I would need to have a statement, an invoice, a proper receipt and a declaration of origin.

'Will you pay cash?' he asked, which should have warned me off. I agreed, providing the documentation was in order. He then showed me an official-looking piece of paper with a Ministry of Food heading on it, which looked perfectly authentic. As it turned out he must have stolen this as well, but I was foolish enough to take this false authorization to sell syrup to caterers at its face value.

He introduced me to his partner. They made rather a fuss about being paid in cash, saying that they had a tax problem, but in the end I agreed on the understanding that I would be given a proper receipt. I drew the money from the bank, nearly £1,200, which was enough to buy sufficient sugar syrup to see us through for months. I then drove down with the two men to an address in Kenton, Middlesex.

The house was almost empty and I started getting suspicious. 'Tell me, did you say you've got the stuff stored here?' I asked.

'Oh yes,' he said. 'It's through the back.'

I did not like the look of this at all and was about to walk out when three ruffians burst in, and all five jumped on me. One of them had a lead pipe and anyway I was quite unable to provide much opposition against five assailants. I was hit over the head several times and knocked out, although luckily my hat prevented any serious injury. When I came to a few minutes later they had disappeared. So, of course, had the money.

I had been loosely tied up but I managed to free myself and rushed out of the house, with my head still bleeding, probably about a quarter of an hour after they had gone. Luckily I found a policeman and he summoned a police car which took us back to the house, but of course there were no clues.

A couple of days later Detective Chief Inspector Glander called on me and took down all the details. Did I remember what the men looked like? Yes, I did.

'I am told you put up quite a resistance,' he said.

'I tried to defend myself, the natural instinct of a man being attacked,' I replied evenly. The interview became increasingly unpleasant.

'You know you were not entitled to buy that stuff anyway,' he said.

'Oh yes I was.'

'No you weren't. It was contraband, stolen goods.'

'How was I to know they were stolen goods?' Fortunately I had kept the original piece of paper the man had presented which I showed to the inspector.

'Yes, but even if it had come from the Ministry of Food, you are not a caterer.'

'What do you mean, I am not a caterer?'

'You are a milk bar proprietor.'

'That is catering.'

'You are not a caterer.'

'Look, Inspector, we *are* caterers.' I called one of our staff, 'Bring our licence here.' He returned with the framed document which hung on the office wall. 'Forte & Company Limited. Milk Bar Proprietors and Caterers', the document said. I pushed it over to the inspector, feeling increasingly irritated.

'Well, you are lucky,' he said. I really believe he had come to arrest me.

That was the turning-point and from then on things calmed down. The next thing he asked was: 'Would you recognize these people?'

'Yes, I think I would.'

'I think I know where I can find these characters.'

'Shall I come along and see if I can point them out to you?'

'Would you be prepared to do that?'

'Yes, I would.'

The inspector said he would let me know and a few days later he was back: 'Did these people talk about music to you at all?'

As a matter of fact they had, during the initial conversation. We had discussed opera. It later transpired that both men had played in a small band. Glander had got on to them through an informer. Subsequently I had to identify them and appear as a witness.

In court the judge asked: 'What happened?'

'Well, the gentlemen in the dock . . .'

The judge stopped me: 'Gentlemen? Those hooligans?' Hardly an impartial response. They got a gaol sentence. Needless to say I did not get my money back.

At that time I had a friend who was much older than me. Carlo Micallef was nearly sixty. His name was of Maltese origin, but he was a Florentine and one of the most elegant men I have ever known. He had his suits made at Kilgour & French, his shoes came from Lobb, his hats from Lock. He had an elegant house just off Portland Place in Mansfield Street. He had come to England when he was about thirty and had done well.

One evening I was having dinner with him when he said: 'I think it is time you got married, old boy.'

'So my father and mother keep telling me. Don't you start.'

A day or two later Micallef rang up: 'I would like you specially to come to dinner.'

'Where?' I asked, 'at your place?'

'No, I am giving a little dinner party at the Hungaria in Lower Regent Street.'

About a dozen people sat round the table in a private room downstairs. I had been placed next to a young girl called Irene. But it so happened that I had already seen Irene before, in her mother's delicatessen in Soho. I had walked in one day and saw a girl behind the counter in a neat white overall. She was young, fresh, unspoilt looking with a lovely smile. She was translating a letter into English from Italian for a very old man standing at the counter. I waited for a while, admiring the grace and gentleness with which the girl addressed the old man, who also happened to be slightly deaf. Eventually I interrupted to ask if I could buy some prosciutto. She replied: 'If I had any prosciutto I'd eat it myself. Don't you know there's a war on?'

I was delighted to see her at the dinner party and we got on very well. I knew her surname was Chierico, not a common Italian name. I found her even more attractive on closer acquaintance. She was twenty-one and I was thirty-three. We laughed all evening. Towards the end of the dinner, I said to her: 'What are you doing tomorrow evening?'

'I have a date.'

'Well, cancel it.'

'I can't do that.'

Next morning I phoned her: 'Are we going out this evening?' She said yes – she had cancelled her date.

I took her out the following evening and a week later, when we were dining in the Savoy Restaurant, I proposed to her. She accepted immediately. I always tell her that I had hardly got the words out of my mouth before she said yes. We went to the Embassy Club in Bond Street to celebrate and danced all night. We married a few months later. It was the happiest and most fortunate thing that has ever happened to me.

Irene had been born in London. Her mother had come to London from Italy to accompany her brother who was a naval attaché at the Italian Embassy, and while in London she met an Italian wine importer and they got married. Her mother, an extraordinary character in her own right, ran a delicatessen called the Continental Stores at the corner of Wardour Street. Twenty-six years ago she came for a long weekend – and stayed, I am delighted to say. She died recently, aged over 103. Irene was her only daughter.

It is quite exceptional how well Irene got on with my own mother and father. They took to her in the most loving manner. As I was so devoted to my parents, this was a great joy to me.

We set up house in a comfortable, large flat in New Cavendish Street near the corner of Portland Place. Irene, with some help from Anna, decorated the flat exquisitely. Two years later my son was born. We named him Rocco John Vincent, after my father, Irene's father and a favourite cousin. Rocco was born in Bournemouth because, when my wife was pregnant, I insisted on her moving there to avoid the flying-bomb offensive against London. Olga, our next child (named after my mother-in-law), was born two years later in the Middlesex Hospital. She and Rocco spent their infant years in the flat before we moved to Hampstead.

By now the war was over and we could start thinking in terms of leading a more normal life. But rationing was still upon us. At the beginning of 1946 I was appointed a member of a small consultative advisory committee in the Ministry of Food. It consisted of a few top people in the business to advise the government about the steps necessary to change gradually from the system of wartime rationing to the conditions of peacetime. The chairman of the committee was Mr Hugh Wontner, chairman of the Savoy. He comes into the story again at a later stage.

CHAPTER FIVE

Wider Horizons

THE END OF the war found us a modestly prosperous family concern, with our five milk bars and the food factory and offices in Percy Street. Michael and Anna were still my partners. We had survived the really difficult years together and knew our small corner of the catering trade inside out. It was now time to think of expansion and a better organized future.

Eric Hartwell rejoined us. Peter Burton's ambitions took him in a different direction and he left to go to the United States. I tried hard to persuade him to stay, but failed to do so. He sold his shareholding, which I purchased. I was sad to see him go because, although he was not a dynamic businessman, he was a pleasant associate and one I had enjoyed working with.

My experience so far had been in the field of light catering. I wished not only to expand these operations but also to enter into a more serious side of catering. What were my motives? My main aim was to be the most successful of the Forte clan. In every family, even one as close as ours, a natural rivalry exists, be it friendly or otherwise. Having achieved this, my second aim would be to improve a business which was already being noticed, to make it bigger and better, and to this end I was prepared to work day and night. I have never regarded money, useful and desirable though it is, as an end in itself. It is simply a means to an end and a measure of success, and two of these ends were to make my family more secure and to create a larger and increasingly prosperous business.

So, if we were going to extend our horizons and broaden our operations, we needed to strengthen the management team, particularly on the restaurant side. I put an advertisement in the trade press, which caught the eye of a man called Leonard Rosso. He came to see me.

Rosso was born into the catering business. His father was a restaurateur and when young Leonard left school he served a management apprenticeship with J. Lyons & Co. After training at the Regent Palace, Strand Palace, Cumberland, Trocadero and Marble Arch Corner House, he became the manager of a group of their branches in the West End of London. He is a quiet, gentle-voiced man. He eventually became deputy chief executive of Trusthouse Forte.

He later told me that what encouraged him, at our first interview, to make the move from the prestigious firm which employed him to our still tiny undertaking was the enthusiasm I expressed and the plans I outlined for the future. He felt that he was going to become part of a growth business and this attracted him. He started putting into effect what Lyons had taught him and there was really no better school in the world. They were the kings of the catering industry in those days and his experience and knowledge were invaluable to us. We had been extremely success-ful as milk bar proprietors. Leonard Rosso helped to give us more wide-ranging catering expertise.

Another recruit who joined us at that time and has only just retired from Trusthouse Forte was Jack Bottell. During the war he had risen from private to major, and had won the Military Cross. I had known him before the war and shortly after he was demobbed he dropped in on me.

'I'm off,' he said.

'Where to?' I asked.

'There doesn't seem much to do here and I'm going to Italy to open a small hotel with my sister-in-law and one or two other people.'

'Well, you must be crazy,' I told him.

'Why?'

'There is plenty of work here, join my company.'

So he did, and became a stalwart member of the growing team, an exceptional character, a man who would never let anyone down.

*

We were now actively engaged in looking for new premises and businesses to take over. I often reflect on the frequency with which the right opportunity has presented itself to me at the right time. As mentioned earlier, I had got to know a property agent named Joe Levy, at that time in a modest way of business although he was eventually to become a big property developer and a millionaire.

One day he came into the office and said: 'Look, Forte, would you be interested in Rainbow Corner?' Rainbow Corner, in Shaftesbury Avenue, had been a Lyons establishment until 1942, when the Red Cross had taken it over and turned it into an American Services Club. It was a famous institution and also a landmark.

'Certainly I would be interested, but surely it belongs to Lyons?'

'Yes, it does,' he said. 'But I think we could buy it.'

'Why do they want to sell it?'

'Well, they want to get out of the place. Now that the wartime boom with all the servicemen is over, they are not doing particularly well there.They have a much bigger place, the Trocadero, across the road.'

'What kind of money do they want?'

'Maybe twenty, thirty, forty thousand.'

'You must be mad, Joe. Where am I going to get £30,000 from?'

'I could arrange it for you. You have a pretty good covenant and a good record. You could afford to pay the rent. (The rent was £12,000 a year for the whole building.) If you could arrange a lease-back to someone like the Prudential Assurance Company,' Joe Levy went on, 'I think they would accept your covenant and guarantee and advance you the money to buy the property.'

I was still inexperienced in property deals in those days, but I was learning fast. I had no idea then that such a lease-back arrangement was possible. (In such a deal you sell the property to raise money, but take a lease, thereby remaining in occupation.)

'I think I can arrange that,' said Levy. 'Will your bank give you a good reference?'

'I am sure they will,' I was able to say.

The sum that I envisaged spending was something like ten times as much money as I had ever spent on anything during the period in which I had been building up the business. The incident taught

— • —

me something valuable – indeed it confirmed what my father had often told me – that a good reputation is better than money in the bank because it gives you access to credit. If you have a reputation for meeting your obligations, it could be worth millions to you. Whenever I have required money I have always managed to find it. It is all a question of inspiring confidence. The money is there in the banks and financial institutions. They are as keen to lend as you are to borrow, but of course they have their responsibilities to their employees, pensioners and shareholders. They have to safeguard themselves as far as possible against risks. The first obligation of banks must be to avoid the risk of losing their depositors' money – and after that to make a profit.

What is true now was true then and the deal came off exactly as Joe Levy had predicted. In fact I borrowed not £30,000 from the Prudential, but £5,000. We decorated and refurbished the premises, which took nearly ten months. I let the upper part of the building to the Ontario Government for £8,000 a year, and the balance of the rent payable, £4,000 a year, made a large ground floor and basement a very reasonable proposition for me. We now had the advantage of large premises in one of the finest sites in London, if not the finest for our type of business.

In the meantime, we had acquired by straight purchase another catering business, which brought with it another of my earliest colleagues. This was Rex Henshall, who had come out of the Fleet Air Arm and was acting as the secretary of a company called Pearce & Partners, which had a chain of ten restaurants dotted around the centre of London. We refurbished them and gave them the new name of Variety Fare, integrating them into our management and supply system. They were soon adding their profits to the whole.

Rex Henshall is a delightful man. I am sure that he will not mind my saying that he was a bit of a maverick, who always wanted to go off at an interesting tangent. Occasionally he came up with extraordinary ideas, some of them down to earth and practical, some not. Rex's principal contribution was on the development and property side, with special responsibility for new acquisitions.

With Rex's arrival we completed the team which was to be so

vital in building up the business. We avoided many mistakes because, while believing in the necessity of leadership by one man, I have never seen myself as an infallible captain of industry, taking the right decisions every time. I believe very strongly in the perhaps over-used expression 'the team', a group of people able to think better together and therefore choosing the wisest course of action. The Americans call it group thinking. Moreover, I am not by nature secretive. My immediate colleagues knew exactly what I thought, what I did, what I earned, what my plans were, what I felt.

This constant exchange of information and views is essential for the success of any company. But I have always believed that we should keep our *discussions* secret and in this I have never been let down. My emphasis on secrecy was not based on paranoia, or on a desire to keep my affairs hidden from the outside world. I myself have learnt a great deal about competitors' plans by random information given away, often in a social situation. Information acquired in this way may not mean very much in itself, but it may if connected to something else that one knows or has heard from another source. I have gained some amazing and valuable information in this way.

I was acquiring the insights and management which have stood me in such good stead.

I became a firm believer in the men at the top, even though not directly involved in the accounting process, knowing day by day the precise financial position of the company. This sort of knowledge which, after all, is the measure of the health of a business, should always be taken into account in every act of decision-making.

I was not an ambitious artisan. I never minded if somebody made better coffee than I do, but I did know what good coffee should taste like. I did not try to teach the man making mayonnaise his job — I respected his skill in making it, but I wanted the best mayonnaise. The manager at any level who wants to do everything himself must eventually, by definition, limit his activities. The technique must always be to pick people who can do things for you in the way you want them done, and to instil in them the knowledge that their skills are appreciated and respected.

A good manager must inspire loyalty. But he cannot expect loyalty unless he is respected. At the same time he should only judge people by their achievement, not by whether they appeal to him personally. I am by nature patriarchal and paternalistic. I do not think paternalism is a bad thing. Paternalism means a fatherly attitude and employees being cared for, valued, and noticed, however big the organization may be. It is all a question of finding the right course of action and giving it sincere expression; I have always found that employees respond positively to being cared for and valued.

Another important point which has never ceased to astonish me, is that if a philosophy is not only preached but also practised at the very top of a company, that philosophy permeates down the line and throughout the organization.

Obviously running a successful catering business is not simply a question of understanding and inspiring people. The caterer must also understand and overcome the challenges posed by the basic problems of the business, which remain the same, week in, week out, year in, year out: how much do you pay in wages; what is the percentage of wages to turnover; what is the gross profit; is the purchasing system efficient; how do you buy, where do you buy and what do you buy? The larger you grow, the more difficult it becomes to control all these factors.

We always accepted that success is never based on a one-off transaction; it comes only by encouraging the customer to return again and again. It all sounds very simple; put like this, almost too simple. But it is true. There need not be anything complex about basic commercial prosperity in catering, which, in common with all businesses and professions comes from sound principles rigorously applied, allied to professionalism and attention to detail. Yet in catering profits are not easily come by; indeed they can easily disappear. It always amazes me that people, at the drop of a hat, will start a restaurant or hotel, businesses which need so much skill and careful management. I have been a director of many different kinds of company and I am convinced that the hotel and catering business is the most difficult of all in which to earn a living, but it is to me the most fascinating and rewarding.

In catering it is imperative to avoid waste. Some people regard waste as inevitable, and of course it is inevitable if you do not plan both your day and your purchasing properly. But to suggest that you cannot run a top-quality restaurant under tight control is nonsensical.

I have often been asked for advice by catering establishments which are unprofitable despite their large turnover. Certainly if the turnover is large, they have the means to provide the customer with very agreeable service, but on studying the accounts in detail I have always given them the same answer. You can provide the same value, or even better if it comes to that, but you must cut out waste and manage your expenditure. I often find myself giving this advice to people who have spent a lifetime in catering. Let me be explicit. They may, for example, be paying ten per cent more in wages than they need. I am not saying that you should not pay staff well. On the contrary, I believe in paying the best possible wages or salaries, but they may be using four people instead of three, ten people instead of eight. In other words, use the correct number of people but pay them more. Wage costs as a percentage of turnover should be a maximum of twenty per cent, not forty or fifty per cent. And the cost of their materials is probably too high. Gross profit to cope with overheads should be sixty-five or seventy per cent upwards, not thirty-five or forty. Low gross profit is caused by bad buying and waste, and in the end it is not only the caterer who suffers but the customer as well, for diminished profit can result in lower standards and inadequate service.

It was in this area of cost control that Len Rosso was such a marvellous asset to us. I made him supervisor of the new restaurants we had acquired and he went round every one of them every day, making a personal inspection. He analysed the clientèle we were attracting – who came in for breakfast, who came in for lunch, and who was there in the evening. Were the menus right for each particular type of customer? He would prepare a league table of whatever had been sold. Certain items would be in the top six of his list; others, which had hardly moved at all, came off the menu. Len modestly said that it was all a matter of common sense and so, in a way, I suppose it was, except that it is highly organized common sense. He never went in to criticize and nag, only to assist and organize things better. He ran little competitions for the

managers and manageresses. Those who achieved the highest
profitability or surpassed their budget would get a small bonus.

We introduced the whole system of day-to-day monitoring which
formed the basis of our huge business. If you serve forty pounds of
beef a day and have forty pounds in stock, then you need to buy
very little beef the following day. The same goes for potatoes,
green vegetables, fruit and whatever else makes up the menu.
Steaks have to be kept constantly under review. This is not a desk
job or a pen pushing exercise. The managers had to go round
personally to check the stock itself. The same was true even when
guided and assisted by a computer. We had a comprehensive
training scheme to teach these principles, a programme to which
we attached the greatest importance.

By this time I had begun to make something of a name for myself.
The first ever lengthy newpaper profile about me appeared in
August 1948 in, of all places, the *Methodist Recorder*.

Strangers to the west-end of London are sometimes puzzled by
the ubiquity of the name which is becoming as well known as
the familiar Lyons, ABC, Express Dairy and other stars in the
catering firmament. The name is Forte's. Recent purchasers of
the famous Rainbow Corner in Shaftesbury Avenue, home of
the American Red Cross during the war, the company now has
some fifteen shops in the west-end, some of them milk bars,
some cafeterias and the latest being the intriguing sign of Variety
Fare. The last-named denotes a counter-service restaurant at
which full-scale meals are served. Variety Fare restaurants are
now established in Coventry Street, the Strand, Tottenham
Court Road and there are others being planned.

What distinguishes Forte's establishments from those of its
competitors? Not only the fact that they are modern in decora-
tion and furnishing, with up-to-date accessories and staffed by
efficient assistants, with menus to attract, but because throughout the organisation there is a clear anxiety to 'serve' the
customer in the fullest sense. . . .

Behind the good management lies the personal drive and
initiative of one man, who refuses to be discouraged because the

service he gives to the public is still, in his opinion, inadequate; who believes that Britain is the finest country in the world, could offer its visitors as good catering as any other country; who represents the catering industry, the Milk Bar Association council and the Caterers' Consultative Committee; who serves fourteen million meals to the public a year and has over twenty million customers; a man with a restless temperament, coupled with a big ideal and the vision to achieve it – Charles Forte, a friend of his staff and his competitors, and a man who is making a success and is proud to be doing so.

CHAPTER SIX

'We haven't paid for it – but we've bought it'

MOST PEOPLE AT the head of a business which they have built up to be worth a million pounds would doubtless be content to rest on their laurels. My operation was functioning smoothly; we had an efficient management team and had recruited good staff. The figures were looking good, we could have banked our salaries and started to take it easy. That is not the way I am made. In my case, the million was not rattling round in my pocket; it merely showed up on the balance sheet. At last I had some time and plenty of energy to spare. I wanted to move on to bigger things.

On the south side of Piccadilly Circus stood the building occupied by Criterion Restaurants Limited, a public company. It had banqueting halls on the top floors, the then famous Criterion Brasserie at basement level, and shops, including the sports shop Lillywhite's, on the street. The showpiece was a large, ornate restaurant called the Marble Hall. Its walls were studded with semi-precious stones said to be worth £80 per square foot. The Criterion was an old-fashioned company, perfectly sound and respectable, but lacking energy and drive.

The Marble Hall was almost a separate part of the establishment with its own entrance. Through the catering and property grapevine we heard that the Criterion management would not be averse to leasing out the Marble Hall to someone else as it was losing money, so I got in touch with them. The rent they were asking was £12,000, exactly the same figure we were paying for the headlease of Rainbow Corner, so the transaction came within limits to which we had become accustomed. We took it over, and we opened it up as a cafeteria. Salads cost 2s.9d. (13.5p), Chicken Maryland 4s.

(20p), Ice Gateaux 1s. (5p). Our methods worked right from the start and the enterprise made us a handsome profit.

Some years later, in 1953, we discovered that the Criterion Company wanted to sell out altogether. The asking price was £800,000, twenty-five times as much in the way of capital expenditure as anything in which I had ever been engaged. In proportion to the size of our organization, and even to what we later became, it was the biggest leap I have ever contemplated.

We did our homework first. We looked at the Criterion figures, analysed its turnover, calculated the interest on the loan we would have to raise, added in the ground rent, the rates and taxes, and worked out the running costs according to our catering and purchasing methods, and, in those pre-computer days, put it all through our adding machines. If properly run, we saw that a good profit was to be made. But how on earth, even with my record of financial probity, was I going to raise a sum of money like that?

I went to see the general manager of my bank. I had by then moved our account to Clydesdale Bank, whose top man was Sir John Campbell, the prop and mainstay of our expansionist years. He was a tall, handsome man, very formidable and forthright, with a habit of looking sideways quizzically at anyone who was trying to get money out of him. He was a first-class banker and one who took few risks, although he took some with me. That said, he would interrogate me through every nook and cranny of each transaction I proposed and gave nothing away easily. We became great friends and I held him in the highest regard. Tough and terse he could be, but I always knew exactly where I stood with him.

'I can't possibly let you have £800,000,' he said. 'It is far too much money. You will cover yourself in debt.'

'Look, John,' I said, 'the place is a wonderful property.'

'It may well be a wonderful property but you haven't got the money to buy it. You already owe me money and your overdraft is quite large.' (The overdraft had been incurred by a number of other ventures, which I will mention later.) He was adamant.

'I have always paid you and you have my personal guarantee,' I persisted.

'Yes, you have,' he admitted. But our conversation was at an end.

I pondered on my next move. We already did a certain, if limited, amount of business with a brewery, Ind Coope, which formed part of what was to become Allied Breweries. I rang up the chairman and asked to see him.

'We will give you exclusive rights to the sale of beer in the Criterion complex if you help me to raise the money to buy the property,' I offered.

'How much is it?'

'£800,000.'

'That's a lot of money. Maybe we could lend you a quarter of a million, it could be worth that.'

'But won't you stretch it a bit?'

I think I got him up to £300,000. It was a start at least. I looked at the rental values of the shops which formed part of the property and reminded myself that we would be relieved of the £12,000 in rent that we were already paying for the Marble Hall. I added all the figures up again and went to see my old friend Joe Levy, who had by this time been joined by another great friend of mine, Robert Clark.

'Look, Joe, how do we get this package together?'

'We will have to see if we can get an insurance company to put up the money in the form of a sale and lease-back.'

I was used to this sort of transaction by now and, with Joe's help, got a promise of money out of the Guardian Assurance Company. I agreed the rate of interest I would have to pay to the brewery and went back to see Sir John Campbell again.

'Now John, I have the answer. Look at that.' I showed him a detailed account of the proposed transaction.

'It begins to make sense,' he conceded. None the less he still had endless reservations. He wanted to be sure three times over that his money was going to be secure. He would advance the bridging finance if I got binding letters from everyone else concerned. In short, one way and another, I succeeded in putting the package together, although it was a close-run thing. The bid was successful and I became the proud possessor of the Criterion.

It had been a nerve-racking period for us all. We had worked morning, noon and night on the problems, and had finally convinced ourselves that I had not gone out of my mind with *folie de grandeur*, but that we had a viable proposition on our hands. We kept our heads, made it work, and it inspired us with the confidence to go on to greater things still.

But I have taken liberties with the chronology in telling the whole story of the Criterion. Let us return to the early 1950s. It was the time of the Festival of Britain, which was not only an important trade exhibition featuring products of British manufacture and commerce, but also a symbol of Britain's emergence from the austerity of the post-war years. It took place on the south bank of the Thames and attracted millions of people.

The organizers invited tenders for the two catering concessions. We obtained one, and ABC caterers second only to Lyons, obtained the other. I believe it cost ABC something like £80,000 to set up their share of the concession, but then it was quite a small part of their whole operation, and they could finance expenditure like this out of their own resources. We had to go about it differently. We obtained sponsorship from our suppliers, who in many cases paid a premium for the privilege and publicity of their products being featured in the festival gardens. Others provided their goods at reduced prices.

By the time we opened the concession had cost us very little in the way of cash; we had simply contributed our organization and expertise. It was a frantically busy period but worth every minute of it because it was our first foray into mass catering. We had calculated correctly that there would be tens of thousands of people who would want everything from a glass of lemonade to a snack meal. Despite the size of the venture, it was no gamble. We knew from the start that we stood only to make a profit, and so it proved.

Our method of running the concession differed from ABC's. Their top brass took the operation in their stride, setting the thing up and leaving the staff to get on with it. In contrast, either I or one of my co-directors was down in our concession at most times of every day, ensuring that everything was in order and studying ways and means of improving our performance. We set up two

parallel cafeteria counters with a cashier at the end of each and
were moving thirty-two people a minute. If there was a hitch we
found that the flow dropped from thirty-two to twenty-five. I might
then jump the barrier, go up to a woman with a fractious child,
and say, as pleasantly as I could, 'Do you mind moving on, please?
You are keeping a lot of people waiting.' We were constantly on
the job because that is how we do things in my company. You
cannot get results simply by sitting back and giving orders. You
have to get down to the nitty-gritty of the business. The people
who work with you must be aware of the fact that you know the ins
and outs of the business as well as they do, that you are prepared
to work with them at all times, and that you are not the last to
come or the first to go.

One of the principal administrators of the original exhibition had
been Leslie Joseph, or Major Joseph as he preferred to be known.
He later became Sir Leslie Joseph and was running what in modern
jargon are called leisure complexes. He already had a funfair and
caravan camp at Porthcawl in South Wales and had been
appointed by the government to run that part of the Festival of
Britain with which we were concerned. In effect he was our
landlord.

  When the official festival came to an end, I suggested to Leslie
Joseph that we join forces, make an offer for the concession, which
was in Battersea Park, and continue to run it. I think we both put
up £25,000. Forte's could afford it after our success.

  Leslie Joseph took over the day-to-day management. A very
gifted architect named John Gardner had embellished Battersea
Park with charming landscaping and attractive architectural features. One mistake we made was to dismantle many of the features
of his creation, thus changing the character of the original
exhibition into an elaborate funfair. There was a great outcry by
the press, who protested that it was against the public interest,
inasmuch as we were making a commercial undertaking out of a
public park. This is a view with which I had some sympathy.
Nevertheless Leslie was right from a commercial point of view; the
public loved it and came streaming in.

  The first year went splendidly. In the second year, however, we ran into trouble. The whole operation began to take on a sordid aspect, even though there were certainly some marvellous attractions introduced. (I remember a magnificent water chute which I opened jointly with Margaret Thatcher, then a junior minister, and a very attractive junior minister she was too. I have a photograph of us sliding together down the chute!) Unfortunately we started to attract a certain element of rowdies and Teddy boys. It was not the sort of atmosphere with which I wanted Forte's to be connected, and although we kept our involvement going for three years I became very disenchanted with the project. Eventually the local council, quite rightly, refused to extend the lease and that was that. We closed the place down. I can't say I was unhappy, and I certainly was not proud of this venture. It might have turned out differently, I suppose, becoming something that could have been of permanent value to London, akin even to the inspiration and merit of Disneyland, but it was not to be.

I continued in association with Leslie Joseph. Some time later the Bellevue leisure complex in Manchester came up for sale. We went to see it together. It was a depressing sight and had deteriorated badly. It consisted of a zoo, an amusement park, plus catering and banqueting facilities. There was an arena where boxing and wrestling took place, and which was occasionally used as a concert hall. There were two public houses and a speedway motor-cycle track. We decided to acquire it, organized it as a subsidiary, and put in Leslie Joseph, who had by this time been knighted for his work for the Festival of Britain, as chairman.

Leslie was very interested in wild life and the animal world. He transformed the zoo, providing landscaping and more comfortable quarters for the animals. The other parts of Bellevue were also improved. I supported him in every way possible and Bellevue was reborn. It began to make reasonable profits but eventually we sold it – I have always been chary of anything outside the mainstream of our business. Leslie continued with the company and remained a main board director until recently.

I and my close colleagues were now beginning to apply the classic methods of administration and control. None of us had grown up in the world of big business. No one had worked for any of the major companies, or attended business schools. We had learnt through experience that we had to become a properly organized entity. So from time to time we consulted management experts, and even at one time employed one of them on the premises: Bob Fry stayed with us for several years and from him I learned a great deal of the theory of management. We began to realize what an organization chart meant, and the importance of communication at the top and throughout the company. We have always been prepared to learn and I am happy to say that I am still learning.

The next concern which attracted my interest was Slaters and Bodega, a well-known public company, mainly caterers and food merchants, with quite a mixture of interests. The business was far bigger than Forte's but not as profitable – they had an ice-cream factory, a bakery, a fleet of vans and large warehouses. They were fishmongers, greengrocers, butchers and also had wine shops. They had some good properties around London. The executive chairman was Ronald Field, who was a large shareholder in his own right. I went to see him one day and told him I was interested in buying the company. Would he consider an offer? I mentioned a figure. He listened with interest.

A day or two later our meeting was leaked to the press and the shares went up. Some time later I received a letter from Mr Field saying that he was not prepared to consider my offer. Again this was leaked to the press, and the shares went down. I went back to see him and offered to increase my bid. He requested time to think the matter over. Yet again the press got wind of our meeting and the shares went up again. A few weeks later he wrote to me saying that his board had turned down the offer. This was duly communicated to the press and the shares went down accordingly.

I made yet another appointment to see Mr Field. In the tray on his desk, very careless on his part, there were stockbrokers' slips covering transactions in Slaters and Bodega shares. This man is playing me like a fish for his own benefit, I thought to myself, and became very angry. They call it 'insider trading' these days and it is a punishable offence. It is a practice which neither I nor any colleague of mine, nor my company, has ever indulged in. It is a way of making money on the side out of your own shareholders, like burglary without the risk that a burglar takes in breaking and entering.

Mr Field was a highly respected figure in the industry. If we had been seen together I do not doubt that people would have thought him an honest man and me a dubious go-getter. I decided that somehow I must put a stop to this.

In these negotiations I had also been working with an estate agent called Claude Hershman, who had first mentioned the Slaters and Bodega situation to me. He had appraised the value of the Slaters' shops, restaurants and other properties, and was due to make a fee out of the deal when it was agreed. Claude, as well as being a nice man, was an honest one.

'You know, Claude,' I said to him, 'we will never do a deal with Field, never, unless we force him into it.'

'How are you going to do that?'

'By putting the deal on paper and telling him this is the price we are going to offer. Then we will say, either you accept it and recommend it to the shareholders or we make an offer direct to them, and I am sure that we will get enough shares to gain control. When that happens you will receive no compensation for loss of office.'

'That won't work,' said Claude.

'Let's try.'

I went to Sir John Campbell at Clydesdale Bank. 'Look John, I want to make a bid for Slaters and Bodega,' I said, and I explained the deal to him.

'And how are you going to pay me back?' He was off again!

'By taking lease-backs.' I had learnt a lot from Joe Levy by now. 'We have a valuation on the properties. We will lease the properties back; there is more than enough to satisfy you and if there is anything left over in the way of a loan we will pay you back a little at a time.'

Even though our business was now a substantial one John insisted on a personal guarantee. We were looking at a sum of around £1.5 million.

'You know very well that if anything goes wrong, I wouldn't be able to pay that back for a long time, if at all,' I said.

'I understand that, but it would help to convince my board.'

'All right, I'll guarantee it.'

I don't think all my shareholders realize the personal risks I took in days gone by. But, of course, I knew the value of the assets, and thus knew it was a very remote chance that my guarantee would be called in. The other condition Sir John imposed was that again I should obtain one hundred per cent of the shares. Obviously if I could not get one hundred per cent of the shares, I could not mortgage the company and pay the debts.

When financing had been agreed, I went back to Field but did not tell him the conditions on which the bank were prepared to advance me the money. After all it was none of his business. I had taken the precaution of bringing Claude Hershman with me as a witness.

I came straight to the point. 'Look, Mr Field, I will make a public offer for the shares and I am going to announce this offer tomorrow. I hope you will support me.' I handed him the letter with the terms of the offer spelt out. Again he demurred.

'You know very well that with this offer I will get at least fifty-one per cent of the shares,' I said, 'and will therefore control the company. When I do, you will be out unless you support me.'

What I did not add was that if I only had fifty-one per cent of the shares, I would not have found it easy to raise the money to buy the company.

'Let me think about it,' he replied.

'There's no thinking about it,' I insisted. 'I am making this offer public tomorrow.'

I had been very careful to make the appointment for about four o'clock, which was after the Stock Exchange closed. I was not prepared to let him deal in any more shares.

'Well, what is my shareholding worth?' he asked.

'If you support it, we will pay you whatever your shares are valued at,' I told him.

'I want more than that for my shares.'

'All right, we will pay you compensation for resigning as chairman.'

I made an offer to the shareholders. Field recommended it and sold his shares, as did more than ninety per cent of his shareholders, and I was able to call in the rest. The bank advanced me the money and we incorporated Slaters and Bodega into the Forte Company.

It is interesting to note that raising the £1.5 million for Slaters and Bodega was probably easier than raising loans of lesser amounts for my own company for previous deals. This was because Slaters and Bodega had such valuable properties. By selling some properties that we did not need and leasing others back to the company, we got all our money back and were able to pay back the bank and everyone else. We were left with a thriving business.

Our other major purchase in this year, 1954, gave me more pleasure than almost anything else I have ever done. During those solitary days before the war when I walked the streets of London looking for a site for my first milk bar, my principal pleasure, as I have mentioned, had been to go and sit in the Café Royal and order a glass of lager and a smoked salmon sandwich. For me it still represented the literary and cultural hub of the capital. Even then I suspect I was a decade or two late. It was, however, full of life; and the plush seats, the gilding and the chandeliers gave it an atmosphere which I found nowhere else.

I now heard that the Café Royal was up for sale. It had belonged to the Bracewell Smith family. They had recently sold the Café Royal to a City consortium headed by a very well-known accountant-entrepreneur named Russell Tillett. The Café Royal was, and is, a complex of remarkable restaurants and banqueting rooms. The Grill Room remains exactly as it was a hundred years ago. But the Bracewell Smiths, who should have known better, destroyed the restaurant, reducing it to something very ordinary. It had been losing money, but not at a great rate. It was, however, becoming a little seedy and run down. I made an appointment with Russell Tillett and he was kind enough to give me lunch in the Café Royal Grill. All the emotions of my early twenties came flooding back and I felt that the aura of those artists and writers of the past still lingered. As well as being a practical businessman, I have always been a romantic.

Russell Tillett was exceptionally agreeable. He explained that although his group were still trying to run the establishment, they were not really caterers, relying on the general manager, a wonderful fellow called Jules, a Frenchman by origin, who was doing his best to maintain its standards and character. It was not making any money, however, and they wanted to sell it. Did I want to buy it?

'Yes,' I said, 'how much do you want?'

He named a very acceptable figure. I think it was about £240,000, but by then it was losing something like £40,000 to £50,000 a year. Russell Tillett took me back to his office and showed me the accounts, which I then took away and analysed with my associates. We were in very little doubt that we could turn the whole business round. It was time to see Sir John Campbell at Clydesdale Bank again. This time he was in an implacable mood.

Both I and my company had borrowed heavily with all the purchases I have mentioned, and including one that I will mention later the Café Monico.

'Well, John, how are you?'

'I'm all right, Charles. How are you?'

'Very good,' I said. 'Business is excellent.'

'Yes, I can see money coming into the bank, but I did not know it was as good as all that.'

'Oh yes, it is absolutely first class.' We were in fact doing very well, but I was making the most of it.

'Well, what can I do for you?'

'John, the Café Royal is for sale.'

'Get out of here,' he said. He knew what was coming!

'What do you mean, "Get out of here"?'

'Don't you ask me for a penny. You owe me a lot of money.'

'Please John, I have met all my obligations to you. I have paid your interest. I am repaying all my loans on schedule.'

'Yes, but you've got too much money on loan. I can't look at another thing.'

'John, you must give me the money to buy the Café Royal. It will be a terrific asset to my company and I will pay you back. You know I have always paid you back. I have not had the time to arrange everything in advance for your convenience; you do something to help me this time.'

'Help you?' he said, 'I've done nothing else but help you.'

I would not say that we had a row, because it was between friends, but we had quite a ding-dong argument and I walked out of the bank very despondent, without the promise of even a penny.

For God's sake, I said to myself, what am I going to do now? I had to have the Café Royal. I had more or less intimated to Russell Tillett that I would buy it and he was getting all the documents ready. I had told him I could not pay all the money at once, but he had told his colleagues and obtained their agreement. They were laying out all the papers on a particular day and I had to sign the agreement. It taught me another lesson. Never move a step until the money is there and never count the money until it is in the till or you have got it in the bank.

I had discussed the purchase thoroughly with my colleagues and we all agreed that it was an exceptional deal. So I went back to see Russell Tillett. I was finding that I had a lot in common with him. He was a man of great humour – he had to be, dealing with me at that time! He was a marvellous businessman, but one with feeling.

'Look,' I told him, 'I can't do this deal of yours unless we do it on the never-never principle.'

'What do you mean exactly?'

'Well, can I put some money down – the least possible – and pay you over five years?'

'How much down?'

I did not have the courage to say 'nothing'. 'Fifty thousand.'

He thought about it. 'That's a reasonable sum of money. All right, and you will pay me the interest on the balance.' I agreed.

'Right, then we will draw up a contract for that. I want to sell the place; it is losing money; you are the chap to run it. I like you and . . . all right, you pay me fifty thousand and pay me back over a three- or five-year period.'

The day arrived for signing the contract. A meeting had been arranged with the accountants Shipley and Blackburn, solicitors Paisner & Co., Russell Tillett, and two of his partners. Unfortunately I was still running round looking for the money.

On the morning of the meeting, I said to Rex Henshall, then the company secretary, 'Rex, how much do you think we can draw from the bank without John Campbell shooting us?'

'Ten thousand?'

I told him to write a cheque for £15,000. I put the cheque in my waistcoat pocket and rushed down to the City in time for the meeting. I went to Russell's office where he was sitting at the head of the table, together with the solicitors and accountants. 'Russell,' I said, 'can I have a word with you?'

He looked at me suspiciously. 'Why?'

'I must talk to you urgently, in private. I cannot talk to you here.'

'Privately?' he said, 'these are my colleagues.'

'No,' I said, 'I would like to talk to you on your own, please.'

'Right. Come through here.' We got up and walked to the next-door office.

'Mr Tillett, I have a confession to make. I am here to sign the agreement.'

'Yes, indeed you are,' he said.

I took the cheque out of my pocket and waved it around. 'I can't find fifty thousand,' I said. 'But I have got fifteen thousand.' I waved the cheque in front of his nose. 'As a matter of fact, I cannot even afford to give you this. I was not able to borrow the money.'

'Oh,' he said, 'you can't. Well, that's different, but you know we have gone to a lot of expense and trouble already. The papers are all prepared. Now you say you can't go through with it because you haven't got the money. Why didn't you tell me?'

I told him the story of how I had gone to see Sir John, whom he knew well.

'He wouldn't give me the money. He has always helped me before, but I could not move him this time. I have this cheque for £15,000, will that do?'

'Oh,' he said. 'Much too little. We agreed a down payment of £50,000. That's little enough,' he added.

'But,' I went on, 'quite frankly, I would rather not give you this either, because it is going to be a bit of an effort for the bank to meet it. He will meet it, but I would rather make it out for ten thousand.'

Russell Tillett was looking at me in wonderment. 'But the deal is for a part payment of £50,000.'

'I am sorry,' I said, 'I cannot manage anything more than the

sum I've mentioned or,' – and I blush to this day at my effrontery
– 'could you help find me the money?'

'Me?' he asked.

'Do you know of any of the banks that would lend it to me?'

'Let me try the Bank of America,' he said. He did not go up in
the air. He did not shout. He did not say 'you so-and-so'. He
merely picked up the telephone and spoke to the manager of that
bank.

'Russell Tillett here,' he said calmly. 'I have got Charles Forte
with me.'

The man on the other end obviously said 'Who the hell is
Charles Forte?'

'Don't you know him?' Russell Tillett said. 'He is quite well-
known, the catering man. I have done a deal with him on the Café
Royal, and he wants to borrow £50,000. Would you lend him the
money?'

Obviously the answer was no.

So I interjected: 'Mr Tillett, he will lend me the money if you
will guarantee it.'

'Me guarantee it?' This really shook him. '*Me*? Hold on a
minute: *me* guarantee it? You are buying the business from me and
I have got to guarantee the money?'

'Look, Russell, if you want to do this deal, this is the only way.
You guarantee it and let me have the money. I in turn will
guarantee it to you.'

'But will you guarantee it?'

'Of course I will, personally.'

He looked at me sideways and said into the telephone: 'Would
you let him have the fifty thousand if I guarantee it?' The answer
was yes. 'Well, we'll be round in a quarter of an hour. Thank you
very much; see you immediately.'

He put down the 'phone and we took a taxi straight round to
the Bank of America. There we signed papers guaranteeing the
money, the bank manager gave me a draft and we went back to
the office, where I signed the agreement, handed over the cheque,
put my own cheque for £15,000 back in my waistcoat pocket and
returned to join my colleagues, who were eagerly awaiting the
result.

'We haven't paid for it yet,' I said, 'but we've bought it.'

The Café Royal had been losing money for all the usual reasons. It could not attract enough customers because to do that you have to give value. But it was impossible for it to give value while its management was wasting so much. The management of the Café Royal required reorganizing from top to bottom. The food and the service were adequate, but only just. The controls were non-existent, and controls in an operation of this kind and size are absolutely essential. Otherwise how does one avoid pilfering and waste where expensive commodities like wine, liqueurs, spirits, caviar, and smoked salmon are in abundance?

Moreover, the Café Royal had become a bit shabby, even though it still retained the aura of a great establishment. I felt it my duty to restore it to its former grandeur, which I did, spending a considerable amount of money in the process. As often happens when you make this sort of effort, the business takes off. The Café Royal was no exception. We could afford to advertise and soon we found that we were making a profit.

In the course of two and a half years, I repaid the Bank of America and paid Russell Tillett the balance of the money I owed him, in four instalments with interest. It turned out to be a good deal for all concerned. And it had been possible because I had had the good fortune to meet a man with imagination who trusted me.

It was during this period that I first became familiar with politicians, particularly Hugh Gaitskell. I admired him enormously, and we got to know each other well. It was through him that I met many of the leading lights of the Labour Party, including Alf Robens, who came on to the board during the Trust Houses v. Forte battle and is still on my board.

Though I am not and never have been a Labour supporter, I am a great believer in a good, strong, opposition party. I don't believe in waste and in hand-outs to those who do not need them. But I think the less well-off should be helped without stint, and I also believe passionately in the Welfare State, strange as that may seem. In order to fulfil its obligations to the less well-off, the country must be prosperous, and in my opinion prosperity can only be achieved through free enterprise.

This is why I supported Hugh Gaitskell in his fight against a section of his party's attempt to impose a high degree of nationalization on British industries. I also agreed with much else he was trying to do, and admired his personal and political integrity enormously. It was a tragedy for the country and for the Labour Party when he died.

Hugh showed his gratitude to me for my support in many ways, including this letter he wrote to me:

My dear Charles,

I have been meaning to write to you for some time. As you know, things have gone remarkably well inside the Party. And for this a very large amount of credit must go to our friends of the Campaign for Democratic Socialism, which you have helped so generously. Indeed it is no exaggeration to say that without this organisation in the field we would never have succeeded.

I want you to know how deeply I appreciate all that you have done. It is easy enough [to be] friends when all is going well – but the ones who really matter are those who are most closely by you in the most difficult hours. Thank you for your ever staunch support, which in no small measure contributed to what I believe may have been the saving of the Labour Party.

Love to you both
Hugh

At the end of the 1950s, Alf Robens paid me a visit on Hugh's behalf. He told me that Hugh, as Leader of the Opposition, was entitled to nominate four peers and wanted me to be one of them. I told Alf that I was not a member of the Labour Party, and had no intention of ever becoming one, and could not see any possibility of ever voting Labour. I was a hundred per cent for free enterprise and nought per cent for socialism. So while I was deeply moved by Hugh's offer and most grateful for it, I could not see how I could accept it.

Alf was persuasive, and said that it did not matter that I was not a socialist. I could always sit on the cross-benches. I must admit that I liked the idea of being a lord: as an honour from my adopted country, it would have meant a great deal to me. I would have been 'established', if not part of the establishment. I was tempted, but I told Alf I would like to think about the matter. I consulted my father, who told me he did not see how I could accept. My mother was pleased, but told me I had to make my own decision. I asked Irene, who was amused at the thought of my being a socialist peer. And finally I consulted Eric Hartwell, who advised me to accept. In his opinion, it would have been good for the business.

However, I decided in the end to turn down the peerage. I would have felt under an obligation to Hugh Gaitskell, and however much I admired him, he was still Leader of the Labour Party. At any rate, I have always treasured his gesture, and, indeed, my friendship with this extraordinary man and politician.

CHAPTER SEVEN

My First Hotel

AFTER THOSE FOUR hectic years of acquisition and breaking new ground, my partners and I could have been forgiven had we engaged in a period of quiet consolidation. It did not work out that way. We had acquired a mutual confidence. We had satisfied ourselves that our management techniques worked, our systems of financial and administrative control were successful in practice, our purchasing methods were soundly based, and that we were recruiting and training the right sort of staff. We had, in fact, established a method of working which meant that we were capable of greater expansion. The momentum was continued.

Another property which we acquired was the Café Monico, situated on the corner of Piccadilly Circus. This formerly fashionable restaurant had been shut down and I purchased the headlease from the Express Dairy Company, who at that time had substantial interests in catering. We took over the Monico, opening up a top-class restaurant downstairs and banqueting accommodation on the first and second floors, and converting the top floor into a new set of offices.

It made an agreeable change from Percy Street. Leonard Rosso remembers the move well. I had teased him: 'I am going to give you an office at the top of the Monico, so that you can get plenty of exercise and stay fit and healthy.' His office on the sixth floor was pleasant and spacious, but there was no lift. Occasionally he dropped a remark about this, while I persisted in reminding him that it was good for his health!

My activities were occasionally featured in the press and people were now beginning to recognize my company as up-and-coming caterers. We certainly ran some well-known establishments, and it was at this time that Patrick Sergeant, who now writes for the *Daily Mail*, gave me the soubriquet of 'Mr Piccadilly', in recognition of all the properties we had obtained in the area. I did not like the title, but I did find that it helped with business and made people even more aware of the firm's presence.

One initiative which obtained a certain amount of publicity was my suggestion to the National Sporting Club that they move their events to the big room on the fourth floor of the Café Royal. The club was an old-established institution, dating back to the nineteenth century, which staged formal boxing matches, with the patrons, club members and guests in dinner jackets. Complete silence was maintained during each round, and in the old days a shower of sovereigns was thrown into the ring after a particularly good bout. The club's popularity was in decline and it was operating out of not particularly suitable premises in Berkeley Square. With the decline in membership, the club's finances were in a bad way. The secretary and factotum, John Harding, had been attempting to hold things together financially. He eventually asked me to take over what was, in fact, a limited company. I did so for two reasons: first, because I could see the commercial advantage in having the club at the Café Royal; and second, because I was very interested in sport and the revival of such a distinguished club intrigued me.

The members of the National Sporting Club were pleased to make the move. It gave the club a shot in the arm and, indeed, it remained at the Café Royal for some time. I am not a keen boxing fan, but was most honoured to be made president by the members. When the National Sporting Club and the World Sporting Club amalgamated, and in view of the size of the new club, it transferred functions to the Great Room at Grosvenor House, where it met under the chairmanship of my friend Jervis Astaire.

Another exceedingly pleasant involvement of mine at this time, the memory of which I still treasure, was with Winston Churchill. I had been approached by Edward Martell, the then editor and proprietor of the *Recorder*, who had formed a small organizing body to collect money for the Churchill Fund, to present Sir Winston with a large cheque on his eightieth birthday. I was one of the contributors and also played an active part in the general fund-raising, having become friendly with Edward. We succeeded in raising what in those days was a huge sum, something like £325,000, and Edward and I were invited to 10 Downing Street to make the presentation.

I had never been there before and was thrilled. It seemed a long way from Alloa! Sir Winston came in, looking pink and fresh, and, although rotund, very elegant in his black jacket, striped trousers and silver-grey tie. 'Pray be seated, gentlemen,' he said courteously. The butler came in with champagne, and the great man put us at our ease.

In the commonly held belief that Churchill was a rich man we had written to him before we launched the appeal asking if he would nominate how the funds donated were to be spent, to which he agreed. As the donations poured in, however, we were asked by one of his closest associates, Sir John Colville, if some of the money could be set aside for Churchill's personal use, and we learned that far from being wealthy he was so short of funds that he had put his London house in Kensington up for sale. Most of his earnings from his writings had gone into a trust for his children. It will be recalled that after the First World War Lloyd George and other war leaders were voted substantial sums by Parliament. No such presentations were made after the Second World War.

We told Sir John, of course, that the money being subscribed by the public was for Churchill to spend exactly as he chose. When we asked if he would agree to such a course, he was by no means displeased and Edward was present when the estate agents were telephoned and the house taken off their books.

I remember thinking at the time what an extraordinary situation had been disclosed to us: here was a man who had been instrumental in saving Britain at her time of deepest need, but who had been forced to put his house on the market for lack of money. I wonder whether this could have happened in any other country.

We therefore presented him with a cheque for £150,000 for his personal use. It had been inscribed on vellum by the College of Arms. The balance of the money, which had come in from nearly half a million subscribers, went to a number of charities and to help finance the founding of Churchill College at Cambridge.

But to return to business. We were soon putting our accumulated knowledge and experience to further good effect. The new London Airport at Heathrow was in the early stages of being built – it sometimes seems to me that it still is. Nevertheless I am always astonished by the enormous amount of activity and the huge flow of passengers it copes with so efficiently. The airport invited tenders from catering organizations and we were successful in acquiring one of the concessions. This was the beginning of our airport operation, which now services fifty-three restaurants and buffets, forty bars and eight VIP lounges at fourteen European airports as well as over one hundred airlines with inflight catering. Such catering is hard work. People simply don't realize the demands of the job, striving for perfection twenty-four hours a day, 365 days a year. It is always easy to criticize the caterer's efficiency in such situations, but efficiency is difficult to achieve. However, if anyone achieved it, I believe we did.

The British Airports Authority struck a hard bargain, demanding a rent and a percentage of our turnover. The initial period was extremely difficult. The main building was only partly constructed and there were no lifts in the restaurant. We had to peel potatoes in the basement, haul churns of them up three flights of stairs, and adopt a hand-to-mouth type of management which was definitely out of character for Forte's. We survived all the growing pains of Heathrow catering, but got little thanks for our efforts. Being a public body, the authority had to re-offer the tenders at regular intervals. A rival offered better terms and we lost the concession. Fortunately for us, and I say this without malice, the complaints then trebled and quadrupled, so back the authority came to us.

At this time I also acquired a somewhat unusual outside directorship. In 1956 I joined the board of Sidgwick & Jackson, the publishers, who were responsible for the first edition of this book. The chairman was then Jimmy Knapp-Fisher, my old partner nearly twenty years previously, who had put some capital into my early milk bars and had then stood bond for me when we ran into a brief cash flow crisis shortly before the war. Jimmy had a house in Wilton Crescent, which he also used as his editorial headquarters. Nearing retirement, he wished to guarantee the future of Sidgwick & Jackson. The firm needed a loan to give it a new lease of life so I provided £50,000 of my own money and joined the board.

In fact I eventually more or less took over the company and gave Jimmy a guaranteed income for life. We remained close friends until his death in 1976. When he retired I brought in new management, which succeeded in turning the firm round. Jimmy was sufficiently grateful to go round telling everyone the story. I felt it was the least return I could make for his kindness in helping me when I needed it.

This involvement with the literary world which I enjoyed (and indeed still enjoy) did not take my eye off the mainstream of my business. One day in 1957 I was having lunch with Bernard Delfont, who is the impresario, and one of the famous Grade brothers (Delfont was actually a stage name). The London Hippodrome was coming to the end of its days as a music-hall and Bernard wanted to take it over and convert it into a theatre restaurant. It was a marvellous site and his idea seemed sound. So we went into partnership, bought the restaurant and changed its title to 'Talk of the Town'. Bernard was responsible for the theatrical side and Forte's for the catering and general administration. It was a great success and remained one of the main popular attractions of central London for the next twenty-five years.

The Hungaria Restaurant in Lower Regent Street was another acquisition. It was a handsome establishment, well run and reasonably profitable, but the owners wanted to sell. We bought it, redecorated it, and continued to maintain it as a luxury restaurant. In due course we changed the name to the Hunting Lodge. This was something of an experiment on our part. We wanted to see if we could move up-market. With the exception of the Café Royal most of our restaurants were popular ones and we tried to make the Hungaria one of the most fashionable and luxurious places to dine in London. We succeeded for many years, but eventually had to give it up because the original lease came to an end and the terms of the new lease were beyond the capacity of any luxury restaurant to meet. Running a luxury restaurant in isolation can be difficult because of the space required and the cost of that space in a key position and we now prefer to maintain our high-class restaurants within our hotels, where we can charge ourselves a reasonable rental and where the management expertise is available on the spot.

To be really outstanding a luxury restaurant must be individualistic. It must reflect the personality of *le patron*, the man who is always there, who knows and greets his customers, who caters for their special requirements as well as their palates, who makes them feel that they are in a private home. He must also be a professional restaurateur of the first order, with an intimate knowledge of *haute cuisine*, and a recognition of good design and décor. To achieve all this requires a touch of genius and the best restaurateurs have always been rare indeed, and so are first-class restaurant managers.

John Quaglino was such a restaurateur. He and his brother Ernest created a restaurant before the war which I believe has never had its equal. It was very expensive. Although I could hardly afford it I used to go for its exquisite food, beauty and atmosphere. On one occasion I remember the clientèle included the Prince of Wales, King Alfonso of Spain, and King Carol of Rumania. Only John Quaglino could have managed that combination. Royalty, even minor royalty, require great skill to handle correctly. They must be treated with respect but without fuss.

John was a short, plump man, immaculately turned out, with an attractive, frog-like face. Ernest was younger, taller and very good looking. John's genius was born out of experience. He had worked in the grandest hotels in Monte Carlo and Cannes. At seventeen he was *maître d'hôtel* in the famous Martinez at Cannes.

The brothers had come to England and worked at the Savoy and several of the better hotels in London before eventually opening their own restaurant. Everything about Quaglino's was superb – the food, wine, décor, comfort, linen, glassware and silver. It is difficult, perhaps impossible, to achieve perfection in our trade, but John came nearest to it.

His manner was perfect too. Every guest was made to feel that he was the only person who mattered. 'How marvellous to see you,' he would say. 'Why don't you sit over there? You know you are my best customer. I do not let anyone else have this table. Even if the Queen came in, she would have to sit somewhere else.'

That was the atmosphere he established and you left his restaurant feeling on top of the world. He gave good value, marvellous service, first-class food and made a lot of money.

Before the Second World War Quaglino's became a public company. With the money thus realized John and Ernest bought the Normandy Hotel in Knightsbridge. Quaglino's itself became part of Queen Anne's Hotel and Property Ltd, which in 1964 became part of Trusthouse Forte.

Like me, the Quaglinos suffered during the war because of their Italian nationality. Reluctantly they chose to return to Italy rather than be interned on the Isle of Man. They were later imprisoned in Italy for anti-fascist attitudes and, in view of this, it is all the more surprising that after the war they were not permitted to return here. A pompous politician whom I approached said: 'Well, they backed the wrong horse, didn't they?'

I replied: 'I haven't come to discuss horses; I have come to discuss two human beings.'

John Quaglino was allowed back into England only for short periods and he could see that his business was in a bad way, sorely in need of his constant personal supervision. Moreover, some unscrupulous operators were trying to pick up the business for considerably less than its real value. They even tried to involve me in these designs.

I felt so strongly about the Quaglinos that I managed to arrange an appointment with the Permanent Secretary at the Home Office, an impressive man called Sir Frank Newsam. He listened carefully to my story: I explained the Quaglinos' anti-fascist background, what useful and talented people they were, and how I felt that they were in danger of being cheated if they did not return. Sir Frank asked me if I was their agent, business partner or solicitor. I told him that I was none of these things, simply making my representation out of friendship, and also to see justice was done. I am glad to say that Sir Frank acted promptly and the Quaglinos returned to run their business.

As a contrast to the Quaglinos I am still reminded of another very famous *patron* named Stocco, who ran the Café Anglais in Leicester Square. It was a lovely place but it gradually went downhill because Stocco had the wrong manner. He was a handsome, well-turned-out man in his Savile Row suits, but he was a big talker. 'How nice to see you, do sit down,' he would say and then, knowing that I was in the profession, he would add: 'you know, yesterday I did two hundred covers here.' He had not; he had done fifty and you knew he had done fifty. Then he would go on: 'Where you are sitting now, I had Princess Margaret sitting yesterday.' I don't doubt that he had told *her* that the Queen had been there the day before. And if it was a baron sitting down, the fellow sitting there previously would have been a viscount.

But to return to the Quaglinos. They came back to Britain, and after a short while the Normandy Hotel flourished again, going from strength to strength, with John and Ernest presiding and ministering to customers with their inimitable good taste. Eventually John and Ernest sold the hotel for a considerable sum of money.

In 1958 we involved ourselves in what was perhaps our most significant venture so far. It was made possible by a fortunate conjunction of events. I was first approached about the purchase of the Waldorf Hotel in the Aldwych. At the same time Jack Cotton indicated to us that his redevelopment plans for Piccadilly Circus were reaching an interesting stage and that he would like to acquire the lease of the Monico site from us so that he could incorporate it in the great piazza which the American architect had designed for him.

The Waldorf was a respectable upper-middle-grade hotel with its own freehold site, part of Frederick Hotels Ltd, an old-established hotel company which was controlled and directed by Sir Stuart Goodwin. Stuart was also chairman of the Neeps End Steel Corporation. He was in fact more of an industrialist than a hotelier, hence his reasons for making the sale.

Forte's was then concerned solely with catering and entertainment. I was intrigued by the hotel business. I wanted to broaden the character of our activities and indeed I believed we could apply the methods which worked so well for us in our current business to the running of hotels. I also felt that the addition of a hotel would make us a better balanced concern, although I knew

Just arrived from Italy: 'The Immigrants,' my parents,
Uncle Alfonso (*standing*), and me.

My birthplace, *Monforte*, with the Abruzzi mountains
in the background.
Inset: On one of my rare visits.

(*standing*) Cousin Charles, Anna, me, Uncle Alfonso;
(*seated*) Mother and Father.

TWO CONTRASTING FAMILY GROUPS, MANY MILES AND
MANY YEARS APART.
Above: *Monforte.* Uncle Alfonso surrounded by relatives and friends.
Below: *London.* Irene and me surrounded by our family, *from left to right*, Portia,
Giancarla, Robert Burness (husband of Marie-Louise), Olga, Rocco, Irene,
Marie-Louise, John Danilovich (husband of Irene), and Michael Alen-Buckley
(husband of Giancarla).

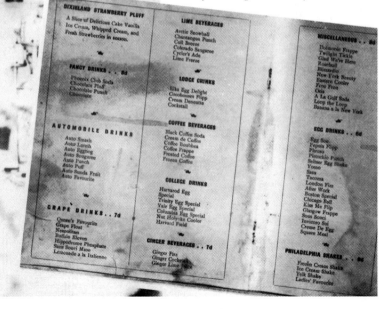

Above: Uncle Alfonso's shop in Loanhead,
in which my father was a partner.
Below: The menu in the *Savoy Café*
at Alloa.

Left: Making coffee in my first milk bar.

The Waldorf – my first hotel. *Inset*: The famous Grill Room in the *Café Royal*'s wine cellar and Rocco working in the *Café Royal*'s wine cellar.

Hotel bid by milk bar king

Star Reporter

MR CHARLES FORTE, THE RESTAURATEUR, IS THE MAN BEHIND THE TAKE - OVER BID FOR THE WALDORF HOTEL IN ALDWYCH.

The offer was fore-shadowed yesterday by Sir Stuart Goodwin, chairman of the Waldorf.

Mr Forte said this after-noon:

"Sir Stuart Goodwin will announce my terms next week.

'My plan . . .'

"I plan to carry on the Waldorf as it is now more or less on the same lines as at present.

"While I have no definite plan in mind at the moment I certainly would be interested

Mr Charles Forte.

in further hotel businesses if opportunities arose."

nothing about the running of hotels at that time. My only experience was limited to staying in them.

I do not know how my name and activities had come to the notice of Sir Stuart, but it was probably through the press. He invited me up to his Sheffield home. I remember that this was not a luxurious residence, but comfortable and nicely appointed. He was a modest, straightforward man with a most agreeable personality.

He came straight to the point: 'I would like to sell the Waldorf. I have already made up my mind about the price I want. I am not going to put it up for auction and I do not want to bargain about figures. If you agree the price, you can have the hotel.'

The price he named was £600,000. It was a wonderful opportunity. There were many companies and individuals who would have been glad to have paid that for the Waldorf and I am still mystified as to why I was his choice. My company did not have the capacity to borrow £600,000, the equivalent probably of about £5 million today. So my next conversation with Jack Cotton about the Monico lease was both timely and very important to me. Of course, I entered our negotiations without any overt signs of enthusiasm.

'Look, Jack,' I said, 'we are doing well here and I don't want to leave. We have spent a lot of money in getting this place up to standards.'

'How much have you spent?'

'Oh, something like a hundred thousand.'

'Well,' he said, 'I'll give you a profit on your lease.'

'How much?'

'What about half a million pounds?' he replied.

I could hardly believe my good fortune. This transaction would realize all but £100,000 of the purchase price of the Waldorf. I knew that I could raise the balance of the money and, indeed, more money than I needed to refurbish the Waldorf on a sale and lease-back arrangement, which I quickly managed to achieve with the Prudential Assurance, who bought the freehold from me and granted me a ninety-nine-year lease. And so I acquired my first hotel.

Looking back on my early career I can see that my ability to raise money at decisive moments was of crucial importance to me. I had already successfully used the sale and lease-back arrangement to finance some purchases, and I had also negotiated loans and credits to finance others, such as the Café Royal. It is worth stressing again that my reputation for financial probity and for being professional and hard-working was, and would be, crucial to my success. Although sale and lease-back arrangements have gone out of favour today, the reputation of the borrower or the lessee is still paramount.

The Waldorf was the precursor of more than eight hundred hotels that we later owned, leased, or managed, and its purchase opened a whole new chapter in our lives. My first priority was to obtain a top-class manager. After due enquiry I engaged John Lee, who had been the general manager of the Dorchester. He was the complete hotelier and I learnt a lot from him. I now understood the economics of running a business but there was a lot I had to learn about the hotel trade, which is a world on its own, involving the complicated transactions of bookings, sales, contact with agents and general running of the hotel. John Lee carried me through step by step and it is largely due to him that the ins and outs of the hotel business are now second nature to me.

The Waldorf was a major step forward but we were still laying foundations in other areas on which we have subsequently built. The motorway era was coming to Britain, thirty years later than in Germany and America, but it was about to revolutionize the country's communications. Motorways usually ran through the middle of nowhere, skirting towns and villages, bypassing the existing hotel and inn network. The planners had realized that a pause for rest and refreshment on these long journeys would be essential and tenders were invited, under very strict control and conditions, to build and operate motorway restaurants and petrol stations.

The idea intrigued me and I suggested to my colleagues that we should become involved. We obtained the figures from the Ministry of Transport of the number of vehicles they expected to make use of the new M1 and it soon became clear that this would provide an important new market for us. Travel is an essential part of our lives and even if people were going to halve the time spent travelling long distances, they still needed refreshment and comfort on the way.

We put in our tender, having carefully estimated the income. We offered a fixed basic rent and a percentage of the turnover. This met with the approval of the authorities and we were allotted our first site at Newport Pagnell in 1959. We were prepared to make a major investment in the project and erected a spacious building carefully designed to serve thousands of people a day. By the time the motorway network had extended to most of the country, this pioneer establishment served forty thousand people a week with snacks and hot food. The effort involved in providing such a service is tremendous.

At that time our name became identified with the whole motorway service area operation and we were criticized for inferior food and service and blamed very often for operations in which we were not involved.

At one point we introduced, in common with the other motorway operators, gambling machines – slot machines and one-armed bandits; this against my personal better judgement. The machines in question made a lot of money, but they attracted the wrong type of person and gave the wrong impression of the establishment to our regular customers. Furthermore, a certain proportion of very young people were attracted to these gambling machines. Eventually I had them removed, and though their removal caused a considerable drop in turnover and profit I have never regretted taking the action I did.

One of my first competitors in London was a colourful character called Kenneth Hall. Kenneth and his brother had come over from Australia, and with the help of Hugh D. Macintosh, to whom I had once offered my services, had opened the first of his Quality Inns, which subsequently grew into a successful chain. The first one (just off Oxford Street, next door to the Palladium) opened up at the same time as I set up my first milk bar near the polytechnic in Upper Regent Street. (Their initial advertisement read 'Where is Quality Inn? Next door to the Palladium.' This was shortly changed to the highly successful, 'Where is the Palladium? Next door to Quality Inn.') Kenneth and I used to keep a watchful eye on one another. I would stroll down to Oxford Circus to see how many customers he had and he would walk up towards the BBC to count mine.

I was now in an expansionist mood and wanted to increase the size of our restaurant operations. I asked Kenneth Hall if he was interested in selling and I was delighted to find that he was. It was a straightforward financial deal, but Kenneth said that he would like to remain as an executive for a year to see that the take-over went smoothly. We became very good friends, to the extent that he was still with us twenty-five years later until his resignation on 31 December 1979. He died three years later.

He was a rather stout man, overweight for his height which was average, but he managed to preserve a considerable elegance with suits from Savile Row, shoes from Lobb, hats from Lock: he was a thorough *bon viveur*, liking the best cigars, wines and food, all of which he knew well.

In the course of carrying out his inspectoral duties for us he was once down in Brighton, in the Bodega restaurant. He found his lunch appalling and summoned the manager to give him a dressing down. The manager, shaken by the tirade, asked him who he was.

'I am a director of this company, Kenneth Hall. Don't you know me?'

'No, sir.'

'Well, don't you serve this rubbish any more.'

He came back to London a few days later to lecture me about improving our Brighton restaurant. I took the wind out of his sails when I told him that we had sold it the previous year. Kenneth eventually became a member of the main Trusthouse Forte board, never as a full-time executive but more as a senior freelance supervisor and critic. We did not impose any set rules on him, but he had lunch most days at one of our restaurants, entertained quite extensively, knew a lot of people and would draw any shortcomings to our attention. He was a friendly man and, despite the touch of abrasiveness he had about him, he was always popular. I valued his views and advice.

*

In 1962 we decided that the company should go public. Our entire growth up to that point had been within the framework of a private family concern. I was still the majority shareholder with other members of my family and, for some time my co-directors, apart from Eric Hartwell, had been employee executives of the company. However, as the business grew I enabled them to acquire shares, thus making them partners, which they had earned with their hard work and loyalty. My colleagues from those early days became wealthy men.

I was interested in expanding the company but found, however, that there was a limit to how fast and how large a private company could grow. A public company can raise capital much more easily, and without that, capital expansion is difficult. I had only to look abroad to see American hotel companies, such as Conrad Hilton's, building hotels all over the world. I could see clearly that my determination to pursue a policy of vigorous acquisition and expansion could only be achieved if the company went public.

I was influenced in this decision by a conversation with Sir Edward Beddington-Behrens of the Ocean Trust, who suggested the methods we might employ. I also had a number of serious talks with a highly regarded accountant named Tony Burney, now Sir Anthony Burney and one of the top men in his profession. Tony tells everyone that the first time he met me I was doing a handstand on my desk as part of my continuing effort to stay fit. He was undeterred by this unusual first meeting and recommended unequivocally that we should go public.

It was one of the most successful flotations in the history of the Stock Exchange until then. We put 600,000 5s. ordinary shares on the market, coupled with the purchase of 7 per cent preference £1 shares. We priced the package of two shares at £2. We were offering forty per cent of the shares in the company, my family, co-directors and I retaining sixty per cent. This issue was over-subscribed forty-three times. The ordinary shares promptly jumped up to 30s., thus making the whole concern worth about £10 million. It was just ten years since I had been told that I had made my first million.

What was satisfactory, but not all that common, was that the beneficiaries were the people who had actually built the business up, including my brother Michael and sister Anna. However, I have to say here that I had drifted a little apart from them. They had a few disagreements with other directors but I suspect the main cause of the problem was me. I had been a bit too forceful, even dictatorial, which younger brothers and sisters are the first to resent. I am sure I should have listened to them more than I did and tried to understand their point of view, although there were probably faults on both sides. They went their separate ways. Michael became a successful independent hotel man and one of his interests, which he sold, was the St George's Hotel in Llandudno. Anna came back with me again, working with my daughter Olga in the vital role of supervising the design and décor of our hotels. Both Michael and Anna remained substantial shareholders in the company, our disagreements long-forgotten.

CHAPTER EIGHT

Take-overs

ENRICO MATTEI WAS one of the most extraordinary and invigorating men I have ever met. He was the head of ENI, the nationalized Italian petrochemical conglomerate, one subsidiary of which was the chain of petrol stations called Agip, which have the distinctive trade mark, seen all over Italy, of the six-legged dog. ENI was an enormous company, one of the biggest of its kind in Europe. Mattei was a true *condottiere* in spirit, full of aggressive competitiveness, and something of a thorn in the side of even the largest international combine in his field. He was a man of great, almost overwhelming, charm, and I greatly enjoyed his company.

We had first met through a mutual friend. Mattei was fascinated by salmon fishing and, knowing that I was also a fisherman, wanted to know if I could find him some sport. At that time I was renting a stretch on the Dee in Scotland, and used to go up there regularly. Mattei joined me for a few days' successful salmon fishing, and immediately fell in love with the Dee Valley, which is one of my favourite spots in the world.

Not long after this he asked me to join him at a somewhat primitive, but comfortable fishing lodge, in the hills above Cortina d'Ampezzo, on a lake which provided good sport in the form of mountain trout and other freshwater fish. It was an enchanting spot thousands of feet up, and I became a regular visitor.

On one of my visits we were having a delightful break when the weather closed in on us and we had to retreat to the lodge for shelter. Mattei always travelled in style. He had a three-engined American jet that took him all over the world on business and on fishing expeditions, but even that could not get him up into the Dolomites. There was only a short landing strip near the lodge, so he had left the jet down in Milan and we had come up in a small Dove aeroplane that he used for short flights.

It was essential for Mattei to be back in Milan that evening, because he had an important board meeting the following morning.

'Enrico,' I cried, 'you are surely not going up in this bloody weather, are you?'

'I've got to.'

'You're mad.'

Then the pilot came in. 'You're not really taking off in this weather, are you?' I asked him.

'Well,' he said, 'it depends on the boss.'

'Can't you refuse?'

'Refuse? I don't think he will want to fly in this, though.'

Mattei was a man of courage. An hour or two later, the gusts of wind had let up slightly and they took off. The 'plane went up more or less sideways. My God, I thought, they are going to kill themselves. But the pilot was a very skilful man and on this occasion his luck held.

That was Enrico Mattei. He would bulldoze his way through anything.

In Rome on one occasion he said: 'Come to dinner.'

'But of course.' I said. 'Delighted!'

It was only then that I discovered that he was having dinner at the Quirinale with President Gronchi, and he was taking me along as a gate-crasher. I demurred at first, but he insisted and I was made warmly welcome. The Quirinale is the former Italian royal palace and I have seldom found myself in such elegant surroundings.

Mattei exhibited his buccaneering confidence throughout his career. When he was about twenty-four or twenty-five, and the fascist government was in control of Italy, he had thought up a plan for the oil and petrol industry which he wanted to put to the powers-that-be. He organized an introduction to one of the senior men in the government, and went along to find this same powerful figure waiting for him in a conference room, together with about a dozen advisers. Mattei outlined his plan, quietly, patiently and logically, and at the end the minister said to him: 'Young man, I don't like it. I don't think it will work.'

Mattei exploded, declaring with passion, 'You say it won't work, but then you haven't understood a word of what I have said, have you?' The friend who brought him along grabbed him by the arm and tried to pull him away. But Mattei was not to be silenced. 'Of course you don't understand; you are completely ignorant of the subject!'

'Get out of here,' ordered the minister. His friend dragged him off.

One of his most extraordinary exploits took place after the war, when he had become head of ENI. His warehouses were full of artificial fertilizer – a by-product of his oil refineries – and he could not get rid of it. The warehouses were bulging at the seams. He weighed up the options, as he always did, and came to the conclusion that the only country that needed fertilizer in this quantity was China. 'Let's go to China,' he proposed to his associates. 'But *Ingegnere* Mattei [he liked being called *Ingegnere*, which is a great term of respect in Italy and the highest degree that any university can grant], the Italian government does not even recognize the Chinese. How can we deal with them?'

'Let's go to China,' he insisted. So they went. His fame preceded him and a large government luncheon was held in his honour with three or four hundred people present. After it he was asked to make a speech. He got up and thanked them. Then he took the Agip flag with its six-legged dog and planted it on the table in front of him. 'That is the Agip flag,' he said. 'Italy may not recognize you, but Agip does.' He sold all the fertilizer he had in his warehouses at a very good price.

Next it was my turn. 'Charles,' he said during one of our fishing trips, 'I want to come to Britain. I want to establish a chain of filling stations and I want to start building them now. You have got to help me.'

'I will certainly give you any advice that you want,' I replied. 'I could help the man you appoint and could vet many of the sites that would be useful to you.'

'Will you become chairman of the company?'

'No, I am very sorry. I am not an oil man. I know nothing about it. I am not prepared to devote time to anything except my own company. I am too interested in what I am doing.'

But Mattei's charm and drive made him a formidable force. One day the telephone rang in my office and his voice was on the other end, 'Congratulations, *Signor Presidente*,' he said.

'*Cosa Presidente?*'

'We have formed a company in London, backed it with one and a half million, and guess who the chairman is?'

'No don't tell me, because I am not going to do it.'

'You *are* the president of the company, the chairman, and you have got to do it, you have got to do me a favour: do it for a short while.'

There was no way of resisting this man. 'All right, Enrico,' I said, 'I will do it, but I will do it for twelve months and not a day more. Another thing, let me tell you this on the telephone now. You have been making enemies all round the world for yourself by undercutting the price of petrol. I am going to get one thing straight from the start: there is going to be no price cutting here. We will charge the commercial price of petrol, as charged by Shell, Esso or the other oil companies. Either you agree to that or I will not agree to anything.'

'Do as you like. I agree.'

I was probably responsible for saving the petrol companies a lot of heartache.

The next time he was in London we talked in greater detail. I told him I did not want a salary as chairman, but that I was very willing to take some shares in his British subsidiary. 'No,' he said, 'but I will tell you what I *will* do. The thing may not go well and you may lose your money, but I will give you an option on twenty-five per cent of the shares.'

I thought that was generous. No money changed hands, and we did not put anything in writing. It was a gentleman's agreement to be honoured in due course. The operation went extremely well. We took over some very good sites and the work occupied relatively little of my time. Mattei had put a first-class man in as general manager, Signor Belli, who worked intelligently and hard. I liked Belli very much and we worked well together.

— • —

At the end of the first twelve months Mattei asked me to carry on. I could see that I was being of use, had become interested in the development and agreed to stay. I still had done nothing about the option. I trusted Mattei implicitly and there would be time enough to draw up a suitable document once the company had really established itself.

One morning at home I took an early call on the telephone. Enrico Mattei had been killed in an air crash together with his pilot – the same one I had known at Cortina d'Ampezzo. I was in bed at the time. My wife sat up and looked at me, and could not understand what had happened because for half an hour I could not get a word out. I was absolutely stunned by the news of his death. He had been such a vital and exhilarating person to be with, and now he was gone.

His death affected the whole enterprise. His successors in the main conglomerate in Italy were less enthusiastic about the British subsidiary. It was agreed to dispose of its assets and interests. I helped with the sale of the Agip stations we had built. Esso bought them for about £12 million. Agip had spent in the region of £5 million to £6 million, so there was a large profit. My share of the option would have been about £1.5 million. Of course, I never saw a penny of it. I never asked for it and I never missed it. What I missed was the friendship of this great man. As long as was necessary I continued as chairman of the rump company, dealing with the sale of spares and accessories, and I resigned at the first opportunity.

The Forte Company spent most of the 1960s consolidating, diversifying and expanding. Whenever an opportunity arose we added a further component to the concern, provided it fitted in with our general scheme. Above all, I was looking for more hotels; but this took time and patience.

Our first new acquisition was the Kardomah company, which included coffee shops and a wholesale coffee company. We also bought Fuller's, its several restaurants as well as the chocolate business. In 1963 we bought the long-established firm of Joseph Terry & Sons of York for £4.3 million. Terry's make the best quality chocolates in Britain, and always have done so, but their

balance sheet had started to look threadbare, with profits only in
the region of £200,000 to £300,000 a year, very small when related
to the capital employed in the company.

I put in a young general manager, Ian Johnston, who had come
to us with the earlier acquisition of Fuller's. He was a Scot, an
enthusiastic and hard-working man, and with the instinct I think I
have for singling out effective people, I felt he was the man for the
job. We kept Terry's as a separate subsidiary, but Noel Terry, the
chairman, was a man I liked. I could see that he was reluctant to
leave the chairmanship of the company, which after all carried his
name, so I asked him to stay on as chairman, and he accepted with
pleasure. He retained a beautiful corner office looking out on the
factory, and we remained great friends until he retired, of his own
volition, a few years later, after which I took on the chairmanship
myself.

Our first job in Terry's was to introduce new machinery and
methods, which dramatically increased production. On top of this,
we had to reduce the number of employees from 3,600 to 2,300.
This we did easily, offering good redundancy payment and early
retirement.

Gradually output was increased and we were able to employ
more people – but this time more productively. It was not long
before the profit was up to £2.5 million to £3 million. Terry's
remained a successful part of our company for a number of years,
but as our expansion concentrated increasingly on the hotel and
catering side, Terry's became the odd man out. We sold it for £19
million in the 1970s, thus showing a very good capital profit
indeed.

Our next purchase went badly wrong. A firm in Ipswich called
Burton Sanders had built up a successful business making and
marketing ice cream under the brand name of Mr Whippy. We
already sold a lot of ice cream and so were naturally interested in
the proposition, as to all intents and purposes it appeared to fit in
well with our other concerns. I may also have been influenced by
the memory of Pacifico Forte and his early ice-cream ventures in
Scotland!

Our accountants studied the figures and recommended the purchase. I was also impressed by the chairman and managing director of the company. But I had made a mistake. As soon as I bought the company, the management seemed to lose all interest and it was not long before Mr Whippy was losing a lot of money. I decided to cut the losses and we sold out to Wall's, who were no doubt glad to eliminate a competitor whilst increasing the size of their own operation.

The losses on this deal were over £500,000: it was a complete failure and in many ways a salutary experience. It proved to us that we were by no means infallible. It also taught me a very good lesson – never acquire a business, however good it may appear to be, unless you are either guaranteed continuity of management or you are in a position to replace the management immediately with people in whose capacity you are confident and whom you can trust. In the case of Mr Whippy, I had no one available with the necessary kind of experience. It is something I have never forgotten.

The property business has always interested me and whenever I have ventured into it I have usually been very successful. In fact, I think I would have made far more money in property than in hotels and catering. Nevertheless, I know I would not have enjoyed it; neither do I consider it a particularly creative or satisfying way of earning money. But on one occasion I managed to pull off a coup in the property market which turned out to be immensely useful to my company.

I have already mentioned my friendship with Isaac Woolfson. He always took a friendly, occasionally slightly amused, interest in my business. One day he approached me about a property he had near Oxford Circus: 'Why don't you buy it off me, Forte, and put in one of your cafés serving real butter in the sandwiches?' (We were then beginning to advertise sandwiches made with real butter.)

I had a look at the building, but I did not think it suited our purpose. But I did feel that there was some money to be made here, even though it was very rare for Isaac to miss any trick in

property or any other business. I calculated that if I could get two
first-rate tenants on long leases for the building, I could then sell
the property for considerably more than Isaac was asking.

After a bit of research I managed to find two clients who wanted
such premises: Alitalia and South African Airlines. Alitalia was
desperately looking for prominent premises in Regent Street and
so were South African Airlines. I was friendly with both companies.
Having got their agreement to a lease, I then bought the building
from Isaac, signed the leases, and resold it several years later to
the Prudential Assurance Company at a very considerable profit.
If only all the money I have ever made had been earned so easily!
This transaction was done entirely on my own behalf and had
nothing to do with the company. However, it served the company
well in enabling us to make our next acquisition.

In 1969 we bought Lillywhite's, the world-famous sports equipment and clothing store in Lower Regent Street. Having nothing
whatsoever to do with catering and hotel keeping, this acquisition
might at first sound as if we were diversifying for the sake of it. But
we did have a good reason.

We had already acquired a long lease on the Criterion building,
of which Lillywhite's formed part. There was a strong possibility
that the Criterion block could be redeveloped, in which case it was
essential that we controlled every part of the building, including,
of course, Lillywhite's. Lillywhite's was not by any means a bad
business, and it prospered within the Trusthouse Forte Group. But
our motives for acquiring it were solely to consolidate our property
interests in the Criterion building.

With the Mr Whippy saga behind us, business generally was
going well. The airport and airline catering side was thriving under
Jack Hollingshead, as were the motorway service areas.

We had formed a Leisure Division under my old friend, Sir
Leslie Joseph, my partner from the Festival of Britain days. He was
a genius when it came to revitalizing piers. We took over the North
Pier at Blackpool and two more – at New Brighton and Llandudno.
In any seaside town the pier occupies a wonderful position, usually
in the centre of the main promenade. Leslie utilized these
frontages not only as an entry to the pier itself but also for
attractive shopping arcades. This gave us very valuable and profit-

able retail outlets at a moderate price. Of course, the main money was made by improving the piers themselves, in their facilities, fabric and general appearance. Paint and effective lighting added brightness and glamour. Moreover, Bernard Delfont, who was on the board of the Leisure Division improved the quality of the entertainment – a form of popular culture which had in fact been dying out.

We continued to expand fast. We opened the Serpentine Restaurant in Hyde Park and took over the Henekey chain of wine bars. We also absorbed Ring & Brymer, the City caterers who have organized the Guildhall banquets and much more for a couple of hundred years.

The real breakthrough in the expansion of our hotel business was made possible by the excellent Sir Stuart Goodwin, from whom I bought the Waldorf. His company owned a substantial hotel group called Frederick Hotels, of which the Waldorf had formed part. He got in touch with me, and told me he had reached the stage when he would like to retire. Was I interested in buying his hotel business?

I told him I was more than happy to consider the proposition.

The negotiations were conducted in the same simple, direct way as in the sale of the Waldorf. Again, Sir Stuart said that he was not going to bargain. He put what he considered to be a fair price on the hotels, which included the Hotel Russell in Russell Square. The price was not unreasonable, so we concluded the transaction. We refurbished and re-equipped all the hotels, with the exception of one small hotel in Hull, which we sold off, (many years later we built a large modern Post House in Hull). We managed to raise the standard of the hotels quite considerably, and as a result we made good profits. We had by this time also built and opened the Excelsior at Heathrow and a Motorlodge near Oxford. So we now had the basis of a major hotel division.

One year later, we took an even bigger step in the development of our hotel business. It had become public knowledge that three of the very best hotels in Paris – the George V, the Plaza Athénée, and the Trémoille – were available. The George V was a beautiful hotel, well patronized by Americans, on a large freehold site in

the Avenue George V; the Plaza Athénée was one of the most
prestigious hotels, not only in France, but also by international
standards; and the Trémoille was a smaller hotel, maybe less well
known than the others, a French version of our Browns Hotel in
London. However, since the death of their owner, François Dupré,
these hotels were not making much profit and were beginning to
look, and were indeed becoming, run-down.

Monsieur Dupré had met his wife in Yugoslavia when he was on
holiday. She was, in fact, what was then known as a taxi-dancer,
someone who worked in a dance hall and would, for a fee, dance
with any partner who paid her. The two must have got on well
together, because when Monsieur Dupré left Yugoslavia he gave
his card to his dancing partner and asked her to call on him at the
George V if ever she was in Paris. She took him at his word the
next time she happened to be in Paris, and presented his card to
the porter of the hotel. However, the porter was somewhat
suspicious and took a certain amount of persuading before he
contacted Monsieur Dupré on her behalf. But she did get to see
him, and again the relationship developed. Eventually he married
her.

Max Joseph had been endeavouring to acquire the hotels from
Madame Dupré but, according to the newspapers, had had little
success. Max and I were competitors, but friendly competitors. I
liked him, and I believed the liking was reciprocated. I asked him
whether he had really dropped out of the Dupré deal and, if so, if
I could have a go myself.

I never made a bid in competition with anyone else. I would
only be sole negotiator, and always refused to put myself in a
situation where one bidder is played off against another — or
indeed spoils another person's bid. I have also, with one exception,
never made a hostile bid; that is, a take-over bid against the wishes
of the chairman and board of the company in question — the
exception being the Savoy Group, and there were very good
reasons for this, which I will go into later.

But to return to the Paris hotels. Max told me to go ahead; he
said that he found it impossible to do business with Madame
Dupré. 'She keeps changing her mind,' he told me. I had never

met the lady, so I wrote to her, suggesting an appointment. She
agreed to meet me.

A few days before the rendezvous I received a little note, saying
that she was very sorry but she had a bad cold and would have to
cancel the meeting. From such enquiries as I could make, she
seemed to be running true to form. I saw this as part of the
preliminary game of playing hard to get. I took no offence, and
wrote back a nice note saying how sorry I was to learn that she was
not well, that I hoped she would be better soon, and I accompanied
the note with flowers.

This must have pleased her, because she wrote again making
another date and I duly turned up at her house. She was a very
charming, elegant and attractive lady, of about fifty years of age.
Her house was as elegant and impressive as she was, and at one of
the best addresses in Paris.

We got on well from the start. The transactions we were talking
about involved the payment of something in the order of $22
million. 'But you know, Mr Forte,' she said after the social
preliminaries were over, 'everybody wants to buy my hotels with
my money.' That is to say, they wanted to buy her hotels on credit.
It certainly gave me a clue to Max's difficulties!

She very properly asked me the source of my funds and financial
backing. 'No problem,' I told her. 'I have a letter from my bank
giving all the necessary guarantees, and you will have a cheque on
the table for the full amount when we have agreed terms.'

She read the letter and seemed happy enough with the contents. Then she said: 'The Clydesdale Bank?'

'Yes, the Clydesdale Bank.'

'I do not know the Clydesdale Bank. I know Barclay's or the
Midland.'

'This is a subsidiary of the Midland, and a very large subsidiary too.'

'All right,' she said. 'It is a bank.'

So we were over the first hurdle.

Of course, before we reached this stage we had done a lot of
careful and detailed homework on the hotels. We had inspected
them thoroughly and made detailed calculations – which seemed
to show that we could obtain a return of at least twenty to twenty-

one per cent on our investment. I was so elated that after leaving
Madame Dupré I went again to walk around the properties. The
hotels seemed just as elegant and exciting as on first acquaintance.

My next meeting was more formal, and with our lawyers present.
Madame Dupré's *avocat* was a famous member of the French legal
profession. He again brought up the name of the Clydesdale Bank:
'I do not know the Clydesdale Bank, does it exist?'

'Look, *Maître*,' I said. 'You are a very famous man in France, but
a lot of people in Britain who do not know you would wonder
whether you exist.'

'Oh, yes, I exist.'

'Well, so does the Clydesdale Bank, only you don't happen to
know it.'

'I will make enquiries.'

Of course, there were no problems about the Clydesdale Bank
and the deal went through.

But we also had to deal with the question of minority shareholders, who had forty per cent of the shares.

'Do not give them anything,' said Madame. 'They are no good.
Give them nothing. I hate them.'

In fact, I did a deal with the minority shareholders too, who, it
transpired, were extremely charming people and quite naturally
upset at Madame Dupré's habit of riding roughshod over them.
They were, I might say, very pleased to get their money out.

Anyway, I liked Madame Dupré and offered her a seat on the
board, and she attended meetings regularly. She brightened up
the whole proceedings and turned out to be quite useful. She told
me a little later: 'For the first time I have been able to go into a
jeweller's shop and spend what I like. When I was married to
François, he used to say to me: "Don't spend too much. I need the
money for business." So, after he died, I was very rich on paper,
but I could never spend any money because I did not have the
cash. Now you have made it possible for me to go into a jeweller's
shop and spend millions of francs on jewels if I want to.' And she
did, too.

But Madame Dupré was not well, although one wouldn't have
guessed it from her appearance. She remained actively involved in

her racing stud, and in Paris society, but only two or three years later she died. By that time I felt that I had lost a real friend.

The amount of money that we had raised to buy the Paris hotels was extremely large in relation to the size of our business then, even though this had grown substantially. But the company had done a wonderful deal in acquiring one of Paris's most prestigious hotels at a reasonable price.

The obtaining of this loan was made much easier for me by bringing in British European Airways as a co-guarantor and as a partner. The airline thus acquired forty per cent of the business. The association with BEA alarmed certain members of the French staff, who thought the hotels would be flooded with tourists on package holidays. However, they soon found that we were good employers and hoteliers. We improved the hotels considerably by investing money in them, maintaining their traditional character and running them with flair, discipline and consideration for the employees – hallmarks of our company.

To strengthen our international side, we also acquired about this time three firms involved in the travel business. The first was Hickie Borman, who were also forwarding agents; the second was Milbanke Travel, which had built itself up very quickly and successfully by paying special attention to the travel requirements of companies and professional organizations; and the third was Swan's, who then, as now, ran very superior organized tours, concentrating on historical sites in the Mediterranean, with talks by archaeologists, architects and historians on the various places of interest which form the itinerary. Eventually, however, we found that our *forte* was not the travel business, so with a certain pang of regret I sold these firms.

We ventured further afield with our hotel purchases. In Cyprus, we bought a hotel, which we ran extremely successfully. We became interested in further development there, not only because of its climate, but also because good staff were easy to find. We were offered a wonderful site adjacent to a section of beach known as the Golden Sands, very near Famagusta. This development was in fact financed by the Church in Cyprus, at the instigation of

Archbishop Makarios, head of both the State and Church. At my
first meeting with him I made a slight *faux pas*. I was explaining to
him that we had been recommended to build our next hotel in
the Seychelles, but we had chosen to stay on in Cyprus. I asked the
Archbishop whether he knew the Seychelles. He looked at me very
pointedly, and said: 'I know it well – as a guest of your government.' He had in fact been confined there during the struggle for
Cypriot independence.

We became very friendly, and we developed the 450-bedroom
hotel together. We entered into a lease at a very reasonable rate
with a participation in the profits with the Church. It was a fair
arrangement, and it promised to be a considerable commercial
success for both parties. Makarios was very interested in developing
further the tourist influx to the island.

I vividly remember the opening day in Famagusta, in brilliant
sunshine. When the Archbishop arrived to declare the hotel open,
he was surrounded by a wildly enthusiastic crowd anxious to talk
to him, to touch him, even just to see him. We both had to be
rescued by the security men.

Sadly, the Golden Sands Hotel is not open at present. It is in
the Turkish part of the island, and when the Turks took over they
closed it down. However, they have not damaged it and the hotel
and its contents are well protected by an armed guard.

Although Makarios had his share of troubles with Britain, I
personally never heard him say a word against this country. I
believe, that although a great patriot, he always admired Britain
and the British way of life. When he died I was sad indeed.

We also did business with Sir Harold and Lady Zia Wernher, who
lived in great style at their stately home, Luton Hoo in Bedford-
shire. Among Sir Harold's many interests were three hotels on
Bermuda, but as he and Lady Zia were both advancing in years,
they decided that the time had come to sell. We were happy to
acquire the hotels and the transfer could not have been more
straightforward.

The Wernhers kept up a private apartment in one of their
Bermuda hotels and, when we had completed the deal, I said to
Lady Zia: 'This has gone so well, that I would like you to continue

using your apartment with my compliments.' I said that we would like to redecorate the apartment and incorporate a further room on one side.

'No, no,' she said. 'Why? It is quite comfortable as it is. I don't want you to spend a lot of money. As long as I can go there for a few weeks in the year and play golf I will try to be the least possible trouble to you.'

Lady Zia was a very great lady, descended from the Russian royal family and a notable favourite with our own royal family. I can quite see why. She had immense charm and the most exquisite manners, and organized the splendours of their great house effortlessly. As far as the apartment in Bermuda was concerned, she took no advantage of our private arrangement at all. She did not order champagne and caviar on the house when she was there; she was very parsimonious and self-restrained. I was both impressed by and devoted to her, and when she died I felt very sorry to lose such a good friend.

Lady Zia was also a friend of Lord Mountbatten, but the fact that she could be as imperious as he could did not seem to affect their relationship. On one occasion my wife and I were having lunch with Lady Zia and one of the guests was Mountbatten. He told Lady Zia that he wanted to see her urgently after lunch. When Lady Zia told him that she could not see him, Mountbatten looked rather startled: 'But I have come especially to see you.'

'No, I cannot see you. I am going to the hairdressers.' At that she got up, leaving him standing there. Lord Mountbatten was then at the height of his fame.

It was in her house one day that I had had a most alarming experience. I had been invited to lunch there, and found myself sitting next to Lord Mountbatten. We got involved in a vigorous argument about the merits of a certain politician, whom I was denouncing roundly and he was defending. I got so carried away that I began to choke on a piece of meat. I rushed from the room, but my wife saw what had happened, followed me, and banged my back hard. The meat was fortunately dislodged. When I returned, I found that Mountbatten had taken the whole event extremely seriously. He had had a friend in India in the army who had died in such a way and he advised me always to keep a large glass of water by my plate to avoid any recurrences. When I next went to Broadlands, his home, the vital glass of water was by my plate.

About this time I undertook a development which gave me as much pleasure as any commerical enterprise I had undertaken. I had a relative by marriage, Francesco Sanna Randaccio, who was Leader of the Liberal Party in Italy. (My sister Anna had married Emilio, his brother.) One day Francesco said to me: 'Charles, you ought to do something in Sardinia. There are some beautiful spots there. Why not put up a hotel? And there is one particular spot I would like you to see.'

He took me to the site, a place called Santa Margherita di Pula. It had a wonderful view with a pine forest stretching to the sea, a spectacular beach – one and a half miles of clear sand – hills in the background. A small paradise. There was a beautiful old stone building, but there was no sign of any habitation at all.

'Look, Francesco,' I said, 'there's no electricity here, no roads, no water. We can't put up a hotel here.'

'We can give you grants and the region can be very helpful. If you want a dam, we can build you a dam to supply you with all the water you need. We can certainly bring a road here. We can give you cheap money.'

'How cheap?'

'Four, four and a half per cent.'

This was certainly intriguing, and with the twenty per cent of the cost that he said was available in grants from the Cassa de Mezzo Giorno I could see there were distinct possibilities. When I had thought about it I told him I did not want to build a hotel there, but a de-luxe holiday village. He was, of course, extremely enthusiastic; such a development would bring employment in the area and bring visitors to Sardinia.

The dream created between us became a reality. We built our village. There were two hundred beds in the chalets, with the Castello, converted into a hotel, as the centre-piece. We planted five thousand flowering shrubs, created a children's playground and nursery, and provided every possible amenity. I laid down several rules. One was that there should be no noise, because at most holiday resorts abroad one is constantly assailed by the noise of motor cycles, cars and shouting. I ensured that deliveries should be made at certain times, and then only by electric trolley.

The local people were extremely enthusiastic about the village and we obtained every assistance we could hope for. However, there were teething troubles. The union muscled in; we found we had a gang of ten to fifteen so-called members of the union who bullied the local management, all in the name of the union which, I am convinced, did not even know what was happening. They imposed their will, and generally told the management what to do.

I had also laid down that no local people could come into the village without a permit, because I did not want gangs of paparazzi or other undesirables. But the shop stewards managed to let in whom they liked.

This went on for three or four years; at first we tried to negotiate with the people concerned and with the unions, but we were wasting our time; we were losing a lot of money in all manner of ways and getting complaints.

Eventually my patience became exhausted and I saw that we had either to close the place down or get rid of our tormentors. I discussed it with Giuseppe Pecorelli, who was then in charge of our Hotel Division, and he put in his brother, Franco Pecorelli as general manager. Franco enlisted the co-operation of the local mayor and local police chief. The police co-operation was particularly important: the *carabinieri* are tough, disciplined and an admirable body of men. By strict enforcement of the law, and by strong management within, the agitators were expelled overnight. They stood outside the gates with banners proclaiming: 'Forte slave driver', 'Forte colonizer', and so on. As long as they were outside the gates, they could say what they liked: we got on with the business and the protests faded away.

The holiday village was enormously successful and we had no better staff in the whole of our organization. We got constant praise for it. Franco Pecorelli ran the development comprising two thousand beds, immaculately and profitably. I was convinced that the village could pay and pay handsomely, and I was proved right.

CHAPTER NINE

How We Grew

BY THE END of the 1960s, the Forte Company had nearly 16,000 employees, a far cry from the fifteen or sixteen people who had helped me in my first milk bar thirty-five years earlier.

In the preceding fifteen years our growth had been rapid and, I believe, impressive:

	Pre-Tax Profits £	Net Assets £
1955	20,900	224,617
1956	12,500 loss	1,459,671
1957	58,200	1,318,630
1958	224,500	1,971,192
1959	211,000	1,973,155
1960	262,600	3,218,422
1961	451,100	3,556,732
1962	603,400	3,972,348
1963	1,342,800	13,842,196
1964	1,695,200	24,249,848
1965	1,624,000	24,884,000
1966	1,640,000	27,606,000
1967	1,933,000	27,589,000
1968	2,564,000	34,066,871
1969	4,044,000	44,664,226
1970	5,571,000	73,023,062

It might seem to the reader that the story of the company during this period has been one in which success came easily – that everything we touched turned automatically to gold. I have certainly had my share of luck, but I believe that our success came primarily through good management. This book records the high points of my career, the decisions to buy and to sell, the crises, the successes, the conflicts, the turning points. But it obviously cannot record the demanding yet vital day-to-day activity which contributed to our success: the hard work and professionalism of our staff, the unremitting attention to detail, our capacity to learn, the careful application of tried and trusted systems. *This* is what enabled us to succeed. It may sound glib to say this, but over half a century spent in business has convinced me that this is true. But I would also add that we have not always been able to practise what we preach, and we certainly have never been infallible. Moreover, our principles and practice of management were those that worked for us – there are other firms which are run differently and are just as successful. I simply operated what I would call a management of common sense, as applied to our own particular industry and my own circumstances within it.

Hotel and catering is big business, and one which includes many large and international enterprises. This was true in the 1950s and 1960s, and everything I say still applies. These enterprises are often very different from most other firms of their size, because they are the sum total of numerous and often varied component parts, which are frequently very small businesses in themselves. To succeed, its parts have to be run with all the skill, application and attention to detail that make a small business a success.

Our trade is characterized by numerous small transactions, all the year round, twenty-four hours a day. It is labour intensive to the extent that success can only be achieved by the individuals involved giving customer satisfaction. But it is not merely labour intensive, it requires an intense application of individual skills. They are very special skills, employed by very special people, and I believe that our staff represented the cream of the working population of this country or any country.

Nevertheless, success rests first and foremost on the activities of the manager on the spot, whether of a hotel, restaurant, café, or motorway area. It is his or her ability to run the enterprise effectively and to inspire and guide the staff that is decisive. A hotel or restaurant is only as good as its manager. If the manager is good the staff is good, if the staff is good the hotel or restaurant is good.

At the same time an enterprise cannot grow and develop without strong central direction and support. Thus, by now, the activities of our numerous individual units were backed by strong central services: finance, personnel management, training and marketing.

We always insisted on strict but simple financial controls. I found that the financial principles of running a large hotel and catering group differed very little from those inculcated by my father. Indeed, our systems were more or less a sophisticated extension of those used in my first milk bar. Whether running a large hotel or small café, management must keep in view the required gross profit figure (the difference between the sales revenue and the cost of its raw materials), which will enable the operation to cover its fixed costs such as lighting, heating and rent, then its wages, and leave a small profit at the end. The manager must be constantly aware of these requirements and analyse his operations with them in mind.

When Eric Hartwell first joined me to open the fifth establishment in Leicester Square, I said to him: 'If we can keep our gross profit at sixty per cent and our wages at twenty per cent, this place will make £2,000 a year.' Eric wrote this down on a piece of paper. In our first year we made exactly £2,000 net profit. I believe Eric Hartwell still keeps this piece of paper as a souvenir.

As much effort must be put into quality control as financial control. Success or failure can stem from the kitchen and it is a myth that a good kitchen is an untidy kitchen. The best chefs are always meticulously tidy and keep everything spotlessly clean. They are better organized like this and they can ensure that the food tastes exactly as they want it, uncontaminated by any other extraneous flavours.

Whenever I could, I conducted the tours of inspection that saw us through our early years. My first test in a kitchen was to open the refrigerator and see how it was kept. Was it clean? Was the fish in a separate box from the other items? Did they keep onions in the 'fridge so that everything else tasted of them? If everything looked neat and tidy, then I knew it was a well-run kitchen. If everything was higgledy-piggledy, I knew it was a badly-run and wasteful kitchen. This constant discipline had to be maintained.

Our people were taught how to store things, how to look after things, how not to waste things. In a business where the main stock-in-trade is made up of small perishable items, to waste or lose them, or have them pilfered, is the way to bankruptcy. It is quite easy to take a bottle of whisky out of the back door. So unless we controlled pilferage we ended up in the red and not in the black.

There are, of course, scores of thousands of successful caterers, particularly the smaller establishments. The owner of a business working for himself is very conscious of what he is doing, he pays a lot of attention to it. He is there on the spot: owner, manager, preceptor all in one. Very often his wife is there to help him and they see to it that there is no waste. They may have a country hotel, with twenty or thirty bedrooms and a good restaurant, and they are able to give it their personal attention. They see to it that the bedrooms are clean and tidy and well kept. They buy in the best possible market, at the best possible price, and maintain and increase their custom.

I believe that the individual hoteliers are the grass roots and the seed corn of the business: they run the majority of hotels in this country and they are marvellous trainers of staff. I would even go so far as to say that they are the heroes of the business. I believe our group has been and was a protective influence for them, in standing up to unfair demands by unions, maintaining standards, and helping to bring tourists into this country through our international marketing and advertising campaigns.

The hotel industry is now, as it was in the 1960s, primarily a conglomeration of small businesses. Although we were the largest company in the United Kingdom by far, owning two hundred plus hotels in Britain, we were still a very small part of the whole, which amounts to about fifty thousand establishments. This made it quite ridiculous to talk of a monopoly and also pinpoints very dramatically the importance of the individual hotelier.

We ran our hotels not as a chain, but as a group of individual units, with centralized services and individualistic management. I am not saying that large cannot be beautiful. I admire the Waldorf-

Astoria enormously. But with three thousand bedrooms, it is like a city or busy railway station; it must take a major-general to run that sort of hotel and maintain its standards.

Nevertheless, the basics of running the business are the same. I always told my people that we must remain artisans. We must act as if we were running a small shop round the corner, not a big corporation. We must remain in total control at all levels of our operation, while making the greatest possible use of the skills of the accountant, financier, lawyer and any other relevant specialist.

The directors must also stay very close to the trading end and to its detail. For example, I remember that in a short time one of our sections had several complaints about service. I went up first one Sunday morning, and then on a Saturday evening, when it was busy. I could see what was glaringly wrong. In fact, I said that Forte's was beginning to go down the drain right there; when you begin to lose touch with the detail of a job, it is the first sign of a company going into a decline. I was exaggerating, but there was nevertheless some truth in it. This was nothing, a small section, but we had lost touch with it.

Why? Because it was being controlled by a good administrator who was not a caterer, therefore he locked up at five o'clock and went home. We continued to employ him as an administrator, but to get the service right, the solution was to send in one of our younger men who knew catering backwards. Eric Hartwell stayed in touch with that operation and I was in touch through him. It simply is not true that at the top of a large company you don't have to take care of the details. At the top you must be very much aware of the detail – of the necessary detail.

Not that we were super-efficient, or anywhere near it. In a company which has growth as its objective, you cannot be influence for them, in standing up to unfair demands by kept well channelled; the lines of communication must be adhered to. This means trying to put the right person in the right place and keeping in contact with the detail along the lines of communication. My duty as chairman was to know the detail, not to deal directly with it.

You can try to do this through very strict management rules and regulations. But the human aspect in a business is vital; you can

keep drawing squares and lines, but within these squares you must
have people and the people must be the right people and they
must be deeply involved with the business. If this does not happen,
then the lines and squares and the diagrams mean nothing.

New developments in management ideas or in business circumstances obviously changed our way of thinking and changed our
management structure. For instance, the group has become separated into more autonomous divisions. But the principle of
divisionalization is that the man on the job must have as much
responsibility and as much authority and freedom as possible, but
on a very long string. The string, however, must still be there; at a
certain point we just pulled it a bit.

Good staff relations are crucial in our business. I am glad to say
that we achieved this from our earliest years. One of my greatest
pleasures has always been to hear people tell me when they visited
one of our establishments that they were received with courtesy
and kindness by the staff.

The industry has been criticized for having a high turnover in
staff, but this does not imply staff dissatisfaction. Statistics are
distorted by the seasonal nature of a lot of our employment. Many
people in our business only want to work for a part of the year, or
part of the day or night, and the hotel and catering industry is
thus ideally suited to them.

Good staff relations begin from the top and I always tried to set
an example. First and foremost, you have to treat your employees
as individuals. When you say: 'How are you?' to someone, you
should mean it. Whoever that person is, whatever he is doing, he
has a life to lead, as you have. He is another human being, with all
the faults, misery, expectations and hopes that you or I experience.
I think this approach means a great deal to a lot of people.

People are not all made the same way. They are not all rounded.
Some are angular, some are difficult, and you have to fit in with
them and their personality. I have always said that the type of man
does not matter as long as he is not consciously bullying, or rude
and bad-mannered. What matters is what he has to give and this
applies all the way down the line. It does not matter what tie he
wears, what colour he is, what his nationality or religion is, where
he comes from, where he does not come from, what school he has

been to. What matters is whether he is an honest, hard-working, decent fellow. That is the only criterion that counts with me. I do not mind if one of my associates or employees is French, Italian, English, Scottish, Chinese or Middle Eastern. I only wanted people around me who conform to our philosophy and give the results.

I am not anti-union. We were among the first people in the catering trade to allow the unions to come to talk to our staff. This was their right and it was our employees' right to listen to them if they so wished. We had many unions represented in the company. But we never allowed them to dictate to us. I would not allow the unions to bully our management or staff, or tell us how to treat our employees. Moreover, I do not recognize or approve of the concept of two sides of industry. It is the manager's sole responsibility to see that his staff are properly looked after and happy in their work.

I do not like bullies, and will not tolerate them in any shape or form. On the other hand, I have no time for yes-men. All my colleagues and associates were asked for their views and opinions before a conclusion is reached and group discussion has always been my preferred method. I tried always to be fair to people at all levels and trusted they would return the compliment. Without true team spirit no enterprise can succeed.

Leonard Rosso remembers one exchange from the early days when he came to me and said: 'I am so sorry I have made a mistake.' 'No, you have not made a mistake,' I replied. 'We have made a mistake.' On another occasion, when we were starting to attract public notice, we held a small press conference. I was asked what the company's main assets were, so I told them: 'My colleagues sitting around this table.' My constant objective was to create a cohesive team of people.

Team spirit is a delicate plant to maintain and that is why the background of a family business is so useful. If we called in an executive director or senior manager for discussion and review of his or her part in the operation, it was essential to create an atmosphere in which any criticism takes the form of seeking information, not trying to do the person down. They had to feel that everyone else was there to help and that solutions jointly arrived at would be supported.

I always imbued my people with the spirit of the enterprise by talking to them. If I had a problem, I liked to sit round a table with five or six people. I did not like pondering over a problem on my own and I was not good at it. There are other leaders in industry, with more ability than I have, who have a different system. If they have a problem, they sit down for an hour or two and think it out. Of course I did that too, but I only half thought it out. I did not come to a conclusion, or very seldom, unless it was a conclusion that came to me spontaneously. The idea of airport catering came to me at about three o'clock one morning, for example, and I could not sleep for the rest of the night.

When we sat down in a group, I would often exaggerate the nature and problems of a project in order to get a reaction. One of my partners then contradicted me. Should a new hotel have a hundred rooms or five hundred rooms? Where is it best sited? One of my partners would then point out that there was no week-end business, or very little business travel, or it was seasonal, or the cost of the land was excessive. After two or three hours you ended up with a totally different conception of the whole idea. Some of our best developments started as projects that I was absolutely set against, and then had to suffer the embarrassment of outsiders saying to me: 'That was a marvellous idea of yours.' In the end we get it right because I have the facility to listen to people.

Management by common sense means that you do not have constant meetings. We had one meeting to consider major projects, not ten. I preferred a general review once a month to once a week. Every meeting means extra work for somebody.

The secretary of the company has to prepare the agenda, write up the minutes, people have to leave the job they are doing to attend. I studied the regular reports from our departments, looked at the figures, I caused enquiry to be made into some operation that did not seem to be running smoothly, but our main purpose was to take decisions and apply principles.

I delegated whenever possible and I tried to give the person to whom I delegated complete authority, with the responsibility the delegation brings. I tried not to interfere. Only a very conceited man feels that he is the only one who can do a job properly. Thus the very conceited man remains very limited in his field of activity.

If he is always interfering with people he is limiting his time to do other things. He can only develop his business to a limited extent, because he does not trust people to do things properly. In return, he gets very little sympathy from the people with whom he is dealing. He must learn that perfection does not, or can very seldom, exist, and that he himself does not do things perfectly. People ask me what level of efficiency I aimed at. I aimed at being seventy per cent efficient. I knew that I could not reach one hundred per cent, but I was all the time trying to improve.

Nevertheless it is amazing if one sets a target how easily one hits that target. Unfortunately, I learnt this at a very late stage; I wish I had known it consciously before, instead of only subconsciously. If a manager says, 'This is my objective in two years time: we want to reach that turnover and make that profit', it is quite amazing how often he does it – given that such an objective is possible.

No one must say that he is going to jump eight feet, because that is out of the question. You'd break your neck. But what is the record? Six feet seven inches? Try and jump that. When you have succeeded, put it up another quarter of an inch. The art of reaching business targets is not to aim at the impossible, but to aim at the championship level – which you already know to be possible.

We stressed the importance of understanding when to report back, not of course deluging a superior with small and detailed problems, but knowing the problems which demand the attention of higher authority and greater experience. This resulted in a lack of mistakes, essential in a successfully run business.

Consistency is another vital quality. People must know where they are with the person for whom they work. He need not be perfect, but he should be the same all the time, even his defects must be the same. If he is volatile and changeable people won't understand how to work with him.

I didn't like to see a manager leave a cluttered desk, either, not because of an aesthetic approach to management, but because of what it symbolized. It meant not only work delayed in completion, but more often than not problems postponed. Sometimes, of course, things do look differently the next day, but usually I found

Early colleagues: some members of my board and Forte executives.
On my left: Eric Hartwell. *On my right*: Anna, Rex Henshall, Len Rosso.
David Lavender is extreme left and Jack Bottell is extreme right.

Above: Michael, Anna, Irene and me.

Below right: At Giancarla's christening with Marie-Louise, Rocco and Irene.

Facing page: My wife at twenty
(I took the photo).

Below: At home in Hampstead with
Marie-Louise, Olga and Rocco.

Forte's and Trust Houses in a £113m merger

BY OUR BUSINESS NEWS STAFF

It took Lord Crowther and Mr. Charles Forte just under one hour yesterday evening to sketch out their plans for a mammoth £113m. British hotel, catering and ente...

this as a vehicle for acquiring catering concerns.

To an astonished hotel establishment, the bastions of Brit...

TRUST HOUSES F

Crowther declares w

BY AZIZ KHAN-PANNI

OPEN WAR has now been declared in the quarrel between the Trust Houses and Forte factions in Britain's largest hotels group, Trust Houses Forte.

This weekend, Lord Crowther

sides of the board." he told me. "is not just a personal squabble. If it were, it would have been settled long ago. It is about fundamental principles of management, efficiency and behaviour. Nor is it confined to the boardroom.

directors to res
we? It is n
divided the bc
vantage of cha
make fundan
arrangements
at the time of

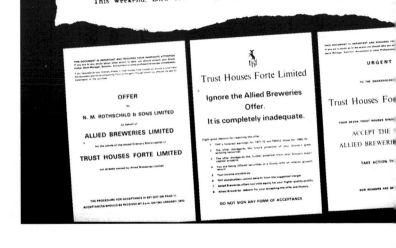

Printed mementoes of a bitter battle.

THF
o study
plan

Following the meeting, a letter
was despatched to Mr Joe
Thorley, the Allied Breweries
chairman, replying to his original
approach

Allied bid is
ridiculous–Sir
Charles Forte

BY ARTHUR SANDLES AND KENNETH GOODING

SIR CHARLES FORTE last night share would no

ord Crowther ousted as chairman of
THF: Lord Thorneycroft takes over

ir Charles
pends £5m
n buying
HF shares

A. Goodrick-Clarke

ir Charles Forte, chief executive
Trust Houses Forte, has per-
ally spent almost £5m buying
rly 2.9m shares in the company
ce July when the deep board-
m rift at the catering and hotel
up became publicly known.
This is disclosed in the detailed
ence document which has now
n sent to THF shareholders. The
ority of THF directors those
o support Sir Charles and Lord
orneycroft, who replaced Lord
wther as THF chairman—and
o together hold 5.51 per cent of
shares say they will not accept
150m takeover bid from Allied
eeries

Forte wins
power
game

CHAIRMAN Lord Crowther was last night
ousted from his £16,000-a-year job at the
head of catering giant TRUST HOUSES
FORTE by his arch-rival Sir Charles Forte,
the combine's millionaire chief executive.

With Irene by my side. I am wearing the sash of the Grand Cross of the Italian Republic.

A private audience with Pope John Paul II.

such postponement stemmed from a lack of willingness to grasp the nettle.

I would not tolerate lack of consideration for others in our managers. For instance, I hate to see people kept waiting. I once became very annoyed with one of our very senior managers because he had allowed someone who had come to see him to sit upstairs for an hour and a half waiting while he was busy on the telephone. I said to this manager afterwards: 'Don't ever do that again'. His reply was: 'One man?' And I told him: 'That is all the more reason why this man should receive a good example from you.' The senior manager in question is no longer with us.

There is no foundation for the myth that women are not suitable for top executive jobs because they are more temperamental than men. A man can be just as moody as a woman, and I have often been exasperated by men bringing their rows with their wives, temporary moroseness, or chips on their shoulder into the office.

A woman can certainly be a good enough judge of character to be able to spot the weaknesses and strengths of the people working for her and not ask anyone to work beyond their capabilities. But she must also know when to reprimand.

Executives must be big enough to give loyalty to their staff so that they gain loyalty in return. They must be considerate, recognizing when a job has been well done and praising whoever did it, and I think this may come more easily to women than to many men.

But it is an interesting fact that there were few women in the highest executive reaches in our business, or indeed still today in any business – perhaps through lack of opportunity or not enough single-mindedness?

In the catering business, the lack of management makes itself felt more quickly than elsewhere whatever the sex of its executives. Management that is weak, incoherent, badly organized, or uncommunicative, can ruin any business. There must be one hundred per cent discipline, but it must be firm and it must be fair. If it is not fair, it will not work.

I do not believe any top management job taxes an executive more than being general manager of a great hotel. He or she must

be a composite executive, know the figures as well as every other
detail of the business: electricity, heating, ventilation, cleaning,
food, linen, etc., etc. He or she must be a leader and very much
able to deal with people, because ours is a people business. A good
general manager is a thing of wonder.

The man at the head of a great enterprise has above all, to have
people with him whom he respects and trusts, who know what his
ambitions are, who share those ambitions and the same view of
things, together with a certain degree of idealism about what they
are doing. You have to impart this to your colleagues and they
must believe you. It is no use saying to somebody: 'Look, we want
to do this very well because we wish to give good value and good
service,' if they think you are only doing it for the money. Money,
of course, does matter – but in our business profits result from a
job well done.

You must also tell people the truth. They must always know the
facts, so that they have confidence in what you are doing.

These, then, were our principles and operating methods. They
were simple, but they seem to have worked. At the end of the
decade we were a thriving business.

By this time we owned, or had interests in, thirty-eight hotels,
with eight thousand beds. In Paris we had the French hotels and
in Britain the Waldorf and the eight other Frederick hotels,
including the Hotel Russell. We had four airport hotels in London,
Birmingham, Manchester and one shortly to be opened at Glasgow. We were developing in the Caribbean, with hotels on
Bermuda and Jamaica; in the Mediterranean on Malta, Cyprus
and on Sardinia, where the imaginatively created Forte holiday
village was shortly to open. We also had substantial leisure interests:
the Talk of the Town, our piers, and so on.

Yet first and foremost we remained caterers, a catering company
with substantial hotel and leisure interests, and the bulk of our
profits and turnover still came from catering, in which we were
definitely leaders in our field. Our range of operations included
the Café Royal, the Criterion, and hundreds of units in operation
at all levels. In catering the name of Forte had become nationally
established. I would say we were second to none.

The next decade was to see a fundamental change in our business. By the end of it the bulk of our profits would come from hotels, although catering still played an important part. The story of this change is, I think, an exciting one. For me it provided some of the greatest dramas of my business career.

CHAPTER TEN

The Merger

MY NEXT DECADE started agreeably enough. Out of the blue came a letter from the office of the Prime Minister (at that time Harold Wilson) asking whether I would accept a knighthood. I understand that the offer was in connection with the financial help I had given to various charitable and cultural enterprises. I was delighted to accept. I have a strong sense of history, and it was pleasing to me to be linked to the Crown through an ancient order of chivalry.

The ceremony itself was touching and moving. I had gone to Buckingham Palace with my wife and one of my daughters, Marie-Louise, to be dubbed by the Queen Mother, deputizing for the Queen. As I went up to receive the honour, the Queen Mother said to me with her sweet smile: 'Everything all right?'

'Yes,' I replied, 'thank you.'

Before it came to my 'turn', I had noticed that the Queen Mother had had something to say to each person who went up. This made me rather curious. So when I went back to my seat, I asked the man who had been knighted before me what the Queen Mother had said to him. 'Oh, she asked me whether everything was all right,' he told me.

Perhaps it was just as well that my morale received such a boost, for I was about to enter one of the most trying and testing periods of my life. What had started out as an attractive-looking merger between Forte and Trust Houses, that could have made us into the largest hotel and catering business in the country, involved me in a long-drawn-out boardroom battle, which was to drain most of my energy and tie up almost every penny I possessed in defence of my position and that of my shareholders.

By now my own hotel and restaurant business was flourishing, and I was keen to expand it further. At this point a proposal was made that Trust Houses and Forte should merge. It made a great deal of sense for both companies, which were of similar size and complemented each other. Trust Houses controlled about two hundred hotels, including such great London institutions as Grosvenor House, the Hyde Park Hotel, Browns and the Cavendish. The management was anxious to expand and diversify both at home and abroad. It had already forged a partnership with the Travelodge chain of motels in the United States and had begun to move into catering. We did not have so many hotels, but our strength abroad was impressive; we had hotels in many of the leading holiday resorts as well as in Paris. Of our hotels in Paris I would say that the Plaza Athénée had already established the reputation of being one of the finest, if not *the* finest hotel in the world. In banqueting we were well-established, too, and had gained a reputation in the popular catering field. We had also developed a thriving leisure side. So a merger between the two firms seemed both sensible and advantageous. Our size would be doubled, our operations dove-tailed, and the whole would constitute something very much greater than the parts.

You might well ask why at this time in my life, running a highly successful business and with sufficient money to meet any foreseeable needs of myself and my family, I was prepared to make such a dramatic change in my business life. The answer is simply that I have always been prepared to enter into a new venture, however large, if I believed it would benefit the business and its shareholders.

The idea of a merger with Trust Houses had occurred to me some time earlier in 1970. I remember mentioning the possibility of it to the chairman, Lord Crowther. His response was not encouraging. Far from sharing my vision of potential benefits, he was coolly patronizing. He had carved out a comfortable niche in the competitive world of business and did not care for the prospect of being disturbed by restless entrepreneurs such as myself. I distinctly remember a brief conversation with him on the subject when we were walking out of the Cumberland Hotel. Geoffrey Crowther was clad that day in a curious old long coat. 'Trust

Houses,' he pronounced, 'is a very different sort of company from yours. I greatly doubt whether we could do business together.'

There the matter might have rested, with an unpleasing rebuff, but other characters were about to enter the drama. I always think that in business, as in politics, the attitudes and reactions of people can be decisive, and subsequent developments were to show the soundness of this conviction. One of our executives, Kenneth Hall, who had brought the Quality Inn chain into our group, had formed an acquaintance with Michael Pickard, at that time chief executive of Trust Houses. Kenneth had gained the impression that Pickard was keen on doing a deal and so Kenneth suggested that we should meet. Recalling the somewhat supercilious reaction of Lord Crowther, I was naturally cautious and less sanguine. 'Pickard,' I remarked, 'may well be interested, but Pickard is not the chairman. The man who matters is Crowther and he has turned me down more than once.' Kenneth conceded my point, but countered with the view that Pickard was close to Crowther, that Crowther listened to him and could well be influenced by his views. I was still mildly sceptical, but told him to go ahead and set up a meeting between myself and Pickard.

I still carry a sharply-etched picture of Pickard in my mind. Aged under forty, tall (he must have been six foot three inches in height and towered over me), hair carefully brushed, he was clad in a neat black jacket and striped trousers, and sported a waistcoat across which a gold chain was draped. He was a grand and striking figure. By training Pickard was an accountant with an impressive way with figures and a sharp mind. He was one of the talented new breed of corporate executives who were then emerging from our public schools. His manners were easy and his speech fluent and persuasive. I was impressed. When I first met him, it was in an enormous suite used for entertaining. There was a sideboard loaded with drinks and with aplomb he offered me a whisky. When we took over the management, we abolished this arrangement and let the suite at a rent of £50,000 a year.

I later sensed a certain tension between him and Crowther – perhaps there was a degree of jealousy on Crowther's part, or maybe Crowther was simply jealous of his own authority. But whatever their differences were before they met, circumstances dictated that they should become close allies.

The conversations with Pickard were cordial and went well. We both accepted that the merger was logical and would be beneficial to both sides. A further meeting was arranged, this time with Lord Crowther present, and although there was a certain reserve in his manner, I could perceive that he was not entirely against a possible deal. This conversion must surely have been influenced by Michael Pickard, who also saw his advantage in the deal.

Although my relations with Crowther were to become strained and eventually poisoned by conflict and bitterness (I believe he behaved towards me with an unscrupulousness which pained and surprised me), I always recognized that he was a man with a brilliant mind and impressive achievements to his credit. After leaving Cambridge, he embarked on his chosen career as a financial journalist, joining the *Economist* at the age of twenty-five in 1932, when I was managing an establishment in Weymouth for my father. In six years he became its editor. He revived the paper, which had fallen somewhat into the doldrums, and turned out to be its most distinguished editor since Walter Bagehot. Journalism, however, did not really satisfy him and he was anxious to enter the world of business and commerce. He joined the board of Trust Houses in 1946 and was appointed chairman of the *Economist* Newspapers and a member of the board of such prestigious organizations as Commercial Union Insurance, London Merchant Securities and the Royal Bank of Canada.

The negotiations with Crowther lasted three weeks and we succeeded in keeping them wholly secret. The business world had no inkling of what was afoot and when our plans were announced they caused a sensation. At a stroke we had created the largest hotel and catering company in Britain, and one of the largest in the world. Trust Houses Forte, as the group came to be called, had combined assets of £120 million. Together we owned 215 hotels in the United Kingdom, as well as others in thirteen different countries overseas, with a total of 18,200 rooms. On the catering side we ran 250 restaurants and coffee shops, 1,500 industrial and staff restaurants, 45 licensed houses and 7 motorway

service areas. We provided catering facilities at 17 airports serving
50 airlines. Our entertainment division comprised 4 theatre restaurants, 4 amusement parks and 10 piers. On the manufacturing
side we had Kardomah and Terry's, and also an extensive organization for purchase and supplies. There were the Forte travel
companies, and Trust Houses had a large stake in both Travelodge
International of San Diego, California, and Travelodge, Australia
– hotel companies with a strong presence throughout North
America, Australia and the Pacific.

Lord Crowther had been shrewd enough to see the commercial
advantages of the merger, and had become increasingly keen. In
an interview published shortly after the arrangement was finalized,
he declared:

> The two companies do fit in very well together – remarkably so,
> considering how big they both are and that they are in the same
> industry. We found that there were hardly any points which
> were in direct competition. Trust Houses was a hotel company
> which had gone into catering. Forte's was a catering company
> which had gone into hotels.

I also believe that Crowther accepted the merger because he
thought that the terms were advantageous to Trust Houses, and
he felt confident that, whatever arrangements were agreed, he
would remain in control. *The Times* quoted him as saying, rather
unnecessarily I thought, 'Forte has got to learn to live with me'. I
limited myself to the emollient remark: 'I think we will fit together
very well.' By temperament I am sanguine, get on well with people,
and enjoy good personal relationships. If I had doubts, I repressed
them. I was hoping for the best and was determined that we should
make a success of the venture.

Trust Houses had an interesting and unusual history. It had not
only commercial objectives, but aesthetic and moral ones too. The
company first emerged in 1903 as the brain-child of the fourth
Earl Grey, whose family had been responsible for inspiring the
famous Earl Grey blend of tea. Its purpose was to modernize and
restore attractive country hotels, inns and pubs. With such a
background it is not surprising that most of the people on the

board, apart from Brian Franks, were not hoteliers as such, but businessmen and corporate administrators. Franks was once to tell Kenneth Hall: 'I hate Charles Forte even more than I hate Crowther.' I am not sure why. There was no one with any basic knowledge, or even, as far as I could see, love of the business of hotels and catering. My own board, by contrast, was seasoned and professional. They knew the hotel and catering industry inside out through years of practical experience and were dedicated to it.

Rather unusually, neither side employed a merchant bank to examine their side of the transaction, check the figures, or value the assets. It was instead agreed that we should ask Sir Charles Hardie, a prominent accountant, to act as an honest broker and work out equitable terms for the merger. Charles Hardie had had a distinguished career, holding such positions as the chairmanship of BOAC, the British Printing Corporation, and Metropolitan Estates. He was a valued friend of many years' standing and, indeed, for a period in the 1950s had been on the board of Forte's.

In effect Charles worked out the terms over a weekend, in Brook House in the Metropolitan Estates' boardroom – a room which used to be the Mountbattens' drawing-room. We concluded the arrangements about 3 p.m. on Sunday; none of us had any lunch. Crowther sent out for some lunch from the nearby Grosvenor House, but the kitchen was closed. I then offered to try the Café Royal, but that kitchen had by then also closed – so we went hungry for a bit.

The terms of the merger were simple: a fifty-fifty amalgamation. We exchanged nine Trust Houses ordinary shares for eight Forte ordinary shares and one of the 'A' shares. The transaction was favourably received in Monday's press and in the City. Together with my family trust, I ended up with by far the largest single share of the equity and was appointed vice-chairman. It was agreed that Geoffrey Crowther would remain as chairman for a year and that I would then succeed him.

Crowther was later to quibble about the meaning of the words in which the agreement was set out. But I know, and so did Charles Hardie, and so did Crowther, that Crowther's verbal agreement to resign after a year was absolute, unequivocal, and explicit.

Michael Pickard remained as chief executive and Price, Water-
house, the Trust Houses accountants, became accountants to the
group. The Trust Houses financial director also became financial
director of THF. Trust Houses had nine directors on the board
and Forte's had eight, although I reserved the right to appoint
one further member. The company secretary, Donald Durban, was
also a Trust Houses man. From this structure it will be seen that
Trust Houses were apparently the dominant partner in the merger.
It was also evidence that we at Forte's entered into the arrangement with trust and confidence in our future partners – too much
trust and confidence as it turned out.

My own team on the board was made up of familiar names – Sir
Leslie Joseph, Eric Hartwell, Jack Bottell, Kenneth Hall, Jack
Hollingshead, Leonard Rosso and a relative newcomer, Dennis
Hearn, a chartered accountant who had spent two years with us as
a management consultant, and who had joined the board of
Forte's as marketing director the previous year. Another old-
stager, Rex Henshall, preferred to retire, but I am pleased to say
that he was later to return to the company.

In theory, the merger made excellent sense, but in practice
things were very different. Differences between the two sides
emerged rapidly. Instead of harmony there was discord. I do not
wish to blame any one individual for wrecking what began so
promisingly: the truth is that there were deep differences of
management philosophy and style, exacerbated by incompatibili-
ties of temperament. When battle was joined, it ranged from
conflicts as to the basic principles of how to run a company, to
disagreements over major commercial decisions, and petty squab-
bles over unimportant details such as office accommodation.

Those of us with a Forte background soon realized that the
methods of Trust Houses were totally different from ours. We had
relied on human contacts, discussion, and personal supervision,
with paper work reduced to a minimum. Trust Houses were run
on bureaucratic lines, accompanied by mountains of paper and
bulging files. The air was filled with salvoes and counter-salvoes of
complicated memoranda. At Head Office everybody stopped working at 5.30, when you almost got trampled in the rush of people
leaving – *we* were accustomed to continuing to 8.00 or 9.00. We

stuck by our personal approach, but Lord Crowther never ceased to harp on the fact that we were now a large concern and that Forte methods were an anachronism. Between our approach and the Trust Houses approach it soon became apparent that there was an unbridgeable gulf.

The uncomfortable situation caused me to examine in more detail the Trust Houses management methods. I soon realized that if we were to continue along this path, it was certain that we would not be a very successful company. The more I studied the detailed figures of the Trust Houses operation, the more my dismay and apprehension grew. The gross profits of the various hotels differed enormously; no consistent principles of management applied; overheads were excessive and I was appalled by what I considered to be ostentatious expenditure at the top.

One early source of friction was minor enough. We had agreed that I should move into the Trust Houses offices in High Holborn and that suitable accommodation should be found for me there. Meanwhile I continued to work in the penthouse I had over the Café Royal. The office provided for me at Holborn was quite inappropriate, without even room for my secretary. I have no taste for luxury, but I am very aware of what is fitting, and also that I have to work in an office for twelve hours a day. In the event, I never saw the office. I refused in fact to move and it was turned down on my behalf by Jack Bottell, who was horrified by what he saw. Eventually a proper office was obtained for me, but the implications and the insensitivity were not completely lost on me.

Rather more important was the proposed purchase of the Sonesta Tower, which was later known as the Carlton Tower. Just before the merger, I had been engaged in negotiations to buy the Sonesta, a hotel occupying a prime site in Sloane Street. I had struck what I considered an excellent bargain to obtain the hotel for £3.5 million. The deal had not been finalized by the time of the merger and I proposed that Trust Houses Forte should now buy the hotel. Both Lord Crowther and Pickard opposed the transaction and maintained that the price per room was too high. They made a lot of involved calculations to prove their point. I thought that their attitude was commercially unsound and bordered on the absurd, but I had to accept their judgement. I

resented their not only turning down a good property, but the
arrogant way in which they did so, particularly at the beginning of
our relationship when more tact might have been exhibited.

I was so convinced that the Sonesta deal was a good one that I
even contemplated buying the hotel with my own money and
bringing it into the group when I became chairman. Eric Hartwell
strongly counselled against this course, since he feared it would
strain a delicate situation. He was right, and I refrained, but my
commercial judgement was subsequently vindicated. Lex bought
the hotel for £4 million and later sold it for £18 million, retaining
in addition a lucrative management contract probably worth over
£500,000 a year.

Other proposed purchases were also a source of friction. Trust
Houses directors insisted on buying the Apollo in Amsterdam, a
good hotel which I had in fact brought to the board's notice.
However, I was completely left out of the negotiations, and in my
opinion we ended up paying thirty or forty per cent too much for
it.

Yet another source of friction arose over the finance committee.
When we were discussing the original merger agreement, I had
pointed out to Crowther and Pickard that we were giving everything into their hands, the managing directorship, chairmanship
and so on. I was then offered the chairmanship of the finance
committee, Pickard contending that the man who controlled the
finances of the company was in control of the company. I
remember saying: 'Well, of course, in this case I don't think he is,
because the board always controls the company. But at least that is
something.'

When I raised the question of the finance committee on several
occasions – by now I wanted to bring some order into the firm
financially – the agreement was never implemented.

But I waited patiently. I thought that I would soon be chairman
of the company as a whole. But it rapidly became evident that
Lord Crowther had not the faintest intention of resigning after
the initial year. When I tackled him about this, he maintained that
there was no enforceable agreement for me to succeed to the
chairmanship, 'only an intention that I should'. I was deputy
chairman, and two deputy managing directors came from the

Forte stable, but in practice this gave me no effective say in the managing of the business. The rules of the others prevailed. I was bereft of all control, and my experience and knowledge of the hotel business was cavalierly thrust aside. This caused me great distress, as did it to those who had come with me into the business.

I believe that I was quicker than my Forte colleagues to discern that there was a concerted plan to remove every form of effective control from our hands. Very often when, through experience and knowledge of the business, I made suggestions they were discarded. Being elbowed aside like this did not please me: I am not made that way — nor are the people whom I had brought into the company with me.

This situation was all the more unbearable because I had brought considerable assets with me into the business. Also, I felt an obligation to protect the interests of the former Forte share-holders whose goodwill I had earned.

Yet we tried to make the merger work. I was still very excited by its possibilities. We now had the opportunity to create a company that could compete world-wide — the only one in Britain capable of doing so. The Trust Houses assets were ripe for exciting developments, and I could see that many of the management systems introduced by Michael Pickard were logical and useful, if applied properly, within a larger system of management by common sense. Such a system means, among other things, close contact with colleagues and staff, and extensive discussion on important points, which should be detailed, careful, informed and informal. Decisions reached in this way are often better than those reached by highly-structured committees, or someone making snap judgements on his own.

Nevertheless, irritations and frictions continued. At the time of the merger we had handed over all the Forte records and documents. I later learned that Crowther's people were going through them in great detail, hoping to find some pieces of evidence of malpractice and incompetence on our part with which to confront me. There was another bizarre incident, more relevant to a James Bond novel than that of the world of English commerce. Outside my office was a cupboard in the corridor let into the wall. Jack Bottell was on his way to visit me one morning, crossing this corridor, when, to his amazement, the doors of the cupboard were flung open and a secretary of a former Trust Houses director scurried out. Jack peered inside but the cupboard was empty and he subjected it to a quick examination. On joining me he observed: 'You had better be careful about anything you say in here. Every word can be heard in that cupboard outside.'

This episode was odd enough, but an even odder one was to follow. Arriving at my office early one morning, I found that the whole place had been ransacked. No papers appeared to be missing, but clearly everything had been gone through. I was so outraged that I went straight to Lord Crowther's office to have it out with him: 'Geoffrey,' I said, 'the situation's becoming impossible. We did a deal with quite clear conditions, but I see no sign of their being fulfilled. Even worse, I am being subjected to eavesdropping and harassment in my own office.' Later I raised the question of ransacking with some indignation at a board meeting. Crowther said pompously: 'You are not accusing *me* of ransacking your office?'

It was now definite that Lord Crowther had no intention of resigning after the initial year. I tackled him again about this. He repeated that there had been no agreement for me to succeed to the chairmanship, only an 'intention'. For good measure, he added that the real reason he was not going to resign was because 'the staff don't like you'. I said that, if necessary, I would take him to court.

'By all means take me to court – but you won't win. I have already taken good legal advice on this matter.'

'You can be sure that I will sue you,' was my reply.

But Crowther blustered on and I did something which is rare for me – I lost my temper. I started thumping the desk with my fist. 'Stop that banging,' he shouted. 'I'll bang your head next,' I replied.

I think he thought by then I was actually going to hit him. But I walked out of the room and, to relieve my feelings, slammed the door of his outer office so hard that the handle came away in my hand. I came back into the office grasping the handle and saw from the look of alarm on the face of Geoffrey's secretary that she really thought I was about to bludgeon her boss. I went over to her desk and said: 'Excuse me, dear. I hope I haven't frightened you. Do you mind handing this back to Lord Crowther with my compliments?' I laid the handle down in front of her and left the room. The next morning I sent her a large box of chocolates.

It was quite clear now that Crowther's dislike of me was developing into a profound personal animosity. Eric Hartwell remembered attending a dinner some time later at which Crowther was present. Afterwards they went back to Crowther's flat to have a talk; Eric's intention was to see if any reconciliation could be made for the good of the company. During that discussion Eric told me that Crowther went red in the face and began to shake and shout: 'I'll ruin him, I'll ruin him, I'll ruin that bloody man's reputation socially, financially, and morally.'

Not long ago my wife was talking to a member of the Cabinet. He told her that he had received a very pleasant surprise when he came to know me well. His previous information about my character, he said, had come from Crowther.

At any rate, I decided it was time I exercised my option to appoint a further director. I chose Peter Thorneycroft. He had been Chancellor of the Exchequer during the late 1950s in the Macmillan government, and acquired a number of City directorships before becoming a life peer in 1967. I had known Peter for many years as a man of complete integrity and outstanding ability. Irene and I had first met him through his wife Carla Roberti, then fashion editor of *Vogue*. After their marriage in 1949, she introduced Peter to us at a concert in the Aeolian Hall in Wigmore Street. We remained in touch with the Thorneycrofts during the whole of Peter's ministerial career.

Although I had strengthened my position, the situation on the board approximated to a stalemate. Crowther and his associates were still able to block any constructive proposals coming from our side. I was frustrated and decided to talk the whole matter over with Charles Hardie. He was very sympathetic. Then to my surprise and delight he said: 'You know, I think if you intended to propose me for the board, they would have to accept me.'

'Charles,' I said, 'they can't possibly accept you. They know very well that you are a friend of mine.'

He replied: 'I feel sure Crowther won't refuse my appointment.'

'Are you sure of that?'

'Absolutely positive.'

The board accepted Charles's appointment and it proved to be a turning point. To this day I have no idea as to the reasons why the Trust Houses directors agreed to this appointment of an outside director who would in effect have a casting vote. What I do know is that we now had on the board a man of intelligence, integrity and consequence, who had been instrumental in drawing up the terms for the merger and who would judge the issues, the personalities, and divisions from an informed standpoint. At first Charles was neutral, but eventually, when he became fully aware of what was going on, we received his full support when we needed it.

Despite the appointments of Peter Thorneycroft and Charles Hardie, the situation was still unhealthy. The board was as deeply divided as ever, which is not the basis on which to run a successful business. By now I could see no hope for my company other than for me and my colleagues to take control of it.

The next major event was fundamentally to alter the situation; it strengthened our position on the board, but also escalated the conflict into another dimension in which outside forces came into play.

On 14 July 1971, the newspapers were full of a report by the Board of Trade into the International Learning Systems Corporation Ltd, a joint venture in which the British Printing Corporation had become involved. The report had been carried out by Owen Stable, QC and Sir Ronald Leach, senior partner in Peat Marwick Mitchell, chartered accountants. It was highly critical of the way the affairs of the International Learning Systems had been conducted. Michael Pickard had been closely involved with International Learning Systems through his previous post as finance director of the British Printing Corporation. He was named and criticized in the report.

At the time I was shocked by these criticisms, which received wide publicity, although it must be said that Michael Pickard was later able to refute them. I, at any rate, needed very little stimulus to act upon them. I believed that for the good of the company Michael Pickard should go. I could see that there was no way that the Trust Houses directors were going to allow me to take over as chairman, and at the same time I believed if the objectives of the merger were to be achieved, I had to succeed to that office.

Fate played into my hands, as one of the Trust Houses directors, C. A. Greenway, of Travelodge in Australia, was going to be absent from the forthcoming board meeting on 23 July. This would give us a voting advantage, and I determined immediately to propose that, in view of the inspectors' report, Michael Pickard should be dismissed as managing director.

The board meeting was long and dramatic. There were two adjournments of forty minutes each, but my motion was carried. All of the seven original Forte directors, plus Lord Thorneycroft, voted against Pickard. There were seven Trust Houses directors present, but Michael Pickard was obviously not entitled to vote on this motion. Charles Hardie, who was at this time chairman of the British Printing Corporation, voted for Pickard, though I understood and respected his reasons for doing so. In the event we won the motion by eight votes to seven.

Pickard took the dismissal well. Perhaps he was relieved to be out of what must have been becoming for him an impossible situation.

At the same meeting, after the motion on Pickard's dismissal, it was agreed that, for the time being, Crowther and I would be joint managing directors, dividing the running of the company between us. But it was also agreed that this would only be a temporary measure, until we could find a new managing director.

Naturally I was happy at the outcome of the meeting, but not so happy about the methods that had had to be used. It was against all my inclinations to have to carry a motion like this through a bitterly divided board. Crowther made the most of the position by putting out a press statement dissociating himself and the Trust Houses directors from Pickard's dismissal.

Shortly afterwards the board met again informally. We agreed on the responsibilities of the new managing director and that a committee of the board be set up to search for one. Pickard was still on the board, but it was my intention to remove him as soon as possible, principally because he was a vote on the other side. At the next board meeting, Pickard said that he was prepared to resign from the board as soon as two conditions had been realized. The first was that he should receive adequate compensation and the second that the replacement director should be acceptable to the Trust Houses directors. The board accepted the first condition and we commissioned the company's lawyers to negotiate a possible settlement. We tabled the second for consideration later. I believe that the settlement which was eventually agreed was a generous one, but Michael Pickard did not resign until January of the following year. By then he had no choice.

I soon saw that I would have to take the executive reins fully into my hands, and at the next board meeting in August it was proposed that I should become group managing director. The Trust Houses directors said that this was not acceptable as the remaining three executive appointments – i.e. group managing director and the two deputy managing directors – would be from the Forte side. It was therefore proposed by them that M. R. Matthews be appointed group managing director. We discussed this proposal at length but my Forte colleagues were determined that our proposal should be implemented; we wished to lose no time in coming to grips with the problems of the company. After a long discussion, my appointment as chief executive of the company was agreed, but Michael Matthews, of the Trust Houses group, was appointed joint deputy group managing director in place of Eric Hartwell, who volunteered to relinquish this position. He hoped that the directors would now be able to work together as a unified team, a sincere wish that was shared by everyone on our side.

However, relations continued to be uneasy and it did not surprise me to hear rumours that the Trust Houses directors were hoping to restore their position with outside help, and that informal discussions with Allied Breweries Limited were taking place.

This news filled me with alarm. My colleagues and I were only too aware of the unfulfilled potential in the group; we knew of the under-developed assets, the value of which was much higher than that represented by the share price. But I also knew that in view of my large family holding and that of my friends and co-directors, we could mount a highly effective defence against a bid. Nevertheless, I saw that this was the worst possible time to have to fight one; I did not wish us to be distracted from our efforts to put the business right.

The formal approach from Allied came on 18 October 1971. They asked for a meeting to discuss the possibility of a take-over bid, and looked to us to provide facts and figures about our present and future performance. Allied Breweries was a large drinks and leisure conglomerate with a turnover of around £400 million, then about three times our size. They had become involved in the hotel business, with forty-eight hotels in Britain. Allied pointed out the fact that their company operated in three more or less autonomous groups and that they envisaged Trust Houses Forte becoming the fourth, and/or the fourth and fifth.

The Allied Breweries approach was discussed at the board meeting on 22 October. It was agreed that no facts and figures should be provided to Allied, and that any merger between the two groups should only be considered in the light of detailed proposals from them.

At the same meeting, Sir Leslie Joseph pointed out that, with the board so obviously divided, it was very important to unite in the face of the Allied bid. He thus proposed the need for a strong outside director and that Lord Robens be appointed to the board.

Of course, we had discussed this at length before the meeting took place. Alfred Robens was in fact an old friend of mine, and again, as with Charles Hardie, I was certain that when he had sized up the situation and had perceived the rights and wrongs, I could be sure of his support. He was a man of great experience in public and industrial life and was just stepping down as chairman of the National Coal Board.

Crowther, though unaware of how well I knew Alfred, was not keen on the proposal. He announced his intention of talking to him before the next meeting. His real intention was to discourage him. At that meeting, on 25 October 1971, Crowther reported that he had seen Lord Robens, had explained the position, and had said to him that although he, Crowther, considered it desirable to appoint an additional outside director, it would be unfortunate if one was appointed on a split vote. Lord Robens, Crowther claimed, fully understood this and wanted his name to be temporarily withdrawn, saying that he would speak to me. However, Crowther then had to report that Lord Robens had telephoned him shortly before the meeting to say that he had decided to withdraw his previous decision, and would like his name to go forward without any conditions attached.

At the end of his first conversation with Crowther, Alfred said that he wanted to think about the matter in view of what Crowther had said. When Alf spoke to me, I simply told him to take no notice of Crowther whatever. Alf's appointment had the full support of Charles Hardie and he was duly elected a director at the same meeting. The board was considerably strengthened by another man of stature and integrity, much against Crowther's wishes.

On 29 October, Allied formally withdrew their interest in a take-over bid, but the tiresome bickering went on. This was something to which my colleagues and I were simply not accustomed. In the past we had never dealt in rows; we had had the most harmonious associations. However, worse was to come. Crowther made an outrageous and, in fact, a very stupid move – but by now I think he had clearly seen that he had lost the day. On 21 November, he publicized the boardroom differences with an article in the *Sunday Times* under the headline 'CROWTHER DECLARES WAR'. Among his allegations he claimed that I was attempting to purge the Trust Houses directors (certainly, by that time, I would have been glad to see the back of them); that I had begun the quarrel by sacking Pickard (which was nonsense – the quarrel had started long before), and that the Trust Houses directors were alarmed by the Forte management methods. The latter statement presumably referred to our attempts to improve the performance of the areas of the company that had been originally the preserve of Trust Houses. And we were being successful in these endeavours; a high proportion of our profits in the future were to come from the proper development of the assets within Trust Houses, and two-thirds of our profits derived from this source.

Two days after Crowther's article, on Tuesday 23 November, Allied Breweries launched a new take-over bid, worth 164.5 pence a share. An emergency meeting of directors was called. Eric

Hartwell proposed in the light of the article in the *Sunday Times* and other matters that;

> The tenure of office of Lord Crowther as chairman of directors be hereby determined; that all executive and other powers delegated to him be likewise determined, and that he hereby be removed from membership of any committees of the board of which he may be a member.

In other words, the message was that he should be fired.

Charles Hardie suggested that, in the circumstances, Lord Crowther should resign. Needless to say, Crowther did not think it was in the interests of the company for him to go, but he was outvoted. I then moved that Lord Thorneycroft be appointed chairman, and this motion was carried. It was one of the best appointments our board ever made. After all that had happened, I thought it would be invidious for me to step immediately into Crowther's shoes. It would have smacked too much of triumph. I knew Peter Thorneycroft would make a first-rate chairman, and I wanted to be completely free to reorganize the company and to get on with running the business.

At the same meeting, measures to oppose the Allied Breweries take-over bid were discussed. A few days earlier I had denounced it as totally inadequate. The bid of 164.5 pence valued the firm at £128 million. My view was that the absolute minimum acceptable figure was 260 pence a share. I was not at all happy at this price, or at any price, but I would have been forced to negotiate at this level, because of our shareholders.

Crowther supported the Allied bid and we had it out in a tense session.

'This bid is not good enough,' I told him.

'164 pence – of course it is a very good bid.' (Crowther had very few shares in the company.)

'It may be good for you, Geoffrey, but it is not for the shareholders – or for me, for that matter.'

'It is more than good enough,' he insisted. 'I am not going to recommend anything more than that, and I am supporting the bid.'

'In short,' I said, 'you are supporting the enemy against our shareholders, and I am going to fight it.'

'Very well, you fight it.'

Soon after, I had a meeting with Keith Showering at his request. Showering was the chief shareholder in Allied and the most powerful man on their board.

'You are not offering enough money,' I told him. 'I am going to oppose this bid. I will not sell my own shares at any price, but I will recommend the deal to my shareholders if you offer the right amount.'

'What is the right amount?' asked Keith.

'The right amount is nearly double what you've offered up to now.'

'Ridiculous.'

'Well then, I will oppose your bid, but I will accept 300 pence and recommend it to the other shareholders and it will give you control.'

Then came the most extraordinary exchange of all. 'Crowther is in favour of the bid because he expects to return as chairman,' said Keith, adding: 'would you agree to support our bid, if we made you chairman?'

'Under no circumstances. The price is what matters.'

'Well, we can look at the price a bit.'

'Not a question of a bit, Keith, it is a question of another 135 pence a share. I cannot possibly recommend your price to the shareholders.' And we left it at that.

So the battle lines were drawn. It was a vigorous combat, fought very much in public. Immediately after the bid our share price began to rise. Because of its continued rise, Allied were eventually forced to raise their bid to 186.5 pence. This was still grossly inadequate. But I could see that I would have to put all my resources – money, time, energy and business acumen – into what was now a major battle.

Our defence had to be conducted in a number of ways. I saw that I would have to spend every penny that I possessed or could borrow to buy Trust Houses Forte shares not only to keep the share price up but also to keep as many shares as possible out of Allied hands. Most of my wealth was already invested in shares in the company, so to buy these extra shares I had to borrow to the limit of my capacity, mortgaging all my possessions. My colleagues also encouraged our friends and business associates to oppose the bid and to buy shares. Most importantly we had to see that as few shares as possible were sold to Allied – we did this by putting our case in a number of letters to shareholders and by personal approaches made to major shareholders.

From mid-December until the beginning of January a series of circular letters to shareholders from both parties rapidly followed one another. They received considerable publicity in the press, and they were the basis of the public debate on the take-over bid. On 17 December, G. B. Thorley, the chairman of Allied, sent a letter to the THF shareholders setting out the Allied offer in detail. He wrote:

> With your knowledge of the wide range of activities undertaken by THF you will appreciate that your company 'fits' with Allied in a way that offers substantial benefits for both. The spread and reputation of THF hotels will directly complement Allied's hotel interests, while THF's know-how in entertainment and catering is directly applicable to Allied's valuable licensed estate. On the other hand, Allied's financial resources, management and brand leadership will be available to support your company's programme of hotel, inn and other developments in the UK and overseas.
>
> With these advantages Allied would in any case have been interested in making an offer for your company. The timing of our approach has, however, been influenced by the much publicised dispute on your company's board, and the real harm that the resulting uncertainty might have caused your company, its employees and the high public esteem in which it is held.
>
> The Board of Allied believes that a merger between Allied and THF will be of great benefit to THF, its shareholders and its employees. There are in my view three strong financial reasons why you should accept the Offer:
> (1) You will receive an immediate increase in capital value
> (2) You will receive significantly more income
> (3) You will become a shareholder in a Group with a larger borrowing base and stronger balance sheet.

Lord Thorneycroft replied on 20 December. He promised a fuller letter to shareholders later, but he gave in this letter our estimate of profits for the financial year ending on 31 October 1972 – £14.4 million before tax. This projection was immediately denounced by Crowther as being unrealistic. (But in the event not only did we achieve it, but exceeded it by £1.3 million.) Crowther also claimed that these figures were entirely different from any that had been put before the board. To refute this statement, we issued a press release containing the following information:

In May 1971 a working party consisting of Mr Pickard, Mr Eric Hartwell, Mr Dennis Hearn and Mr George Hendrie produced a carefully detailed future projection of profits and cash flow. This document was submitted to the Policy and Finance Committee of the board at a meeting on 11 June 1971 when Lord Crowther was in the chair. The detailed projections showed profits before tax of £11.2 million for 1970/71 and in excess of £15 million for 1971/72.

On 30 December, Lord Thorneycroft wrote again to the shareholders with our board's full advice. He repeated the profit forecast and gave a number of other potent reasons for rejecting the Allied bid. The Allied offer, he stated, disregarded the future potential of the group's existing resources, and also the further potential from our major capital projects. The shareholders were being offered shares in a group with a growth record considerably inferior to THF. The present shareholders' income would drop by about a quarter. Too little equity was being offered to the THF shareholders in fact a capital participation of only twenty-six per cent in exchange for an earnings contribution of thirty-three per cent. There was, he pointed out, no evidence that Allied had a talent to improve the management of the group's hotels and other interests. He stressed that the financial advantages Allied suggested were totally illusory.

It was a strong and convicing document and was fully supported by our financial advisers, the merchant bank Warburgs.

We spent a lot of time persuading individuals and firms to invest in Trust Houses Forte shares. Max Joseph even bought some, provided he was guaranteed against loss. But he also sold us a lot of beer through Truman's and thus did not welcome a take-over of THF by a brewer. Other breweries, too, helped us with the purchase of shares. I was heartened by the support of a number of my friends. One of them, Robert Clark, bought two million. Bernard Delfont also supported me generously. But, as I pointed out to everyone, they could not lose by buying THF shares – either the bid would succeed and they would get their money back, or they would have acquired under-valued shares in a company with a great future.

All this activity, coming as it did immediately after the conflicts of the merger, put considerable strain on my family. The activity surrounding the Allied take-over bid was concentrated in two months: December 1971 and January 1972. During this period, night after night, we held meetings at my home, going through lists of shareholders, reviewing our strategy and deciding our next move. My wife was marvellous, loyal, uncomplaining, and staunch, as I knew she would be. Rocco impressed me by his understanding of the situation and his determination to fight. We spent every weekend at Ripley reviewing the situation. I kept nothing from him. He also played an active role himself.

The Allied offer closed on 10 January, and there was a flurry of last-minute activity. On 4 January, the Trust Houses directors wrote a seven-page letter to shareholders, advising them to accept the Allied offer. This was followed on 5 January by another communication from Allied, pointing out that they had increased their offer to 186.5 pence. On 6 January, I joined in personally, writing to every shareholder as follows:

I am grateful to have this opportunity of writing to you at such a vital moment in your Company's history. My family and I are major shareholders in your Company and therefore have an identity of interests with all of you. I want to tell you myself why I consider the Allied Breweries offer so inadequate and why my family and I will not be accepting it.

First and foremost your Company has enormous resources – the hotels, restaurants, etc. throughout the world – which I and my colleagues are very proud to be managing for you. Since the merger in 1970 I have seen more than enough to convince me that the profits from the existing resources of your Company can be greatly improved without detracting from our traditional standards of good service and value for money. I am equally convinced that at all levels we have the management to achieve this improved profitability. Steps have already been taken in the last few months and the recently published forecast of significantly higher profits for the year ending 31st October, 1972 is the clearest evidence that we are on the right track.

Your Company is moving ahead in other directions. I expect you have read the details of our development programme with Lord Thorneycroft's letter of 30th December. It is my wish to see your Company become an even greater force than it is now in the world-wide hotel and catering industry. It is certainly the right industry to be in; the increases foreseen everywhere in standards of living, available leisure time and business and holiday travel mean that the growth prospects of your Company are tremendous. Our development programme will be continuously augmented by new projects and new ideas.

When Allied Breweries made its offer my family and I had no hesitation in deciding that we did not want to give up our entitlement to share fully in the benefits now being derived from your Company's great resources and continuing new developments. It was an easy decision to take as the arguments all pointed in one direction – to ignore the Allied Breweries offer. These arguments are well set out in Lord Thorneycroft's letter to you of 30th December and if you ever have any doubts what to do I urge you to read that letter again. I only want to add that the way I see it Allied Breweries is asking you to sell out on a take-over bid without paying you anything like the full value for the growth potential of your shares.

I have complete confidence in the future of your Company and its management. I believe it to be a wonderful investment. Hence I am determined to defend your Company to the limit. I feel this so strongly that over the last six months but mostly in the last six weeks I and my family interests have increased our investment in your Company by almost £7 million. To do this we have had to borrow substantial amounts of money. I have confidence that this has been the right thing to do and that our investment will prove worthwhile but only if the Allied Breweries offer is rejected.

I deplore the attempts to create the impression that your Company's management was not working properly and your Company was therefore in danger. This is not so. Of the minority of directors on your Board who are being separately advised only one is an executive director.

The management of your Company at all levels is functioning well and is grateful that there is now a clear majority on the Board to take decisions and make any changes necessary in policies and systems to improve profitability and standards throughout. I know this is true – the staff tell me so and I can see it with my own eyes. The forecast of profits for the year ending 31st October, 1972 reflects some of the benefit from these changes. I am content to be judged by the results which we achieve.

Anyone who tried to denounce our decisions, our forecasts and our ability to manage must appear to you not to be acting in your interests as shareholders and should be ignored.

Many shareholders obviously feel the same way as I do about the offer and have taken the trouble to telephone or write to tell me so. I am very heartened by their encouraging support and also by the wide-spread expressions of support from management and staff who naturally fear the outcome of a take-over bid. They believe, as I do, that the future of your Company is far brighter by remaining independent of Allied Breweries. In its offer document Allied Breweries as good as admitted that it needs your Company. Your Company does not need Allied Breweries.

Remember that my interests are the same as your interests. I will not accept the Allied Breweries offer and I advise you also to reject it. Do not sign any form of acceptance.

The battle drew to its close, I felt we were winning – but I still had some anxious moments. Warburgs had appointed Frank Smith, one of their partners, to advise me. This excellent man was very experienced in bid situations. His main advice had been to tell me from time to time to find another million or so to buy more shares!

One Sunday morning I got a telephone call from Frank Smith, saying that to hold our position I personally would have to find another £2 million by Monday morning. My credit was now fully extended, but I told him I would try to find the money. How do you borrow £2 million within twenty-four hours over a weekend? People were out of town and at first I made very little headway. I then telephoned a young friend of Rocco's called Robert Mendoza. My son Rocco and he had been at Downside together and I used to take the boy out with Rocco during my weekend visits. His father, Roberto Mendoza, a great friend of mine, had been the Cuban Ambassador to London, resigning when Castro came to power.

Mendoza Senior had gone to America and made a new life for himself in New York. Young Robert got a scholarship, first to Cambridge and then to Yale and, despite his youth, had become a successful banker with the Morgan Guaranty Company, who had sent him back to London to their City branch. So I asked Robert if he could get hold of Danny Davison, his chief executive, over the weekend. Robert gave me his telephone number.

Fortunately, he was in when I telephoned. 'I'd like to see you urgently,' I said. 'Come and have a drink this evening.'

'I have promised to take my wife out to dinner,' he replied. 'I usually take her out on a Sunday.'

'Well, can you come a bit earlier and have a drink with me?'

So we made an appointment for six o'clock at Chester House. I came straight to the point. 'I need £2 million tomorrow morning. Can you lend it to me?'

'What about your own bank?' he asked.

'I have already imposed upon the Clydesdale sufficiently. They have lent me a great deal – £12 million, in fact.'

'Will you guarantee it, personally?'

'Certainly.'

'What collateral?'

'This house and my estate in Surrey are unencumbered.'

I had hoped to keep these particular possessions out of it. But no collateral was called for – only my personal guarantee. He promised that I could have the money in the morning.

I remember thinking then how right my father had been when

he told me that reputation was more valuable than money. Admittedly Mendoza did some very good business for himself that evening. But I was still flattered by his prompt answer to my request.

On 11 January Allied announced that they had withdrawn their bid. They had only acquired fifteen per cent of the shares; I and my supporters controlled about thirty-five per cent. Allied continued to buy shares on the open market, but the bid was effectively beaten off. (They kept their shares until 1978 and sold them at a profit.) Later that month Crowther, Pickard and their supporters resigned as directors.

Why did we win? Certainly, Allied did not have a strong case for a take-over: there were no obvious major benefits to either party. In a good merger, two and two should equal five; the value of the total should add up to more than the sum of the parts. But most shareholders must have a price at which they will sell, and it puzzled me and my colleagues that Allied were not prepared to pay that price. If they had offered another 50 pence, and even at that price they would have been getting a bargain, I suspect that some of the larger institutional shareholders might have been tempted to sell – even though I would still have opposed such a price. But a lot of our shares were not held by institutions, they were in the hands of smaller shareholders among the general public. They had been with me from the Forte days, had always remained remarkably loyal, and were, I think, prepared to pay very serious attention to my views.

With a higher offer, say another 100 pence, I would have had to advise all the shareholders to accept. At that price the shares would have been correctly valued, as far as our published financial projections were concerned. I had no infallible crystal ball; I could not honestly have forecast the tremendous success we have had. I knew the capabilities of the people working for me, my own capability and the value of our assets; *I* believed in a great future for the company – but the future is never certain, and I could not guarantee it.

Allied were, of course, relying very much on Crowther's valuation of the company, but Crowther did not share our confidence in the future, nor I believe was he even aware of the true value of our assets. Allied were also wary of the situation, knowing full well that our board had been bitterly divided for over two years.

How near were we to defeat? I always believed that we would win. Others may not have been so certain. Rocco tells an interesting story about our financial advisers Warburgs, who rendered a very large bill for their services. He went to see them to renegotiate these terms, and saw one of their founders and senior people, Grunfeld, who recounted an interesting parallel. He told Rocco the story of the man who was choking to death from a fish bone stuck in his throat. A doctor was called to remove the fish bone. Afterwards the man asked: 'How much?'

The doctor replied: 'Half as much as you would have given me if the fish bone were still stuck there.'

We paid the bill! But we were never exactly choking to death. Even so, it had been a hard fight, and I would not like to have fought another like it. But I would have done so again, unhesitatingly, with just as much determination if the best interests of my company and shareholders had been at stake.

CHAPTER ELEVEN

Expansion

AS SOON AS we were able to introduce our proven management methods, we rapidly transformed the finances of the Trust Houses Forte Group. In 1972 the profits reached £16.5 million, which was £5.5 million up on the previous year; and in 1973 we raised the profit figure to £23 million. In this increase we were greatly assisted by the two senior executives on Trust Houses side, whom we had retained in the management team. Indeed, I made no discrimination whatever between ex-Forte and ex-Trust Houses employees. Today we have valued members of management and staff from both sections of the merger. George Hendrie had already proved his worth in Trust Houses and another man was Donald Durban, the company secretary. Once the administration had been reorganized they were extremely helpful. They knew that much work had to be done, so they got down to it and did it. They knew all the ins and outs of Trust Houses – where the water and gas turned on and off – and they were of invaluable service to me and my colleagues in the reorganization of the group.

What I did not know was that George Hendrie was a sick man. It may be that he did not know either. I heard that he took pills to keep down his blood pressure, and told him to look after himself and pace his pattern of work. A couple of years later he and Donald Durban went to the States to look after our expanding interests there. At that time Donald Durban had not been too well, either (I am pleased to say that stayed with me in very good health). I called George Hendrie in to my office. I said: 'George, will you please do me a personal favour? I don't want Donald to know that I have talked to you, but will you keep an eye on him? Don't let him overdo things, look after him – will you?' The day

after their arrival a 'phone call came through from New York.
When I heard it was Donald Durban, I was relieved.

'Yes Donald, what can I do?'

'I have got some bad news.'

'Well, what is it – are you all right?'

'I am 'phoning to tell you that George Hendrie died an hour
ago in his sleep.'

I was deeply shocked. It was a serious loss, both personal and
professional.

The United States had become our main area of expansion at
the time. There was a particularly good reason for this. When you
get to a certain stage in the development of a hotel business (and
we now had nearly two hundred and fifty hotels with a proportion
of them abroad), in order to prosper you need what is known as
referral business, the recommending of hotels to clients across
frontiers. The Americans were more sophisticated than we were in
this and I had been particularly struck by the success that Conrad
Hilton had enjoyed in this field. Hilton had a touch of genius. I
admired and indeed slightly envied the way in which in practically
every capital city I visited I found a Hilton Hotel, usually with a
thousand rooms or more. Of modern hotels, the Athens Hilton is
one of the finest I have ever seen, and that in a city proud of its
architecture.

There was no British hotel company which had sought to
internationalize its business in a big way, but I decided it was time
that we did something about it. It was not because we were
developing elephantiasis or becoming besotted with expansion for
the sake of expansion. It was obvious to me and my colleagues that
the general welfare of the business depended on it. I thought that
if we could establish points of contact from Britain and France, as
we had already done in Germany and in Holland, to various parts
of the world, and particularly to the United States, the whole
would benefit from the activities of the parts.

If guests stayed at the George V in Paris and liked it, it was a
reasonable assumption that they would accept a recommendation
to stay in one of our London hotels, or in one of our American
hotels if we could acquire some. This was particularly true of

Above: In the House Lords with Lord Thorneycroft.

Right: A letter that gave me much pleasure.

Far left: Rocco and his bride Aliai.

Left: Rocco in the London Marathon with THF colleague Neil Kirby.

Below: Irene and our daughters. *From left to right*, Portia, Giancarla, Marie-Louise, Olga and Irene.

Father at *Ischia*.

Mother at Hamptsead.

The Westbury, New York.   Browns Hotel, London.

The Grosvenor House, London.

SOME OF OUR
LEADING HOTELS

Hotel Les Bergues,
Geneva.

The Hyde Park, London.

Below: Our bid to add some more hotels to this
distinguished group.

£58m bid to add Claridges, Connaught
and others to the THF empire

FORTE BID
FOR SAVOY

Three generations.

Americans coming to Europe. If they liked the people who looked after them in America, they might seek them out in Europe.

The easiest first step was to increase our interest in the Travelodge chain, which had four hundred and sixty hotels and motels spread across the United States. We had inherited a twenty per cent interest in their equity from Trust Houses, so I decided that we should buy up the rest. It cost us $28 million. We had always allowed Travelodge a considerable degree of managerial autonomy, while at the same time imposing our own philosophy, accounting methods, controls and type of management.

But Travelodge did not have hotels in the luxury class. We still needed to move up-market, to acquire a flagship hotel in New York. One of my near neighbours at Ripley was Paul Getty. He lived at the lovely Tudor mansion, Sutton Place, not too far away, and we got to know each other quite well. He was not in any way the miserly and grumpy person he was purported to be. On the contrary, he was a very generous, open, agreeable man. Some years previously he had said to me: 'Why don't you look at the Pierre Hotel in New York? It belongs to me and I would like to sell it or do something with it.'

He explained the structure of his holding, which was complicated. The hotel was partly owned by some hundred or more apartment tenants and partly by him. He had the majority shareholding. I went to have a good look at the hotel the next time I was in New York. The Pierre obviously required a lot of money invested in it for refurbishment and at the same time a great deal of personal attention. But Getty's approach occurred before the merger with Trust Houses, and we did not at that particular time have the sort of money available. We were still absorbing previous acquisitions and we were not yet ready to move into the United States. I was obliged to tell Paul that I was not interested. That was probably a mistake. I should have taken the plunge, but timing is everything in this business. I also made a mistake about the Plaza in New York, but more about that later.

Anyway, I did not forget the Pierre and in the 1970s it was brought to my attention again. Would we like to take over the management? Not quite the same proposition, but still attractive,

even though the hotel was losing quite a lot of money. This time I
said yes. Fortunately we had an excellent man available for the job
of general manager, Bertie Gelardi. His father had been the
general manager of the Savoy and he had been born into the hotel
business. Again we applied our philosophy and methods, spent
some money on the hotel, and put in further top staff. Within
quite a short period we had turned the financial situation around
and made the hotel pay against all the odds. It had been losing
over $2.5 million. We produced profits of about $3 million.
Standards also improved, and a number of guide books referred
to the Pierre as the best hotel in New York.

But there was a flaw. Our lease was coming to an end, and I just
could not persuade the consortium of apartment owners to give us
a long lease. They made all sorts of encouraging noises and told
us that we would continue to run the Pierre, but that was not good
enough. We needed to spend a large sum of money on further
improvements, in particular on refurbishing the restaurant and
the banqueting suites. Without a long lease, this was not a practical
possibility, and we also needed the freedom of operation that a
long lease gave. It was an impossible situation to try to manage a
hotel with over a hundred owners round the place, one of whom
wanted a red picture, another a yellow one, the next a red carpet,
the fourth a brown one, and so on.

The old board of management, with whom we got on reasonably
well, was then replaced by a new group with very different views.
They made up their minds that they did not want us, that
economically they would be better off without us, and that they
would bring their own people in to manage the hotel. There was
quite a row because I felt that they were taking advantage of us.
However, they won the day and we came out of the Pierre.
I wonder whether that board still believes it made the right
decision.

It was a temporary set-back. We bought another New York
hotel chain, the Knotts Hotels Corporation, which included the
International at Kennedy Airport, and the Westbury hotels in
Manhattan and Mayfair, and set about building our own hotels in
half a dozen major American cities.

The results were gratifying. The New York Westbury was completely refurbished – embellished with beautiful rooms and a superb restaurant – and was regarded as one of the best hotels in the city, as indeed was the Plaza Athénée in New York, which we opened. We later also had other luxury hotels in Philadelphia, Los Angeles, Dallas, Miami, and Toronto.

But I still remember bitterly the one that got away – the Plaza in New York. It enjoys a superb position on the edge of Central Park; indeed, it is difficult to imagine a better position or structure for a grand hotel. I had made an excellent offer of $22 million, which was being very seriously considered by the proprietors, who had given me reason to believe that it was acceptable. But shortly before the contracts were to be signed, I received a visit in my suite at the Pierre from one of their representatives. He told me that we might have a deal on the basis of the $22 million that I had offered, but at $22.5 million we could definitely have the hotel.

I was irritated by this. I thought that I had offered an excellent price in the first place, and it was thus not necessary to spend a dollar more. In fact, I saw this as a last-minute attempt to squeeze an extra $500,000 out of me. This all happened late on Friday evening. I spoke to my solicitors, who told me that the vendors' solicitors had already made arrangements to sign the contract on the following morning, so I was reinforced in my belief that this was a bit of last-minute bluffing. I also thought that it would be difficult for the vendors to clinch a new sale over the weekend, so I refused to pay the extra $500,000.

On the following Monday morning my New York solicitors rang to say that the hotel had been sold to someone else. It was stunning news. The buyers were the Westin Corporation, a subsidiary of American Airlines. I had obviously under-estimated the man I was dealing with, and had not realized how fast very big business can be transacted, if necessary, in New York. So, for a further $500,000 I had lost one of the most valuable hotels in the world. The Carlton Tower and the Plaza were two missed opportunities, and I suppose with all the excellent hotels we have got, I should be philosophic about them. But unfortunately I will always be irritated – in the case of the Carlton Tower with Lord Crowther and Michael Pickard, and of the Plaza with myself.

It was Rex Henshall, who had by now returned to the group, who first brought to our attention the possibility of buying the Lyons hotels. One day in 1976 he came bouncing into my office: 'Have you heard about the Lyons hotels?'

'What?'

'They want to sell them.'

'Look, they have not wanted to sell them for twenty years. Every now and again there are rumours, but nothing happens.'

'Oh, but this time they are going to sell.'

'These hotels are going to be sold,' he repeated.

'All right then,' I said. 'But let us find out. The best way is to write to Lyons.'

'Give me time to find out what is going on,' said Rex.

So for about a fortnight he beavered away. His sheer tenacity is one of his most admirable qualities. A pattern started to emerge. Not only had the Lyons Group been talking to some American companies, who had turned them down, but also to Max Joseph at Grand Metropolitan Hotels who, at that time, was not interested.

It also became clear that Lyons were over-stretched financially. They had invested heavily abroad and the investments had not paid off. They had borrowed in foreign currency, the exchange rate had turned against them, and the sterling repayments were costing a lot more than the loan they had obtained. They needed to realize some of their assets, and the most conveniently saleable package consisted of their hotels. There were thirty-four of them, including the Cumberland, the Strand Palace and the Regent Palace in London, the Ariel Hotel at London Airport, the Albany hotels in Birmingham, Glasgow and Nottingham, the Royal Hibernian in Dublin and many others. The group had 5,600 beds and would provide a perfect addition to our own 26,000.

Rex had spoken to a senior executive of Lyons and had obtained an indication that the deal might be worked out. Rex then put an outline plan on paper and brought it to me. I thought that the price was far too high, so we had another look at the figures together. We prepared a feasibility study and, having completed this to my satisfaction, Rex made an appointment to meet with the principals, Geoffrey and Neil Salmon.

Geoffrey and Neil Salmon were delightful people to deal with and our discussions were conducted in the most gentlemanly fashion, although they were hard bargainers. We looked at the list of hotels, where they were situated, how many rooms. We went through all the figures.

I asked the Salmons how much they wanted. Their first figure was £35 million. This was by no means an unreasonable estimate, but I knew that we were going to have to spend a lot of money on the hotels, and it was more than my own plans permitted. 'If that is the amount of money we must find,' I said to them, 'we can't do the deal. But I could pay you £25 million.' I told them that we would pay £5 million in cash and the remainder in tranches of £5 million over the next four years.

They insisted that the first payment should be £8 million, to which I agreed. They also asked for interest on the outstanding sums. Interest rates on the London money market at that time were running at about fifteen per cent. 'I can't pay the normal rate of interest,' I told them. 'These hotels need money spent on them. They need new management and restaffing and I do not want the interest charge to dissipate our profits.' We eventually settled on an interest rate of five per cent.

Ten per cent difference on the rate of interest over five years meant a substantial reduction in our indebtedness. I calculated that, with inflation and lower interest, the true price of the hotels was more like £18.5 million; this, for thirty-three hotels with 5,600 bedrooms. To build a hotel in London at the time of writing costs anything between £50,000 to £60,000 per bedroom. Even at that time it would have cost at least £20,000 and we had got the hotels for £5,000 a room.

It had been a good deal and the negotiations had been carried out in the best possible spirit. I think Lyons felt it was the best deal they could have done in the circumstances, which it was, because I could not have paid more, and nor would anyone else. When it was all finalized, Geoffrey Salmon said to me: 'You know one thing I regret about all this?'

'What is that?' I asked.

'That we shall not be meeting any more. I have enjoyed these discussions.'

It was a wonderful moment. All my life I had regarded Lyons as an example. If I had wanted to fire my ambition, I would say to myself: one day we will be as big as Lyons. I never thought it would come, but now we owned all their hotels and had become bigger than Lyons ever were. I must pay tribute to them. They had influenced everything in our business for the good. They had nurtured the trade association, their public relations were excellent. They had influenced the hygiene standards of catering, how kitchens should be planned, and the training of staff. They did great things for the industry, and in particular the provision of good food for millions of people at a popular price. I have always had great respect for them.

It is probably true to say that the Lyons people lost their way on the hotel side and were not fully in touch with their operations. They had become more interested in their manufacturing and food divisions, and there was thus less motivation from the top for good performance in the hotel division.

We went into the smallest details in the Lyons hotels. We sent our own experts into every establishment to look around. Were they overstaffed, were they in some cases under-staffed? Did any of the hotels need renovation or refurbishment? Were the managers right, or not up to the job? Were the requisite artisan skills being properly applied? I use the word 'artisan' deliberately, because I know that it is skilled workmanship, craftsmanship if you like, which can make or break a hotel. The task, like mixing a drink, making a bed or an omelette, can be done well, quite well, or badly. It is the quality of the performance of these and hundreds of other tasks which comprise the running of a hotel which can make the difference between the mediocre and the good, and the good and the excellent.

We also had our tried financial formulae and if the hotel was not producing the ratios of sales to gross profit which we knew were obtainable, then we also knew that there was something wrong and could act on it.

The purchase of the Lyons hotels proved a huge success. We were assisted by the fact that the influx of tourism was increasing in Britain and, of course, during Jubilee Year, 1977, we could have filled all the rooms many times over. We were certainly lucky in our timing, but success came from careful and realistic assessment of the purchase and then painstaking application of professional skills.

Shortly after the Lyons deal, we had some minor outbreaks of trouble with a union, the Transport and General Workers' Union to be precise. We had a very straightforward relationship with the unions. They were not banned from Trusthouse Forte, but our overall approach was that the interests which trade unions purport to represent were not necessarily the interests of our employees. We, the company, believed that we had sole responsibility for the people who worked for us and that it was our duty to look after them, not that of an outside organization. Employment, welfare and the training of personnel was a responsibility that we would never hand over to a third party.

We believed in working very closely with our staff. They were intimately involved in all operations. We had consultative committees in establishments of all sizes; representatives of the staff sat round a table and discussed not only their problems, but the operation in general.

I believe that very often a trade union can subvert the communications between management and staff. We could not tolerate a situation, which occurs in many other industries, where management is not allowed to communicate with staff directly, because the trade union will not allow it and insists that management must deal with its workforce only through the trade union representative.

We believed that when staff consider they need a trade union representation, then we have failed in our job of being good managers. In some areas, like the airport operations, we were surrounded by trade unions. Even there we went to great pains to ensure that we kept in direct communication with the staff. As a result our relationship with them was good and therefore, on the whole, our relationship with the unions was good. We paid well above the Catering Wages Act minimum rates, and we reviewed our rates of pay every year. Obviously, they had to be related to inflation and to the profits we were making.

We kept ourselves very closely informed about union approaches to the company. We were well aware of some of the union methods which might charitably be described as distinctly underhand. We would not tolerate any bullying nonsense, and our staff knew that we would stand up for them. If they decided not to join the union, they would not be victimized by anyone – we would never allow them to be victimized.

These, then, are my feelings about the unions in our business in general. It so happens that our business is not dominated by them. Nevertheless, I repeat that anyone who worked for us was free to join a trade union if he wished to do so. I am a great believer in personal freedom, not only for myself but for others. This, within the law, is the greatest privilege of any living human being.

It was in this context that I viewed the situation which blew up in Birmingham, at our restaurant called The Night Out. The regional TGWU organizer, Alan Law, came along and announced his intention of unionizing the establishment.

'Fine,' we said, 'but what membership do you have?'

'Well, all the staff want to belong to the union,' he retorted.

'But do they?' we asked.

We organized a ballot. Ninety-eight per cent of the whole staff voted against belonging to the union. Law did not accept this and started putting pressure on us in various ways. Matters came to a head when a particular employee smacked a customer on the back of the head with a menu when he could not make up his mind what he wanted to order. We sacked this person, and twelve waitresses out of a staff of three hundred went out on protest strike.

As a result we had five hundred people picketing The Night Out the following day, with lorries blocking the entrance and goodness knows what else. Our staff continued to work. They had to walk through these picket lines and suffer abuse and threats of every kind, but they knew that they had our support and that we would stand up for them. Their views had been expressed, we supported those views and were not going to let them down. Our staff were well aware of this and also realized that in the final analysis the unions did not have a lot to offer them. The action eventually collapsed.

We occasionally had the same sort of thing happening in other places. The unions recruited a few more members but then people saw that they were not getting anywhere and the aggravation all died down again. If the unions came in and started playing rough, we could play rough as well. We did not take any nonsense from them. We were not afraid of unions and they knew we could and would stand up to them if necessary. And we knew our staff were with us.

We had a similar outbreak of militant unionism at the Randolph Hotel in Oxford: three hundred pickets (none of them members of our staff), verbal abuse, etc. But the staff continued to work and the strike collapsed. In 1983, the unions virtually took control of the Shelbourne Hotel in Dublin. The hotel, which was highly overstaffed, became unmanageable. We closed it down, refurbished and redecorated it, and opened it with about sixty per cent of its previous employees. Many of the militant union employees were not re-employed – they were the kind of people who act in the union's name but against its members' interests. After all this, the Shelbourne prospered again and became undoubtedly one of the best hotels in Europe.

In the past fifty years, we had very little trouble indeed with staff problems. We never really had any trouble with the unions themselves apart from Mr Law, who, in fact, was acting in the name of the union only and was really a maverick – not very popular with his own union chiefs.

CHAPTER TWELVE

The Savoy

SINCE THE ACQUISITION of the Lyons hotels in 1975, Trust-house Forte (we changed the name from Trust Houses Forte in 1979), expanded rapidly and successfully:

	Sales £	Pre-Tax Profits £	Net Assets £
1975–6	451,700,000	23,700,000	129,500,000
1976–7	531,000,000	38,000,000	197,200,000
1977–8	613,800,000	55,500,000	301,100,000
1978–9	721,000,000	68,200,000	356,500,000
1979–80	772,400,000	66,000,000	413,500,000
1980–1	833,100,000	52,300,000	559,600,000
1981–2	915,400,000	57,100,000	591,000,000
1982–3	1,012,000,000	82,100,000	654,300,000
1983–4	1,148,600,000	105,200,000	863,600,000
1984–5	1,244,500,000	129,600,000	930,500,000
1985–6	1,476,500,000	136,000,000	1,128,000,000

Expansion had largely been achieved within our existing frame-work; by organic growth, in fact, through developing the successful core of our businesses.

We continued to add to the luxury hotels in the centres of major European cities, such as the Ritz in Madrid and the Hotel des Bergues in Geneva. I love these old palaces of hotels, and delighted in bringing back their former glories.

We had expanded a highly successful Post Houses chain, which caters mainly for the businessman on the move and provides every possible service within this concept. We had also expanded in the United States, and had a strong presence in the Middle East.

We had vastly increased the scope of our industrial catering through Gardner Merchant, and our popular catering through the Little Chef chain and our establishments at the airports and on the motorways.

We had also disposed of parts of the group which may have been successful in themselves, but did not fit in with our policies. We had sold hotels that we thought were too small, that did not have the potential to be renovated up to group standards, or indeed, which were competing with other THF hotels locally.

We sold our Henekey's Inns to Whitbread, for example. It also made good financial sense for us to sell the Leisure Division, with its variety of theatres, theatre restaurants, piers, sporting facilities, amusement parks, etc., to Lord Delfont, who incorporated them in his highly successful First Leisure Corporation. I was glad to see my old friend make such a success out of these assets.

We also, for the same reasons, sold Sidgwick and Jackson, the book publishers, a long-time enthusiasm of mine. I was glad to find it such a good home with the Macmillan Group of publishing companies.

We had disposed of our interest in the travel business, though in the case of Thomas Cook the divestiture was not wholly amicable. When the old firm of Thomas Cook had come on the market – actually it had been originally part of British Rail – the Midland Bank approached us to see if we would form part of a consortium with them and the AA to buy Thomas Cook. The Midland Bank interest in Cook's was because of its travellers' cheques and related banking services; it was the majority share-holder, holding sixty per cent of the shares with the AA and Trusthouse Forte the other forty per cent. It had had the right to appoint the chairman, and I was to be vice-chairman.

Cook's under the new ownership was not at first a great success, but it was eventually showing signs of progress when Sir Archibald Forbes, chairman of the Midland Bank, retired and was succeeded by William Armstrong, former head of the Civil Service. Armstrong decided that he would like to buy out our minority shareholding and that of the AA. He offered me £1.40 per share. I pointed out to him that we had paid £5 for those shares. He told me that the AA were prepared to accept his offer. I replied that I would buy the shares myself at that price and I certainly was not selling ours. Armstrong argued forcibly that since we had bought Cook's it had not made any money and it was going to take a great deal of further investment to put it right. In these circumstances he thought the shares were correctly valued. Eventually, after much strenuous and tortuous negotiation, we obtained £4.25 a share for both ourselves and the AA.

We had attempted to increase our professional expertise, refine our systems, and give even better service to our customers, so that we could consolidate our position as the best hoteliers and caterers in the world. We had won numerous accolades and awards for our expertise, including several for being the best hotel group in Britain.

Our biggest acquisition in cash terms took place in 1986, when we bought the hotel and catering interests of the Imperial Group.

The assets that attracted us were their thirty Anchor hotels, seventy-four Imperial Inn restaurants, seventy-five Happy Eater roadside restaurants, and five Welcome Break motorway service stations.

We had moved very fast when we saw that the Hanson Trust was likely to take over Imperial. Rocco wrote to Lord Hanson shortly after he had made the bid, expressing our great interest in these particular assets. After the bid had gone through, Lord Hanson rang me, said he had received Rocco's letter, and asked whether we could meet and discuss the matter. I invited him to lunch at our restaurant, Ninety Park Lane. Before the lunch, we were given access to the Imperial figures and analysed the potential very carefully. The business had a total turnover of £111 million, with a net book value of £113 million. Of course, by the time we saw Lord Hanson, there were other companies who were attempting to buy the same assets, but we were in there first; James Hanson knew me and we were friends.

At lunch Lord Hanson did tell me that he had a lot of people interested. I said: 'Look James, one thing I must ask you if you and I are going to do a deal: let's do it now. I certainly will not take part in an auction and, knowing you, I don't think you would

either. We either do a deal or we don't. If we don't do a deal over
lunch, then we don't do a deal. You know me, you know my
company, if we do a deal it's a deal, and there it is. There will be
no problem; the money is there and we can finalize the matter
now if you so wish.'

Lord Hanson's asking price was £200 million. Eventually we
settled for £186 million – a tidy sum of money even for James to
discuss over lunch!

Of course, I had already discussed the matter with my executives
and my board, and thus I had no need to go back to them for
confirmation. I had also talked it over very carefully with Rocco,
who was the real instigator of the transaction and who had
convinced me with well-presented arguments and figures that we
should proceed.

Lord Hanson suggested that the arrangement would not in any
way be subjected to a Monopolies Commission inquiry. I said:
'Well alright then, we will leave that out. If there is a Monopolies
Commission inquiry, we will take that as it comes. We won't go
back on the deal.'

Lord Hanson was keen to reassure himself that the deal was
subject to nothing at all. I said: 'It is only subject to your
accountants and ours agreeing on the assets and so forth, and the
balance sheet values, but that is all.' And I went on: 'You will not
sell to anybody else?' James Hanson said: 'The deal is done and I
accept your offer.'

We shook hands on it there and then. He kept his word
absolutely, being the man he is, and I kept mine. I did not go back
to him on anything. Of course, solicitors and accountants always
raise small points, but we insisted, and he insisted that we had
done a deal and that was it. This is one of the few countries in the
world, I think, where anything like this could happen, and it
proved once again, if proof were needed, that James is a man of
his word. He could in fact have sold to higher bidders, because
after we had reached agreement, he had several offers at a higher
price.

The Imperial purchase fitted in well with our existing operations. In recent years we had been expanding very much by the
purchase of Exclusive Hotels. But we were also four-star and three-

star minded. In the provinces we had a lot of good hotels in these
categories; in particular Historic Inns which fitted well with the
Anchor hotels, which were also older properties. In addition, we
are mass caterers, and the Imperial Inns, the Happy Eater chain,
and the motorway services fitted in with that side of our operations
– the Happy Eaters were in fact very similar to our 250 or so Little
Chefs.

The deal was referred to the Monopolies Commission. I can't
think why: it must have been inspired by some petty personal
reasons, and I have a very good idea who it was. But, as we
expected, the Monopolies Commission, which included two trade
union representatives, reported unanimously in our favour, after a
very fair and courteous hearing.

We certainly paid a lot for the Imperial assets; but I am glad to
say that it soon became apparent under our unrivalled management the returns on the investment had turned out to be satisfactory indeed.

We went on expanding in the hotel and catering fields. I believe
that we were probably the most expert people in hotels and
catering anywhere in the world. Any hotel or hotel group we
acquired in due course was improved in performance. Sales went
up proving that people appreciated our service. Occupancies rose
and the bottom line has showed better results due to an enthusiastic, loyal, hardworking executive team. We were interested in
any major hotel or catering group at the right price. With our
record and profit, borrowing money was no problem. Rocco and
our financial director, Donald Main had lunch with Goldman
Sachs, the American bankers. At that time we had in mind a
possible deal in the United States. Over lunch it was intimated that
a loan of up to and over one billion dollars would be no problem
at all, and they confirmed this by letter. It was obvious that our
credit was relatively unlimited.

So, I would say that we seemed to be well on course. But we had
one piece of unfinished business.

I proposed to Irene in the Savoy Restaurant and we spent part of
our honeymoon in the hotel, so I can hardly be accused of not
appreciating its quality and reputation. The Savoy Group with

Claridges, the Connaught, the new Berkeley, the Lancaster in Paris, Simpson's in the Strand and the Forest Mere health farm, still enjoyed the prestige accorded to the world's most distinguished collection of hotels.

The group has played an immensely important part in the hotel life of Britain's capital. For decades, it comprised the most famous of all hotel names in Britain. In the past, it has been the nursery of many of the top class hotel general managers. César Ritz, the Quaglino brothers, and many of the famous names in the top level of the hotel and restaurant business, which is a very exclusive international élite, made their way through the Savoy Group. During most of that time it has had very good restaurant managers, the very best chefs and the most discreet and expert head receptionists. Many of the *maîtres d'hôtel* have become internationally famous personalities: Amanda, Contarini, Vercelli – most of them Italians. The *chefs de cuisine* have been mostly French and the reception staff mostly English. A very British institution, with many nationalities running it.

But I considered that the present eminence of the Savoy Group was not what it had been, and its profitability was far from impressive in view of the value of its assets. I also believed that, overall, the hotels needed to be substantially rehabilitated and refurbished, redecorated and re-equipped, and that the old glamour was fading. They required a massive injection of capital, such as we could provide, and which they had not been able to accumulate because of poor profitability. In the meantime the management who had set itself up as the defender of this great institution, had sold various of their valuable properties, including the part of the Savoy facing the Strand. A reason given for this sale was that it is almost impossible to manage a luxury hotel with more than a few hundred rooms – ridiculous nonsense and in my opinion sacrilege.

The former chairman of the Savoy Group was Sir Hugh Wontner. His father, Arthur Wontner, was a distinguished actor. Sir Hugh had made his way up in the hotel business on the administrative side. He joined the Savoy in 1938, became its managing director in 1941, and finally its chairman. He has presence and influence; he was former Lord Mayor of London, Clerk of the Royal Kitchen, and catering adviser to the Royal

Household. He had become a rich man. Apart from living in the magnificence of fine suites provided from time to time in the Savoy hotels, he owned a Scottish estate of 800 acres, consisting of a substantial house and at least four cottages, and another estate in the Chilterns of 150 acres.

The Wontner Family Settlement owned over 270,000 Savoy 'B' shares which would have a value of over £26 million on present-day stock exchange quoted values − in my view an artificially high value swollen by take-over speculation and not reflecting the earnings record and real net worth of the Savoy.

I first met Hugh Wontner at the end of the war, when we were both appointed to a small government committee to make recommendations for the hotel and catering industry in its transition from war to peacetime. We had a continuing acquaintance over the years, at one time exhibiting a certain degree of warmth. He obviously regarded the Savoy Group as a special institution with standards to maintain, which do not necessarily involve undue profits. All this was hard on the shareholders who had received very little income from their investment, but a hard core remained remarkably loyal. This was flattering no doubt to the current management, but it meant very little because the votes of those who held the bulk of the share capital can have had little influence at general meetings.

Over the years, the real voting power in the Savoy Group had been consolidated under the control of a restricted number of people, including some of the directors; and meanwhile the Savoy had made derisory profits relative to the assets employed.

The unusual variation in the Savoy's capital structure had a long history, going back over thirty years. The first of these arrangements was the 'Worcester Scheme' of 1953. Its object was to protect the Savoy from a take-over bid by property interests, in this case from Harold Samuel. In essence, it removed certain freehold properties from the control of the majority of Savoy shareholders to the control of a trust, making the Savoy Company less attractive to a purchaser. Harold Samuel threatened to institute legal proceedings to have the Worcester Scheme set aside, and indeed requested the Board of Trade to appoint an inspector. Subsequently he agreed to an arrangement under which the scheme was reversed, the properties returned to the control of the Savoy and in which he sold his Savoy shares to the directors of the Savoy, their friends and associates.

While the end of the Worcester Scheme might be argued to have been good, the means were questionable – or such, at least, was the verdict of Mr Milner Holland, QC, who was called in by the Board of Trade to investigate them. He found that aspects of the Scheme were 'an invalid use of the powers of the management'.

The properties in question had been vested in a company controlled by a charitable trust, which was set up for this purpose by the Savoy itself. Trustees have a responsibility to manage a trust in accordance with its stated objectives. As Milner Holland commented prophetically: 'These trustees would have had to consider their position very carefully if they had been offered a tempting price for their shares by someone desirous of obtaining that control. It would have been a difficult decision for trustees owing a duty only to their trust to have refused an offer which represented a substantial capital profit . . .' As we will see, this exact dilemma would face trustees of other such trusts set up subsequently by Savoy directors.

The Savoy directors were not content to let the matter rest there. In 1955 they proposed the creation and scrip issue of a new class of 'B' shares with weighted voting rights as a further defensive measure. Expressed in the simplest terms, the new 'B' shares carried forty times more votes than the 'A' shares – i.e. the old shares. The result was that the 'A' shares which represented 97.7 per cent of the equity, were now to have only half of the votes.

Over the years most of these new 'B' shares were acquired by certain Savoy directors and their friends and, of course, the trusts to which I refer later. All this had been extremely effective in seeing off anyone wanting to take over the Savoy group.

Obviously it had been the concern of the Savoy directors to be vigilant about who had 'B' shares in their possession. An instructive episode was the purchase of the Lancaster Hotel by the Savoy in 1970. The structuring of this acquisition increased the voting strength of the 'B' shares, which by then had fallen below fifty per cent.

To make this purchase, the Savoy issued 92,000 'A' shares and a disproportionately high number of 'B' shares (30,207).

An explanatory notice to Savoy shareholders informed them that the vendor had requested Savoy shares for the sale of the Lancaster. When the transaction was completed, 8,000 'A' shares and 2,000 'B' shares were allotted directly to the vendor. I consider it likely that the majority of the consideration was received in cash within a comparatively short time, from placing or other disposals of the remainder of the shares.

So what happened to the balance of the 'B' shares that had been issued? They have had a complex history. They were allotted to a nominee Swiss bank, and would seem to have ended up with another nominee bank, Childs Nominees, who held 'B' shares representing 5.8 per cent of the voting rights of the Savoy. The Savoy had refused our request for enlightenment as to the beneficial owner.

By these means, Sir Hugh Wontner had held out tenaciously over the years. He saw off a bid from Charles Clore in 1954 and another from Jack Cotton, who got absolutely nowhere. Trafalgar House bought some twelve per cent of the shares in 1970, came up against a brick wall, and sold out to Maxwell Joseph. Even he could not make a breach and sold his holding to the Rothschild Investment Trust, who in turn disposed of their shares to the Kuwait Investment Office.

I well remember one evening in the City, when I sat next to Hugh Wontner. He was then talking about Maxwell Joseph, shortly after Max had bought these shares. He spoke of the man in such scathing terms that I thought then that Wontner would make a very bad enemy indeed.

Some of Sir Hugh's suitors had certainly wished to turn the Savoy into an office block, but whether hoteliers or not they all got the brush off. Sir Hugh Wontner had a great gift for supercilious indifference. This attitude might have been justified if the profit record of the Savoy had not been so dismal.

I had been looking into the situation for some time and must have had half a dozen conversations with Wontner, but each time I got the same treatment as everybody else. 'Oh yes, but it survives as a company on its own. It is something different from anything else,' was his attitude. 'Let's forget about it. This is a unique company. You don't really want to bother with it.'

Sir Hugh did not enquire what sum of money was on offer, or seem prepared to negotiate at all. Such negotiations could have been in the financial interests of shareholders as a whole. The dividends paid were miniscule and the assets in the company's balance sheet were undervalued. I could then, and still do, see the situation of the underdeveloped assets as similar to that which we encountered with Trust Houses.

I had been touched by a delightful letter from Sir Hugh, written to me in January 1980 after dinner at my house, where I had raised the question of a bid. He thanked me for entertaining him in such elegant surroundings, and complimented me on my home and its contents. He said that for him these were rare enrichments of life that are not encountered every day. But I also learned that Sir Hugh later likened my attitude towards him on that occasion to that of Hitler summoning the Austrian Chancellor Dollfuss.

I was talking one day to my merchant banking colleagues at Warburgs, when they said: 'Why don't you do something about the Savoy Group?' 'Well, I have been trying,' I told them. 'Wontner just brushed me off; he doesn't want to know.'

Encouraged by Warburgs, I made a further approach to Hugh Wontner. Again he was not interested. Again no price was discussed. That was that.

Our lawyer then made an ingenious suggestion: that we should concentrate our assault, not through the high voting 'B' shares, but through the 'A' shares. If we managed to get the courts to give us authority to have the scheme approved at separate meetings for the holders of the 'A' shares and the holders of the 'B' shares, and then obtained the support of seventy-five per cent of those voting among the 'A' shareholders, we could have acquired control of the company.

I could now see very clearly that the assets of the company were deteriorating, and to raise cash, the management was selling some of them. Its most recent action had been the mutilation of the Savoy Hotel itself: the sale of part of the hotel, allegedly 'the least attractive part' for development into apartments. These apartments were effectively marketed by the purchasers as the most prestigious and attractive in London. This amounted to selling the seed corn. I estimate that if the Savoy had retained this section, they would have made an extra £2 million or more on their net profit and they would not have mutilated a fine hotel.

So in March 1981 Trusthouse Forte announced a £58 million bid for the Savoy Group by Scheme of Arrangement through the courts. We offered 165 pence for each 'A' share at 125 pence each, or 84 Trusthouse Forte shares for 100 of them, and 5 Trusthouse Forte shares or 975 pence cash for each 'B' share at 700 pence each.

The bid caused a sensation and we had to endure a lot of verbal abuse from the other side. The Savoy managing director, Giles Shepard, even allowed himself to be quoted publicly uttering the tired old cliché: 'On professional grounds we have never thought that a vast combine like Trusthouse Forte, which among other things runs service stations on the main arterial roads and airport catering, is at all suitable to run services of the quality of the Savoy, Claridges, the Connaught and the Berkeley, which must rank among the most renowned hotels in the world.' I had not had occasion to ask Shepard what he thought of our Exclusive Hotels: the George V, the Plaza Athénée, the Hyde Park, Browns, the Grosvenor House, the two Westburys, etc. But doubtless his reply would be along the lines of a letter he wrote to the manager of the George V shortly before we made the take-over bid for the Savoy. He was thanking the manager for 'a really memorable evening' in that hotel. 'What food, what wines, what service!' wrote Shepard. 'What more could one want as a grand finale to a visit to Paris? I was so impressed by all at the George V . . .' Mr Shepard had paid us another compliment in recruiting the general manager of Grosvenor House to manage the Savoy, who had been with us for seventeen years. He was well trained by us and raised the Savoy's standards in the time he was there.

In fact, all this talk by the Savoy people of preserving from our depredations an institution which is part of the annals of civilization is total nonsense. We had always lovingly and meticulously preserved the characters of our traditional hotels, but at the same time have made them better and more profitable institutions.

We took to court the issue of a separate meeting for 'A' and 'B' shareholders, and lost. If we had won, I expect there would have been convulsions in the city, because we would have established the principle that carefully organized, privileged shareholders could be out-voted by the rest.

But we ended up after our take-over bid by actually owning the greater part of the Savoy. The terms were an improvement on the original bid announced in March 1981: 190p for each 'A' share, or 126 Trusthouse Forte shares for every 100 of them, and £22.46 or 15 Trusthouse Forte shares for every two 'B' shares. The Kuwait Investment Office sold us their shares and we got a substantial portion from the public and institutions. At that moment we owned about seventy per cent of the company, but because of the voting structure controlled only about forty-two per cent of the votes. So, when the Savoy people say that our bid failed, they are talking through their hats as usual. Our bid did not fail if we now own just under seventy per cent of the equity of that company. In fact, had we not made the bid, and if the 'B' shares were not controlled by the charitable trusts, so called, the shares would still be around the price we found them at in view of their dismal profit and dividend record over the years.

One of the figures on the sidelines during this long-drawn-out affair was Sir Max Joseph. He hung around in the wings watching events and allowing it to be known that he was interested. That, of course, kept up the price of the Savoy shares. It would have helped us if he had accorded me the same commercial courtesy as I had always accorded him in the past. For instance, when he was negotiating for the Paris hotels with Madame Dupré, I kept completely out of the way. It was only when he had failed to acquire these hotels that I went in and bought them.

Max and I were old acquaintances, not rivals to the extent that might be supposed. I quite liked him. Or, should I say, that I liked him three-quarters of the time, and then he would do something that exasperated me. He was so quick on the draw and never missed a chance. At one time we were negotiating to buy a hotel in Copenhagen. The asking price was far too high, but over the course of eighteen months we managed to bring it down to an economic level and the other side were about to accept our formal

bid when, lo and behold, two or three days later, Max Joseph
bought it. We did all the work, but he had his ear to the ground,
went in and asked what the offer figure was, offered them a few
thousand pounds more and took the hotel from under our noses.
I was not pleased.

His next intervention also annoyed me. We got at cross purposes
with the landlords over the rent review of the Strand Palace Hotel,
which we had acquired from Lyons. It transpired that Max Joseph
had advised the landlords that the rental value of the bedrooms
was not less than £2,000 a year and that they should not let me
have the lease for less. In fact, we got the rooms at £800 a year,
which made all the difference between a prosperous hotel and
one making a loss; I let Max know he had annoyed me and we did
not talk to each other for quite a while. He was not well for a
period before he died and I think this made him mischievous. But
I was sad when he died. He was a great character, and I still miss
him.

To return to the Savoy: we had a situation in which, despite our
seventy per cent stake, no regard or consideration was paid to us
as majority shareholders – we were treated with hostility and our
interests were disregarded. We suggested that Eric Hartwell went
on the board. The proposal was in fact rejected at the Savoy
Annual General Meeting, with the support of the trusts' votes,
even though Eric Hartwell could have brought much experience
and good sense to the board.

I firmly believed that if the fine hotels in the Savoy Group were
to be afforded the international status they deserve, and be better
managed, there would be profits of more than twice those their
present management is able to achieve in their best year. But I
don't include in this criticism many of the departmental managers
and staff, who were of the highest calibre. There were many
employees in the Savoy Group who are probably the most skilled
in the world, but their superb talent appeared to be wasted.

The Savoy Group's plight arose from two long-standing failings
– poor management and unnecessary central overheads. Moreover, the Savoy had allowed its assets to deteriorate through lack
of capital expenditure. In the years 1981–4, according to published

information, the group spent under £11 million in total. Hugh Wontner argued that he spent £23 million, but he had included in this figure running repairs and maintenance. In my view, the Savoy Group needed much more money spent on it, and I have no doubt that such expenditure would produce spectacular results. We spent over £6 million at that time renovating the Ritz Hotel in Madrid, which had resulted in an increase in occupancy of over twenty per cent.

The Savoy's extensive list of London-based properties was included in the 1985 Balance Sheet at £33 million. In 1981, during the Trusthouse Forte bid for the Savoy Group, the properties were revalued at £83 million, and the 1985 Report and Accounts stated that the value exceeded their net book value by more than £95 million. Profits in those years show a poor return on property of over £128 million.

The directors of the Savoy had been and still are protected by the group's voting structure. The Savoy Educational Trust, established as a charity by Savoy directors, then had nearly 250,000 'B' shares. These shares were worth £2.7 million, valued on the basis of the THF bid. If this money had been re-invested at ten per cent per annum, it would have produced for the trust an annual income of £274,000 – the trust's actual income in 1985 was about £6,000. The object of this charity is to enhance the advancement of education in connection with the hotel and restaurant industry. Given the low income received, this is a role which clearly it cannot play with any serious impact.

The D'Oyly Carte Charitable Trust, established by Dame D'Oyly Carte, was another example of this state of affairs. If the trustees had accepted our bid for their 'B' shares, they would have had substantial income to carry out their objectives, one of the most important of which was to support the D'Oyly Carte Opera Company, which produced Gilbert and Sullivan operas. The THF bid came at a time when the D'Oyly Carte Opera Company was failing and must have produced a particular dilemma for the trustees. They held in the region of 324,500 'B' shares. An acceptance of the bid would have produced £3,640,000. This invested at ten per cent would have produced £364,000 per annum against the trust's income in 1985 of about £8,000. The former sum could have been made available to the D'Oyly Carte Opera Company which has now ceased to operate through lack of funds.

Shortly after the hardcover edition of this book was published, the publishers received a long and aggressive letter from the Savoy's lawyers. They denounced me for referring to Sir Hugh's father as being of Hungarian origin, I referred to him as a distinguished Hungarian actor. I made a mistake about the Hungarian origin and I am glad to remove this reference from this edition. They attempted to compare the Savoy profits favourably with those of Trusthouse Forte, but in comparing profit as a percentage of turnover, they were not comparing like with like. The Savoy profits are largely derived from first class hotels in London. Trusthouse Forte profits came not only from our Exclusive London hotels, but from catering and especially from Industrial Catering which comprises a large part of our turnover. In industrial catering, the profit margin can be as low as three per cent and even less.

However, if the Savoy had made a true comparison, it would have been with our top London Hotels (Grosvenor House, The Hyde Park, Browns, and The Westbury). The profit as a percentage of turnover on our London properties was more than twice the very mediocre seventeen per cent reported by the Savoy in 1985; Grosvenor House alone made more profit than all the London Savoy properties combined.

It seems strange that there was no mention in the lawyer's letter of what I have written above about the Savoy Educational Trust and the D'Oyly Carte Charitable Trust, matters which would seem to me far more important than Sir Hugh's family origins. I challenged Sir Hugh to defend his position on these trusts. He knew, of course, that the position was indefensible.

I am often asked whether our Savoy holding, for which we paid £38 million, was not an awkward burden in our balance sheet, as it produced so little income and permitted us no influence in the running of the group. My reply is that the Savoy stake was worth well over what we paid for it; it was an investment for the future.

People have suggested that I wished to acquire these hotels out of vanity, as a climax to my own career. Certainly they would have been one of the brightest jewels in the THF crown. And what hotel man would not be proud to possess them! Nevertheless, I don't need the Savoy Group to crown my career. I have enough already of which to be proud and I have always been more interested in substance than in appearances. I have already made a tiny mark, but a mark nevertheless, in this great country. My greatest ambition was to see Trusthouse Forte continue to prosper under the present young, skilful, and enterprising management team led by Rocco.

Curiously, at the height of the struggle, I met Hugh Wontner by chance when I was walking through Hyde Park. He was carrying a parcel. He looked at me sideways. Then he gave me a half-smile.

'How are you?' he asked. 'I saw a handsome gentleman coming down the road, and I find it's you.'

'Oh, I saw a very nice looking chap coming down the other way and it's you.'

We paid each other a few further compliments.

Then Sir Hugh said: 'You must be very worried, aren't you?'

'What do you mean, very worried?'

'Well, running such a big business.'

'Worried? Everything is going very well, everything is doing fine. I'm not worried.'

Sir Hugh said: 'Of course you can be worried with a small business.'

'Are you worried?' I asked him.

'Yes, at times, you know.'

I then asked him what he was carrying.

'Some wine.'

'What, have you been to the Savoy cellars?'

'Oh, they are samples from the pianist Moura Lympany. She tells me that you buy her wine too.'

'Yes,' I said, 'some of her wine. It's quite good.'

And after that strange conversation, or something like it, we went on our ways.

CHAPTER THIRTEEN

Open Minds and Open Doors

TOWARDS THE END of my career at THF, I asked Eric Howell, my longest standing colleague, how much I had changed over the years. 'Well, you have mellowed,' he said. Obviously one of the things that mellows you is the great difference between going to a bank and trying to get them to lend you a few thousand pounds and being the head of a substantial international company, to whom banks are more than willing to lend money. I must have matured over the years. To outsiders I must appear an entirely different person, but I feel I am still the same person as I was in my early days, with the same attitudes, the same ambitions, the same standards of perfection, and the same faults.

Nevertheless, there is a difference between running a small business and one of Britain's largest companies, with widespread international interests.

There is no doubt that the lessons gained in running a small business are useful, provided you are not limited by them. In a small business, individuals responsible can and do give personal attention to the minutiae of the operation, and can infuse the organization from top to bottom with their drive, wisdom and efficiency. Attention to this sort of detail cannot be given by top executives in a large business. The effectiveness of the THF operation was based very much on getting the detail right down the line. Thus immense efforts were made to instruct and train managers and staff, and to monitor their performance.

I retired as chief executive of THF in 1992, and handed over to my son Rocco (more about that in the next chapter). This is how the group worked when I stepped down. Trusthouse Forte had five main divisions operating at many different levels, and some

60,000 employees. There were over eight hundred hotels in Britain, the United States and around the world; there were well over four hundred restaurants, including those in America; we were responsible for the catering in fourteen airports and in seventy-five international airlines, and our Gardner Merchant subsidiary supplied over a million meals a day to two thousand different clients and establishments. So an enormous amount of detail had to be dealt with.

In Chapter Nine I attempted to analyse the reasons that made us successful by the end of the 1960s. In this chapter there will be a certain amount of repetition because the same system and philosophy were at work in THF on my retirement, but in a much larger and more complex context.

I had always been blessed with sufficient energy to see a deal through, once my colleagues and I had agreed that this was the initiative we should take. I do not enjoy being thwarted from outside and I would not tolerate being thwarted from inside. I have always been loyal to my colleagues and I expect that loyalty to be returned. We all have to be absolutely dedicated to the interests of the company and I could not have people around who were uninvolved, or put their personal ambitions before the development of the group. I didn't mind how long we discussed important issues, but once we had reached an agreed decision, with everyone having had a say, then everyone had to back it. Some of my colleagues, from time to time, joined the boards of outside companies because we had some interest in them or what they were doing. Their experience was that this spirit is by no means universal. They found executives criticizing the main board to newcomers or outsiders. That is a terrible state of affairs and to my knowledge never happened to us.

I am a great believer in oral communications and have a horror of bureaucratic methods, of endless memoranda flying backwards and forwards that nobody reads. Of course, we had the facts and figures before us when matters of consequence arose, but when I called my people together, the discussion was open and opinions were freely expressed. I liked listening to the views of other people and found it quite the best way of arriving at a conclusion.

I could not read all the reports from the lower echelons of the business, and could not visit all the establishments simultaneously. I would have been lucky to get round them all in five years and would have had very little time for anything else, although I did carry out spot checks personally from time to time, whether it was to a Little Chef restaurant, or the George V. But I always warned the manager, or other person in charge, of my arrival.

My door was always open, unless I was engaged in confidential conversation or conference, and we did an awful lot of our talking when we happened to meet in the corridors.

We were, of course, more formalized and institutionalized than that. There was a small *ad hoc* running committee which met a couple of times a week at half past eight in the morning for an hour or two under Rocco's chairmanship, when the day-to-day affairs of the company were discussed. There were usually not more than four or five people there, and those attending varied, depending on which section of the business was being talked about.

Every week I had on my desk the figures for every division of the company, in sufficient detail to show me any strength or weakness, a running summary, in fact, of the operations of the hotels, the restaurants, the airport catering side, Gardner Merchant, and so on. I checked on the turnover, the room occupancy rate and the profit figures. If necessary, I started asking questions. Usually the question had already been anticipated by the responsible person down the line and in most cases they had an answer ready.

These figures were also on Rocco's desk and he may also have wished to raise the matters in more detail with the people concerned. He talked over the problems with me: why the income from banqueting in London was less than usual, why the room occupancy in the American hotels was fluctuating, why one of the hotels in Paris or in London had not come up to expectations. This supervision got projected all down the line, and remedies were applied. If there were problems on the catering side or in administration, the same thing happened.

The four people who still responded directly to me in the family tree of the company were the head of administration, Donald Durban (who had been with the Trust Houses and then THF for forty years); the group finance director, Donald Main; the head of the property department, Michael Silbert; and John Robbins, the head of our public relations. Donald Main joined us in 1981, bringing with him immense international experience gained with such companies as Vickers, the international division of British Leyland, and Mars Incorporated. Each week, Donald and the other three came to see me at least once with a list of subjects for discussion.

Likewise Rex Henshall, the development consultant, also came in most weeks with an agenda for us to go through. Perhaps a hotel in Toronto attracted his attention as a possible purchase, so we went through the relevant facts. What about the city itself, what sort of economy does it have to support a hotel? How many rival hotels are there? Is this hotel in a good position? Ought I to go over to take a look at it? Ought Rex or one of his assistants carry out a preliminary inspection?

We had three formal executive committees. I was chairman of the finance committee, which basically dealt with the strategic and general matters: loans, long-term financing, exchange rates, taxation, cash flow, etc. Charles Hardie was chairman of the property committee: a significant committee as we had such extensive property interests, worth in the region of £1 billion. Rocco was chairman of the executive committee, responsible for the day-to-day operation of the company. But the most important aspect of these committees was that they were only *advisory* committees: they were not decision-making committees. They existed to help the relevant executives with their decisions, not to ratify them or veto them. The executives had their own clearly defined areas of authority and responsibility, in particular the amount of money they could spend on their own initiative. The only committee with authority to approve or disapprove was the board itself. Nevertheless, a good executive knew what problems to refer back to his committee or to his superior.

At these committee meetings we sat down and discussed not only day-to-day matters but the entire policy of the enterprise, where we were going, what we were going to be doing in five years' time. We considered whether our current operations were going smoothly, or whether we should be doing this or that about them.

The main board met monthly. Donald Durban would come to me to draw up its agenda. What further items did I want on it? I would ask if he had checked with so-and-so. A written report on the month's business was prepared, which I saw in advance, took home, and studied so that I was in a position to chair the meeting and had a general idea of our current activities. Most of the proceedings were oral. We talked out the problems and tried to keep paperwork to a minimum.

Every establishment in the group was run as an individual unit. I believe this to be of the utmost importance. I always remember a conversation with Geoffrey Crowther when we had merged with Trust Houses. I said to him, 'You know, Geoffrey, it is an interesting business we are in, isn't it? Everything we do is made up of small things; taking shillings and pounds from customers and trying all the time to give them good value. That is the important part of our business, the individual small unit.' And his reply to me was, 'Oh, Charles, you are in a different business now. You have moved out of that. We are in the multi-million pound business.'

Well, in the hotel and catering field that is death. We were still in the business of small hoteliers and small caterers. Every Little Chef was an important operation. The manageress had got to be right and had to be properly motivated. I believed that if we sat in London and did not take an intense interest in what went on in each of the individual units and from time to time did not go and have a look, the operations would start to flag. We looked at the way they were operating, the products they were selling and the standards they were maintaining. They knew that the board of my company was a hotel and catering board. It was all we were interested in. We did not go outside that field in anything of consequence; everyone talked and thought about hotels and catering. The manager or manageress was the important person on the spot. With a bad manager, it would go wrong; with a good manager, it would go right.

On top of that, we had an intense system of controls. The word is often misinterpreted. I do not mean controls in the sense of cutting down on quality, but of setting standards and seeing that the operation conforms. We needed to determine exactly how many staff were necessary to give a certain level of service, how long they had to work and what percentage of the takings was represented by their wages and salaries. If the food and drink costs were calculated properly, we knew at the end of the day what we should be achieving as far as the prices and the profit were concerned. That degree of control was bolstered by the ancillary services, like marketing and central selling, which helped to support the individual operation, enabling the units to grow and improve. There was not a single person at the top level in Trusthouse Forte who was not continuously thinking about the business and how it could be improved, whether he was at home or in the office.

Our people were integrated into the system from the top. Each senior executive had absorbed and applied the company's philosophy and methods. They in turn educated the people below them and so it went on right down the line. We published our philosophy on the inside cover of our Annual Report and pinned up a copy in all our staff rooms. It may have appeared to state the obvious, but we were particularly proud of the fact that we were the first business concern to declare formally that there would be no racial discrimination in our business. We published this long before there was any legislation on the subject. We were a company that employed an enormous cross-section of people, they all got on with each other and they were treated properly.

The Company Philosophy.

To increase profitability and earnings per share each year in order to encourage investment and to improve and expand the business.

To give complete customer satisfaction by efficient and courteous service, with value for money.

To support managers and their staff in using personal initiative to improve the profit and quality of their operations whilst observing the company's policies.

To provide good working conditions and to maintain effective communications at all levels to develop better understanding and assist decision making.

To ensure no discrimination against sex, race, colour or creed and to train, develop and encourage promotion within the company based on merit and ability.

To act with integrity at all times and to maintain a proper sense of responsibility toward the public.

To recognize the importance of each and every employee who contributes towards these aims.

I would not claim that every single one of our employees was able to recite this by heart, but we did try to get the message over, down to the very bottom rung. One of the main channels through which we accomplished this was our system of consultative committees, which existed in every one of our establishments. Each of our managers or manageresses was trained to chair a regular meeting with the staff, to listen to their suggestions as to how conditions could be improved, and to sort out any problems that had cropped up.

This created a forum for views or even grievances, although there were very few of these. It was interesting to note how these meetings evolved. To begin with, the main part of the meeting dealt with suggestions for improvement in staff conditions, and even some complaints. As time went on much more time was devoted to suggestions on how the business could be improved, how to do things better, more easily, quickly, and efficiently. This was most gratifying.

The main weight of the day-to-day running of the company was carried by Rocco. Each of our subsidiary companies – hotels, catering, airports, and Gardner Merchant – had four board meetings a year, one of which was the budget meeting. Rocco attended each one of these. There was a full report on the company's activities of the previous quarter and projections for the coming quarter. There was a managing director's report, a financial report, a marketing report and a personnel report, then the meetings turned into question-and-answer sessions to sort out any problems.

Every week Rocco had in front of him sales reports for each

individual section of the operation. They were compared with the projected budget, with the previous year's figures, with percentage changes in the occupancy of hotels, with the average room rates, and with the head count of the staff, so that there was a constant basis of comparison.

Every month a profit and loss account was drawn up for each of the divisions, split up into its various parts or various groups of hotels. Rocco checked these back with the managing director concerned, so that we were in a constant position of determining whether things had gone right or, for any particular reason, had started going wrong.

Our main annual administrative operation was to draw up the budget, which produced the basic terms of reference for the financial year, day by day, week by week, month by month. This went into great detail for each of the divisions and all their components. Our various experts picked at it and appraised it. The operating division then presented it, certain parameters were laid down, the financial structure was decided and the operating policies and philosophies for the coming year determined. Each operating division then had to produce the results outlined in its budget.

The company had three deputy chief executives with clearly defined responsibilities: Donald Durban, for administration; Dennis Hearn, for the British and overseas hotels (apart from the United States); and Tito Chiandetti, for catering. Our American interests were part of Trusthouse Forte Inc., reporting directly to Rocco as chief executive.

Outside the United States, our hotels were managed by category rather than by geographical area, with an executive responsible for each category: luxury hotels, four-star hotels, Post Houses, inns, and family hotels.

At unit level each manager was fully responsible for the conduct of the business, the company's customers, the well-being of his staff, and the profits. He exercised direct control, reporting back to the centre through the regional executive.

In the larger hotels we broke down each income-earning area – the bedrooms, the restaurants, the shops – so that we could charge the profitability of each section and make sure that it contributed adequately to the total profit of the hotel. The managers were given operating ratios which we knew were right and which we knew could be achieved. These percentages could be applied to any new operation. It was, in effect, a system of control by proven experience and established norms, with the added advantage of enabling us to compare one unit with the other.

For a hotel to be successful it has to have people coming in through the door to stay. One of our great strengths was that we probably had the most effective sales and marketing organization in this field; certainly the best in Britain and Europe and one of the best, if not the best, in the world. Maybe one or two of the American hotel companies competed at our level, but on this side of the Atlantic we were second to none. Much of this operation was computer-controlled on an international basis and we were able to refer our clients from one hotel to the next.

Often when we took over a hotel, sometimes quite isolated, we saw the occupancy increasing five or ten percentage points overnight. Once it went into our reservation structure and into our brochures, the hotel's occupancy automatically increased. We also had a clientèle which enthusiastically chose to stay in our hotels, and if we added one single unit to the structure, that unit became more utilized overnight.

We had an extremely effective purchasing system. Obviously we could buy in bulk more cheaply than individuals. We spent more than £300 million a year on supplies – over forty million pints of milk, twenty-odd million eggs, eight million loaves, thirty-five thousand tons of meat and vegetables, three million glasses, three million pieces of crockery, six hundred thousand pieces of cutlery and sixty-five miles of carpet, etc. More than twenty-five per cent of this went through our centralized purchasing division, but if our hotels and restaurants thought they could buy more cheaply locally, they had discretion to do so.

We had central kitchens at Dunstable. The tiny establishment at Percy Street in the old days would barely fill the entrance lobby. There was a butchery in South London and a chain of provincial distribution depots. We maintained our own laboratory at Colnbrook in West London, where experts continually tested foodstuffs and collaborated with our chefs over new recipes.

We maintained at the centre a key department called Management Services, which was both a consultancy and a troubleshooting department. If one of our operations started to run into problems, we got Management Services to go and have an independent look and come up with recommendations.

Of course Rocco added his own style and perspective. He reasons things out more than I do and has a slightly different way with people: I think I am more out-going. He has the same feelings about people – perhaps even more so – but he doesn't show them so much. He is more reserved than I am, which of course has its advantages. He is also more temperate than I am. I tend to see the world in black and white: heroes and villains, competents and incompetents. Rocco, I believe, is more capable of grasping the complexities of a situation and he sees the world in black, white and shades of grey.

With his background, training, innate good sense and good taste, I am certain he continued to inspire and expand the company and took it to new heights of achievement. He had experience not only of the operational side of hotel keeping and catering, but also had close contact with the financial director's duties, and with the personnel, marketing and training functions, as well as the experience of working with a large international company with all that this implies.

I had total confidence in his capacity and that of his colleagues – all of his generation, all experienced, skilled and determined.

I do believe the future of the hotel business in Britain is bright. For one thing, we have the most marvellous assets in the country itself: the museums, art galleries, cathedrals, great country houses, the countryside, and of course the courtesy of the inhabitants. But I certainly do not wish to see Britain flooded with the kind of tourists who leave tons of rubbish and very little else. We don't want the cheap end of the tourist market here, but tourists of a calibre that the country deserves.

CHAPTER FOURTEEN

Three Generations

IN THE EARLY days before I was married I used to be out by eight o'clock in the morning to tour our establishments and check the supplies that they had been buying. I would continue the tour at lunchtime to assess the volume of custom. Sometimes I would take the afternoon off and go to a cinema or museum, but three hours later I would be back on my rounds again. At seven or eight in the evening I would have dinner, usually with a friend or some business acquaintances, and then return to my rounds, making sure that everything was operating efficiently.

Even in our New Cavendish Street flat after our marriage the timetable changed very little, although I went out less after dinner unless there was an emergency. When we moved to Hampstead, which was a longer journey from the centre of town, I tended to spend more evenings with my family. The move to Hampstead became necessary because a mansion flat in the centre of London is no place to bring up small children. Rocco and Olga were a lively, noisy pair, to the despair of our long-suffering neighbour in the flat below. Their beds had wooden side panels, which they used to take off and see-saw on. Bang, bang, bang they went on the floor and the poor man, whom the children regarded as an ogre but who was in fact exceptionally tolerant, used to come up to complain, while occasionally offering the two gifts in return for a bit of peace and quiet. We managed to maintain some discipline through a hard-working Italian nanny, who became very tough with the children and gave them several spankings. This did not stop them from loving her dearly.

Greenway Gardens in Hampstead was the solution to our domestic problems. My father saw it first. It was a large house with

about half an acre of garden which I thought would provide ideal
space for the children. It had three storeys; on the ground floor it
had a reception room, dining room, a bar room leading out on to
the garden, and a study. On the first floor there were four
bedrooms with three bathrooms, and further up there were three
more bedrooms. The asking price was £16,000 which was a lot of
money for me to find. My father suggested that I should make an
offer anyway and I managed to get the house for £11,000, having
to spend another £2,000 to £3,000 doing it up. It was 1948 when
we moved in, and we stayed there for twenty years. I understand
that it was sold about twenty-five years ago for £126,000, which is a
measure of inflation in our time.

We had four more daughters after we moved, all named after
relatives: Marie-Louise, after my mother; Irene, after my wife;
Giancarla, after my father-in-law, Giovanni Carlo; and the youngest, Porzia, after my grandmother Porzia Maria Cafolla. In this way
we have preserved the traditional Christian names in the family
for the next generation.

The house was always full of noise and activity but I have to say
that, except at weekends, I only saw the children in brief snatches.
They would come and say good morning to me before I went to
the office and they started off for school, and when I came back at
night I would ring the bell and keep my finger on it until one of
them came and opened the door.

I have to plead guilty to spending more time with Rocco than
with the girls, but then he was our only boy and in any family that
makes for a special relationship. All the children claim that I used
to fuss over Louise more than the others. Maybe this is true. But
she had had an unpleasant combination of whooping cough and
measles when she was one year old. Apparently I always over-
reacted when any one of the family was ill, immediately ringing up
doctors for advice. Irene had the right maternal instinct and took
things more calmly.

Irene was strict with the children. She insisted on the basic
disciplines of family life, the old-fashioned virtues of punctuality,
good manners, obedience and cleanliness. Until they went to
school the children were put out in the garden in the morning
and called back at teatime, and they enjoyed an almost country

upbringing. They had plenty of friends around and they all seem to remember games in the garden as the main element of their lives. Irene held me in reserve as the ultimate source of discipline and they now claim that they were all terrified of being told off by me, but I do not believe a word of it. They also complain that while they were all taken to school in a chauffeur-driven car, they were kept short of pocket money. Irene was determined, however, that they should realize the value of money and not become spoilt.

We soon had not two but three generations in Hampstead – it almost became Monforte-on-the-Heath. My mother-in-law, Olga, came to live with us in a separate flat in the house. Then Irene saw that the house next door was for sale. My father bought it and my parents settled down as part of the family unit. My cousin, Pace, and her husband, Armando, came over from Sutton to keep house for them, so my parents reached the evening of their lives surrounded by the love and affection of their family.

We knocked the garden wall down between the two houses and my father appointed himself head gardener. He had a great gift for gardening and was always pottering around making the garden quite beautiful. Father had his own car and chauffeur and he used to come down to the office occasionally to tell me where I was going wrong. This apart, he took no further role in the business.

I owe my father everything I have and am. He taught me the rudiments of the business, had confidence in me, and after his initial doubts about my breaking away to London, always supported me to the full. More than that, he inculcated in me all the best standards of an upright and hard-working family. He was a model of propriety in business and in his personal life.

There was a portrait of him, aged about eighty-four, in my office, behind my desk. One day someone said to me: 'They've made you look a bit old, haven't they?' We looked very much alike. He was my size and height and had very much the same build. As he grew older, he could not be bothered to go to the tailor any more. Instead he would ask me to have a suit made up for him. I used to show him the cloth, have it made to my measurements, and take it over to him. It would only need an

occasional small adjustment to the collar or trousers. He was a
more relaxed man than I am and was not so loquacious. He spoke
surprisingly good English but you could see he was completely
Italian in his appearance, ways and manner. He was only twenty-
seven years older than me, so age was no great barrier between us.
He was very like me in many ways, and indeed he would have been
far more successful than I have been if he had had a better start in
life. He had nothing like such a good start as me; he came over
here as an immigrant with only an elementary school education –
and that from an elementary school in the backwoods which was
certainly not remotely on a par with the kind of inspiration and
sophisticated education that he afforded me. His achievement was
more meritorious than mine.

He had an imperious presence; you could not ignore him, a
most forceful personality. He was scrupulously honest and he
would not forgive the slightest deviation. My mother was even
more so. She would say: 'Do you know, that person lies – actually
tells lies.' She could not understand how anyone could tell a lie. I
suppose people who read this book may feel I am talking about
perfect people – but I believe they were like that and I hope that I
have learnt from their example.

My father was very free with his advice about everything. He
encouraged me in the basic virtues: 'Don't drink too much, drink
will ruin you. Don't gamble: whatever amount of money you have
you will never have enough to gamble – the more you have, the
more you can lose.'

I used to have a number of vigorous arguments with him,
mainly about the business and sometimes about my brother and
sister, on whom he felt I was too hard; but such articulateness as I
have is derived from my mother, a lively talkative lady. My parents
remained what they had always been, a modest, frugal, and loving
couple from an Italian provincial background. Of course, they had
their occasional rows – my father felt that my mother put on airs
with him as she considered her family a bit better than his.

In spite of his rudimentary education my father had exceptional
taste. Some of the best furniture in my house today was bought by
him and left to me. There is a superb set of Meissen china, one

hundred and forty-six pieces in all. It must be worth a great deal now. It was always used for special occasions and nobody except him was allowed to touch it.

My father was intensely devoted to his family, especially to his grandchildren. At a family party my son Rocco, then aged about three, and named after him, picked up one of the precious Meissen plates and actually started banging it on the table. I rushed across horrified, to stop him. My father was quite cross: 'Leave the boy alone. He is not doing any harm.'

I was shooting one day when one of the farm hands came running over to the line of guns and said that I was wanted on the telephone – an urgent message from home. It was a good mile away, so I got into the Land Rover and drove back to the cottage as fast as possible. The message was unexpected and even worse than I had anticipated. My father had had a stroke.

I drove straight back to London. My father was well over eighty by now but until that day had been strong and in full possession of his faculties; it had come to seem as if he was indestructible. Now he lay crippled and helpless. I could hardly believe it and I took a long time to get over it. But, aided by the great courage and tenacity that he had possessed in abundance, my father fought back to near recovery. He took exercises, regained most of the use of his left side, which had been affected, and returned to walking round the garden again. He had the very best doctors and care and lived on for another five years, dying at the age of eighty-seven.

My mother had died two years before. She had not enjoyed good health during her declining years and was often in bed, but she remained as gentle and sweet as ever.

She had very few friends apart from the family – her English was not good and the family was her universe. I was everything to her and she was gentleness itself. She had also taken to Irene the moment she saw her, and treated her like a daughter, – indeed Irene was equally fond of her. I never heard my mother wish, or do, any harm to anybody. She was also a superb cook. Irene, my sister Anna, and Cousin Pace all learnt their cooking from her and my daughters are equally good. All my relations took every opportunity to sample her wonderful food and she produced the most marvellous recipe for stuffing the Christmas turkey, which I give here. I can recommend it to anyone.

STUFFING FOR CHRISTMAS TURKEY

Ingredients (for a 20lb turkey)

2½ lb white bread crumbs (obtained from stale loaves)

4 cloves garlic

1½ cups picked parsley

4 whole eggs

3 oz. ox tongue (cut in cubes)

½ lb gammon ham (cut in cubes)

2 dessert spoons olive oil

¼ pint milk

salt/pepper

Preparation

1 Finely chop garlic and washed parsley

2 Lightly fry the gammon ham

3 Break eggs into a bowl

Method

1 In a large earthenware bowl, mix the bread crumbs with the chopped parsley and garlic, dispersing the latter well

2 Add 4 whole eggs and two dessert spoons of olive oil

3 Add milk little by little in order to obtain a thick doughy consistency

4 Add ox tongue and ham, and work these two ingredients well into mixture

5 Season with salt and pepper to taste.

Stuff the neck of the turkey only, filling out the breast skin flap well. Tuck the flap well over the shoulders of the bird and lightly sew the ends on to the back.

Roast the turkey as normal ensuring that it is often and regularly basted.

The telephone was for me an instrument of torture during the last five or six years of her life; every time it rang I used to think it must be some medical problem over my mother.

Her heart problems were long drawn out and painful. I remember when she was eighty-two I asked Dr D. Evan Bedford, who was looking after her, who the greatest heart man in the world was.

'There is one man I would defer to,' he said. 'Paul White.' He told me that White was in America, so I asked Dr Bedford to bring him over.

'What, all the way from America? He may not want to come.'

'Well, try – and I will pay his fare and whatever fee he wants.'

Paul White came over to see my mother. He confirmed that she was having good treatment from Dr Bedford, but he changed things a little bit. I asked him anxiously how long my mother would live. Without hesitation he said: 'Under twelve months.' You may imagine my feelings – and he was absolutely correct.

My parents remained Italian to the last but they had become so fond of Britain that in their later years, even when they were still in good health, they never returned to Monforte for long.

'Why don't you go and spend a few days up in the village?' I used to ask.

'Well, yes, I might go and spend a few days,' my father would reply, and that is exactly what he did.

They both lived an absolutely blameless life and had never had any sort of brush with the authorities. I doubt if my father had ever even committed a parking offence. They were upright, honest, hard-working, God-fearing people. Both are buried in Hampstead cemetery. Like Monforte it is on a hill.

The family is an integral part of my existence and always has been because I have always belonged to a tight family unit. I have tried as far as possible to insulate my family from the problems, pressures and dramas of my business career. You cannot put a family first, second or third. It is all important, and I have always tried to make the family important not only to me, but for all its members, too, encouraging everyone to contribute to the unit in whatever capacity he or she is able. Such a contribution makes it easier for the family to give to the individual in return. I have always felt quite instinctively an ingrained sense of duty towards my family, and they have returned it. It has made for an extremely happy existence.

It is my wife Irene who has kept the family unit together and made a marvellous home for us. She is the most perfect wife and mother and I never cease to thank the Lord for my good fortune. She has always been a tremendous source of strength to the family, always there, always solid and always willing to help and to encourage each one.

I praise my wife as all happily married men praise theirs. She and I have been close and good partners all our married life. We have always enjoyed each other's company more than that of any other person. Whenever I have had to bring business problems home I have discussed them with Irene, who has always had good, sound common sense advice to give. She knows the way my mind works and is able to lend encouragement. She can sense if I am preoccupied and will get me to chat about it, but she never takes the initiative in trying to influence me in matters of business. She is the sounding board and solid support whenever I need it. I have yet to hear her make an unkind remark about anyone.

I have always enjoyed being with children, especially my own. I would get particular pleasure from taking Rocco and Olga back to Monforte and to Scotland, so that they could appreciate something of their origin. I took the other girls later as they grew up, though perhaps with less frequency.

Most of my children are bilingual. Their first language was English, but we encouraged them to speak Italian and they have kept it up to this day. Louise speaks Italian very well, but we were less insistent with the others and the youngest, Porzia, hardly speaks it at all. All the children were brought up Roman Catholics, and they went to Catholic schools, always under heavy pressure from me to get good marks, though sadly I found little enough time in which to guide the girls in what they should read and learn.

With Rocco it was different. He was my only son and I took a very close interest in everything he did. Occasionally, I think, he found this attention exasperating. But we have remained good friends. When you think of the tensions which can arise between father and son, and the age difference between us, thirty-six years, it is something of a miracle.

I used to fence a bit before the war and eventually took it up again. I was coached by Professor Delzi, at one time European sabre champion. He was a great teacher and the sport attracted Rocco. So we used to have regular fencing lessons in the Hampstead house, in which Olga joined as well. She cannot have been more than ten or twelve at the time. Rocco became very good indeed at it, and eventually became a fencing blue at Oxford.

I gave a lot of thought to choosing the best school for Rocco. He had the opportunity to enter most of Britain's leading public schools, but I was determined to choose first and foremost on academic standards. I was relieved to be told on good authority that the Roman Catholic public schools Downside and Ampleforth, were among the best, academically, in the country. We chose Downside, thus combining my desire for academic merit and Irene's strong wish for a Catholic education.

Downside is set in pleasant, rolling country in the Mendips outside Bath. It was a four-and-a-half-hour drive down from London in those days and I used to go down to see Rocco every other weekend. Rocco always looked forward to my visits. I would take him out to lunch or dinner with several of his friends, and we would go fishing on the local reservoirs. I enjoyed these weekends as much, if not more, than Rocco did. I am always pleased that I chose Downside, which completely lived up to all my expectations.

I was keen that Rocco should follow me into the business but I was determined not to force the issue. Nevertheless, he showed an interest at an early age and I encouraged this. I often discussed business with him at home and always answered his questions, while taking note of his views. I would let him look at interesting correspondence and letters and I never hid anything from him. But I never pressed the matter of his joining the firm: 'Whatever you want to do,' I used to tell him, 'if it is honest, do it well and give it the best you have.'

I still remember an occasion at lunch in the Hampstead house when Irene used some such phrase as: 'If you are ever as good as your father . . .' I sat down with her afterwards and asked her never to do it again. And she has not, for I explained that that was the best way of creating a rift between father and son. In our case this has never happened and today I can see that Rocco is as quick as I am at grasping essentials, financial or otherwise, if not quicker.

In order to earn some extra pocket money during the school holidays, Rocco went to work in a number of our establishments. When he was sixteen he did a spell down in the cellars of the Café Royal. On one occasion he was taking stock with a wine merchant, who had no idea who he was. Rocco must have made a good impression because the man said to him: 'Look, young lad, if you are looking for a job at any time, come and see me.' When I heard about this, I was amused and delighted.

We certainly used to have the occasional difference of opinion. 'I don't know if you have any idea how old-fashioned you are,' Rocco said on one occasion.

I thought my reply was quite good. 'Remember this,' I told him. 'Five thousand years ago what I am saying was right. In five thousand years' time what I am saying will still be right – cleanliness, honesty, decency, respect for other people, politeness, good manners, integrity – they will never be old-fashioned.' I don't suppose he was grateful – who is, for advice? – but it remains true.

I was very keen for Rocco to go to Oxford. He was not all that enthusiastic, but I was absolutely determined that a university education, an element which had been missing in my own life, should form part of his. I was delighted when he was offered a place at Christ Church, Oxford, but it was only for the following year. Rocco had heard that there were three places available at Pembroke in the current year. He worked immensely hard with no pressure from me and succeeded in obtaining one of these places.

He enjoyed university, though he did not gain any double firsts. As I have said, he got his half blue at fencing, at which he was quite exceptional, and he beat the British champion, Hoskins, three times. There was a good chance that he would make the British Olympic team, but at that time he had started work in earnest and did not have time to train properly.

One story he tells against me, which is perfectly true, concerns his allowance at the time. I had given him £1,000 a year at Oxford, which was a reasonable sum. It was not over-generous, but it meant that he could live comfortably. When he came down he had made up his mind, certainly without any discouragement from me, that he would like to come into the business. It was decided that it would be a good idea if he spent three years getting his articles as a chartered accountant. He went for an interview with my good friend Charles Hardie, and was given a job, with a salary of £700 a year. With the £1,000 a year he had been getting from me, coupled with the fact that he was living at home with very few outgoings, there opened up for him visions of a life of near luxury. We had lunch that day.

'How did you get on?' I asked.

'Oh, I got the job,' he said.

'Very good. What are they going to pay you?'

'£700 a year.'

'That's even better,' I told him. 'I can reduce your allowance to £300.'

The girls have all been family- rather than academically-minded, although I made it clear to each of them in turn that I would be more than happy if they wanted to go on to university. Irene became head girl at St Mary's, Ascot, and had a good scholastic record. She considered going to university, but decided against it. Giancarla, my fourth daughter, went to university for a couple of months but found she was not enjoying it and left.

All the family now complain that they were very strictly brought up and it is true that we preferred to keep them close to home. Olga goes so far as to say that she never spent a night away from home until she was married. That was not quite true because we let her go to stay a couple of times in Italy with great friends of ours, Grete and Enrico Mattei, about whom I have already written. The children could have all the friends they wanted round to the Hampstead house, could organize dances and parties, but they still hold it against me that at about midnight I used to throw everybody out!

Eventually the family home in Hampstead became inconvenient. I was beginning to be asked to one function after another, which

meant rushing back to Hampstead, changing, rushing back to the
West End and getting back to Hampstead late at night. But now,
with my parents' death, there was no reason for us to live out
there.

A lovely residence came on the market, Chester House in
Upper Belgrave Street, just off Belgrave Square, next door to the
Belgian Embassy. I bought it and spent another £100,000 refurbish-
ing it and making some alterations.

Eventually we had to move again, leaving Chester House, as we
required more accommodation. My mother-in-law, then nearly
ninety years of age, lived with us, and our children, not yet
married, were also with us. We moved into a house with more
bedroom accommodation, in a quieter street. I remember that
selling Chester House was a stimulating experience. I sold it to
Prince Khaled, a member of the Saudi Arabian Royal family. His
advisers argued strenuously about the price, which admittedly was
high, and eventually the Prince and I had a face-to-face discussion
at the Dorchester Hotel where he was staying. He was a charming
man, elegant and well spoken.

'We are not bargaining,' I told him. 'That is the price and the
price is reasonable. I have ascertained the market value for the
house and what I am asking you is the market value.'

'Yes, it is an excellent house', he agreed.

I went on: 'The price is what I say it is. I am afraid I won't argue
about it or bargain about it.'

Prince Khaled replied: 'I am not arguing about it. I agree with
the price.'

'But your chap . . .'

'Never mind my chap . . . As a matter of fact I would like to buy
the contents as well.'

I told him that the contents were not for sale.

'But I particularly like the chandelier in the reception room.'

'Well, I will give you that – you can have it.' I later got into
trouble with my wife, as she too liked the chandelier (it was very
valuable and hard to replace).

He was also particularly impressed by the tidiness and organization of our house, and how well everything was kept. He told me

that I must have a very good housekeeper. I said: 'Yes, my wife –
but I am afraid she doesn't go with the house . . .'

In 1966 Olga married: a charming man, Allesandro Polizzi di
Sorrentino, the son of General Polizzi, the head of the medical
services of the Italian Air Force. Tragically he was killed in an
accident some years ago, leaving Olga with two young daughters.
She decided to come and work for the company, and surprised us
all by her considerable talent. She is in charge of décor and design
and she managed to combine creative flair with organizational
ability and exceptional drive. This is a great gift – I have seen
people with considerable artistic talent who have failed because
they lacked business sense, and vice versa. Olga later married the
distinguished journalist, William Shawcross.

Rocco delighted us all by marrying Aliai Ricci in February 1986.
They had known each other for quite some time and her parents
are old friends of ours.

Louise is married to Robert Burness, who works for the company, and Irene, my third daughter, to John Danilovich, who is in
shipping.

Giancarla is married to Michael Alen-Buckley, a stockbroker.

All seem very happy indeed.

I am pleased that members of my family work in the business.
They turn the light out when they leave the room, and they look
after the pennies! In fact, I have a delightful family.

I enjoy quite extraordinary good health, to the point, I am told,
that my family regard me as a fitness fanatic. They say that I am
always trying to stop them smoking or to put them on a diet. I take
a mixture of the generations off to Portugal in the summer on
holiday, and they complain that I make them play two eighteen-
hole rounds of golf or several games of tennis a day, or swim sixty
lengths of the pool, or make them eat nothing but salad.

I like having my grandchildren around. I may turn on them
occasionally and tell them to make less noise, but when they leave
I wish they were back again. I have always been accustomed to
having three generations around me and I infinitely prefer it to
having a dinner party with people of my own age. I am told I spoil
the youngsters disgracefully, always handing out folding money for

them to spend, but I am careful not to overdo it, or let them imagine that it is something that grows on trees.

We sit down to Christmas dinner with at least thirty people, all members of the family, and they have taken to turning up unannounced every Saturday at Ripley when we are shooting.

I said to Olga only the other day that for me an ideal existence would have been to have lived on an enormous estate. We should have sold everything and have bought seven houses, all within sight of each other – in fact like an old Boer farmer. Olga said: 'Then you don't think you behave like an old Boer farmer now, then?'

CHAPTER FIFTEEN

Afterthoughts

HARD WORK HAS always come naturally to me and I throve on it. I maintain what is maybe an old-fashioned view that the man who works a bit harder and longer is the one most likely to achieve success. I have always regarded work as rather like piano practice: the more you do, the better you do it – though I have spent most of my life performing, not practising, sixteen hours a day, very often from eight o'clock in the morning until midnight, probably double the amount of work that the average man does.

Of course I have been inspired by enthusiasm for what I was doing and the realization of the direct benefits my work was bringing to me. I have also been helped by enjoying very good health, a crucial factor in business success. I have found that if you enjoy what you are doing and your work is free from debilitating tensions, you can work amazingly long hours without it affecting your health and that when you get tired you can recover quickly.

For me success lies not only in achieving the financial rewards of my endeavours but also in the satisfaction of doing a job effectively. What is success anyway? I know many 'poor' men with a lot of money. Real success consists not of having millions in the bank but of fulfilment and happiness in the knowledge that you are doing something worthwhile – as well as having no financial worries.

A successful person is in fact one who has a fulfilling job, a loving and happy family, good health and enough money to provide him or her with the basic necessities and pleasures of life. Although money is splendid stuff, and, of course, can provide wonderful security, the single-minded pursuit of it can be brutalizing, and obviously, in itself, does not bring happiness.

There seems to be a general impression that I am a tough character who grew up bare-footed, avid for money. Some years ago I was visiting one of our hotels in Scotland. The manageress, a charming young woman, was there with her husband and over a drink she said: 'Oh, I do admire you, Sir Charles. You really are a wheeler-dealer.' I was not pleased.

'What do you mean, wheeler-dealer?' I asked. 'I am a hard-working hotel and catering man. I am not a wheeler-dealer at all.'

Even this nice young woman had the wrong impression. She thought that I was some sort of buccaneer, one of those people who goes out and makes £2 million here, £5 million there, sells this, buys that. It is all wrong and I don't think any lasting success can be achieved in this way. I do not equate success with accumulating vast sums of money, but there is an exceptional fulfilment for a successful entrepreneur in a life of building up a business from scratch. I have a few observations on successful entrepreneurship, and they are definitely observations rather than prescriptions or a blueprint. They have been culled from my experience, and from observing other successful businessmen; and they may either inspire or deter.

I say 'deter', because the life of an entrepreneur is not for any aspiring executive. Entrepreneurs can be born – and indeed made; they have special qualities which can be inherited, or derived from upbringing, experience and acquaintances, but they are very special qualities – not everyone has them, and yet I suspect more people have them than is fully realized.

But I am positive about one thing: it is that if you can find a solitary excuse for not making a fortune, then you will certainly not succeed.

Let us look at excuses. Age, I suppose, is one. But I believe that an old-age pensioner can make himself rich, if he so wishes. Look at the man who built the Liberty ships in the last war. He was in his eighties before he started making a lot of money developing property in the Pacific. You can argue that he had already made a fortune as an industrialist in America, but a millionaire entering a new field is as vulnerable as the next man – sometimes more vulnerable.

The next usual excuse is inexperience. I can only cite the

example of my mother-in-law, who was left a widow with very little money at forty-six. She immediately went into business and prospered. There are many like her.

Responsibility? A man in his forties or fifties who has sat at someone else's desk all his working life and has a mortgage and a growing family, obviously has to be braver than most of us if he is going to give away his security. But it has often been done, and done successfully.

So may I say as gently as I can that if you feel that the above are real objections, it would be best not to try to make a lot of money as an entrepreneur. Self-doubt is every man's worst enemy. I am not sure whether it is an attractive or unattractive quality, but I must say I have been completely lacking in it.

What about luck? I regard it as an element both to respect and to ignore. I think that too much good fortune too soon is dangerous. It promotes over-confidence, and we all know examples of people who have been overwhelmed by good luck. Fortune turns against people like this; they often crash, not just half-way, but right down to the bottom.

I think it is better by far to remember the parable of the Japanese salesman who, every time a door was slammed in his face, let his smile grow wider. When asked why, he said: 'By the sheer law of averages, the door that will open must be getting nearer.'

What about the special qualities of an entrepreneur? Lasting success does not come easily. Assiduity and dedication are essential. Successful people persist in what they are doing. Normally they are very hard-working and they usually manage to get through work quickly: in fact, they manage to do far more work in an hour than the next man can do.

Take Simon Marks and his brother-in-law and partner, Israel Sieff, who built up Marks and Spencer. I knew them both. I found Israel Sieff fascinating and thought the world of him. Every Saturday he would put on his hat and coat and off he would go to one of his stores, and look round thoroughly – this at the time when he was an elderly man and chairman of the company. He would inspect the goods, look at the customers and the display; he wished to see with his own eyes what was happening.

Hector Laing, who built up United Biscuits, is a rather different example. Irene and I went to dinner at his flat one evening. Peter Carrington and his wife were also there. When I had finished the first course, Hector asked me pointedly if I had liked it. I thought that it was a little curious to find a host asking whether I enjoyed what I was eating. Actually, I had semi-enjoyed it – it wasn't bad. But I said: 'Yes, thanks, very much.'

Hector then said: 'As a matter of fact we make it and it costs £x a gross.'

I said neutrally: 'I see.'

He went on: 'Yes, that is one of our frozen food products. It was good, wasn't it? And I am sure you could use that in your firm.'

My eyes met Peter Carrington's; he could hardly believe what he was hearing.

Exactly the same happened with the next course. 'Did you like that, Charles? You can keep that in the refrigerator for six days . . .' etc.

The dinner party was in fact a selling session. When I left the house my wife said to me: 'What an extraordinary man.'

I said: 'By God, I admire him. I *do* admire him. He is absolutely dedicated to his product. Of course "it is not done", etc. – but what the hell! He was straight and to the point and everything else.'

It was from that moment that I came to admire Hector Laing for his forthright and uninhibited dedication to his business.

Hard work, ambition, dedication, and persistence, make bad bed-fellows but they are essential, as is common sense. They will not work, however, without capital. I started out with some of my own money and a bank guarantee for £2,000 from my father. Jack Cohen of Tesco had only sufficient money to get a barrow and put a few cabbages on top. I would recommend beginning with as much share capital and as little bank borrowing as possible, otherwise you may find you are working for the bank.

I am not a great risk-taker. I suppose risks must be taken, but you must always have an eye to the consequences of the risk. If you take a big risk for a small gain, it is ridiculous. If you take a small risk for a big gain, then you are being intelligent and far-sighted. Ultimately successful business people really do not take major risks. They never take a risk that might wreck the business – never.

Otherwise the business sooner or later is wrecked. You can gamble ten times and get away with it, but the eleventh time can ruin you and the business you have striven with a lot of people, to create over the years.

When you take a risk ask yourself: how much can I lose? Can I lose £5 million? Yes. Can I afford to lose £5 million? Not really, but I can stand it. If it is going to be £10 million, that's going to wreck me. So you don't risk £10 million.

In this book you can read of many apparent risks I have taken. In fact, I don't regard any of the major moves I have made in business as *real* risks. I have always analysed the venture very carefully, until I was confident that it made complete financial sense. And if it went wrong, the venture would never have ruined me.

Another of the keys to success is the ability not to make major mistakes. Judgement, based on instinct, experience, or common sense, is essential – good judgement both of people and of business situations.

Everyone has made mistakes, but you cannot make too many serious ones. Two major mistakes I made, both described in the book, were over Mr Whippy and over the Plaza Hotel. I think, on the whole I also have good judgement of people – but there have been exceptions. I have taken people on, trained them, looked after them well, made way for them, and then they have left me and become the biggest enemies of the company.

Probably the best decision I ever made was the merger with Trust Houses. But during the blackest moments I thought I could have made a mistake: I had misjudged Crowther, who was determined to swindle me out of something I had created.

Any big business is built up by a consistent series of correct decisions. If this were not the case, the business would surely not exist. The fact is that, by a combination of good management and luck, we got most of the things right most of the time. If we had not done so, we would now have no business.

Some people, whatever they do, fail, but I have noticed that those who succeed never blame other people when they have a bit of a failure, because they have got the strength and courage to blame themselves. It takes a lot of courage to blame oneself when things go wrong. An unsuccessful person often blames everyone except the real culprit – himself.

As you head successfully for your target, you may find that your aims have changed. The actual money you are making becomes of little interest. You want more plant, more equipment, a second shop, or a further challenge. This is another of the critical stages; your resources may become stretched, taut, even over-taut. The only thing that will get you over this barrier, perhaps the most difficult of all your hurdles will be your integrity. Your name must be your bond. You must be able to write your signature as if you were Nathan Rothschild.

I have learned quite a lot from consultants, but does one need them? Sir John Harvey-Jones, former chairman of ICI said: 'A consultant is someone who borrows your watch to tell you the time.' I wouldn't put it quite like that – but I would say about five per cent of their advice is useful.

I have left to the last the question of diet and exercise, a favourite subject of mine. Forgive me if I am about to give a homily, but I believe it to be important. I do not believe that you can succeed without positive good health, and the way you look after your body is thus relevant to your success.

I am eighty-nine years of age and I have not yet had a major illness. Part of this good health and activity must be due to my genes – I came from sturdy stock. But it is also due, I believe, to the way I live.

First of all, you should have good feelings about things and people. If you do, you have a chance of being healthier. If you do not, debilitating tension arises. I think positive relaxation is an excellent way of ridding oneself of it. I spend ten minutes a day lying on my back on a settee.

I take an above-average amount of exercise. Every morning I do a Swedish series of exercises, mostly twisting and bending, and then fifty press-ups. At night I also do twenty press-ups before I go to bed, unless I have had more than usual to eat and drink. In the morning I have a hot shower followed by a cold shower. Exercise in the fresh air is essential. I still walk a lot.

I don't believe in a lot to drink: at the most two or three glasses of wine a day, plus the occasional glass of whisky. I try to avoid alcohol in the middle of the day as much as I can, because I find it slows me down. What drinking I do, I tend to do in the evening.

I eat a lot of fruit and vegetables, though I am not a vegetarian – I eat meat three or four times a week, but no more. When my wife and I are on our own, maybe at weekends, we have a lot of vegetables for lunch and a big salad at night, with fruit. I find this does me good and keeps my weight controlled. I avoid fatty things as far as possible, have honey instead of sugar and I have cut out salt and white bread.

All of the above is, I suspect, fairly obvious, but I know that following these rules and routines has given me vitality very much above average for my age, and I believe this vitality is reflected in my business performance.

There is a passage in one of Scott Fitzgerald's novels which goes: '"Let me tell you about the very rich – they are very different from you and me." "Yes, they have more money."'

The very rich may be different from other people – large sums of money bring security, independence, and great pleasure, as well as the opposite. I suppose I am kept happy by not wanting things. I am not really a slippers-and-fire man, nor a hermit. I like beautiful objects. But I have never wanted yachts and harems and villas in the South of France. I like best to be within the family. But if the rich are different from other people, and I am not so sure that I agree with Scott Fitzgerald, they are all certainly different from each other. Wealth gives you the freedom to be yourself, for better or for worse. It positively encourages individuality and self-expression. Millionaires I know are a bunch about whom I would find it difficult to generalize. You could not, for instance have two millionaires less alike than Harold Lever and Paul Getty.

I gather someone once asked Harold Lever: 'What kind of socialist are you? You married your wife because she had four million.'

Harold's reply was: 'I married my wife because she had four

million? I would have married my wife even if she had only two million.'

Paul Getty's meanness was legendary and in my opinion mythical. On a few occasions when my wife and I had dinner with him at Sutton Place, he was far from mean. We enjoyed the best wine and very good food. I still remember a Château Latour 1943. He always provided the best for his guests, and I have made at least two 'phone calls from his office in his house without charge – and yet they tell the story of Paul Getty installing pay 'phones. I did not see a pay 'phone, but if there was one hidden somewhere it must have been installed for someone who saves up long-distance calls for visits to his friends.

Getty was a knowledgeable man on most things, not only commerce and industry but also art and furniture. On one occasion after dinner he insisted that we should go upstairs to look at some innovation in his bedroom. Irene and I went up with expectancy, thinking that we should see some wonderful picture or *objet d'art*; but behind a screen was a stove, a cupboard, a shelf and a small fridge.

'You see,' he said, 'sometimes I come home very late at night – the household is all asleep and I don't want to disturb them. So if I require a hot chocolate drink at one a.m. I can make one for myself.' He showed us this with great pride.

Getty was a man who hated waste of any kind and this quality can be mistaken for meanness. During the rationing period after the war, Getty had invited three friends to dinner at the Caprice. It was fairly late, 9.45 p.m. and they were all feeling hungry.

As they neared the restaurant Getty said: 'Let's walk around a bit before we go in.'

'Walk around?' said one of his friends, 'I am hungry.'

But Getty was adamant. 'Let's wait, it's not ten yet.' Then he added: 'There's a cover charge of five shillings a head, and after ten p.m. they take it off the bill. I don't want to pay an extra pound for fifteen minutes.'

I have been interested by, but very rarely actively involved in, politics. I was made a life peer in 1981, but I am not a natural speaker and do not have a political mind. I might intervene in uncontroversial subjects and see whether experience in my profession enables me to make a contribution.

I have a special liking for Margaret Thatcher. She never wears the company down with political talk and is always forthright in her common sense. I genuinely believe she had a vision of leading this country back to greatness, and I am not talking about an old-fashioned imperial greatness, but a greatness based on the development of this country's true potential; a greatness in a moral and modern context, one in which our traditions, institutions, system of government, and, indeed, the great qualities of the British way of life can be preserved.

Margaret Thatcher is a patriot. She cares passionately for the well-being of all people. She has been called uncaring, but she does care, even though she does not wear her heart on her sleeve. She is not running a hat shop or a dress shop. To lead, one must be forceful and she has proved conclusively that she is a leader. Nevertheless, I do wish that this very great lady always communicated publicly this passionate care which she expresses so movingly in private. She will go down in history as an outstanding national and international figure.

Jim Callaghan is another man who put country above party – a man I have always liked and admired, and who has a good sense of humour. I remember well having had lunch with him and others at 11 Downing Street. He accompanied us to the door and photographers took our picture. He put his arm round my shoulders, saying, 'This will do my credit a lot of good Charles.' I thought ruefully of the large overdraft I then had at the bank.

I admired Aneurin Bevan also. When I first met him, he challenged me: 'You Italians. You took the Tyrol from Austria.' He was referring to what happened after the First World War. I managed to produce quite a good answer: 'We didn't take it, we took it back.' I did remember from my history that the Tyrol had once been part of the Venetian Empire. Bevan was the greatest master of words I have ever listened to in the House of Commons. I wish there were more people like him and Jim Callaghan in the Labour Party.

When Richard Nixon came over to London to help launch one

of his books we gave him lunch. He was intelligent and witty to talk to. 'I bought a bed in Paris which belonged to Napoleon,' he told me. 'It would just about fit you. You must come and see me in California and sleep in it.'

I had lunch with President Reagan when he was Governor of California. I found him an extremely interesting, charming and modest man.

Incidentally, it has occasionally been suggested that my small size provides me with Napoleonic ambition. It has never bothered me. I have only found it a handicap at a football match when I am trying to look over someone else's shoulder. Anyway, a lot of the Napoleons of the world are tall men (such as General de Gaulle).

My own political views are straightforward if rather unfashionable. In this country I believe that we are far too pushed around by an articulate minority. If the silent, hard-working, respectable, kindly majority took to marching, and maybe one day it will, the squares and streets of our cities and villages would be overflowing. The silent majority comprises every section of our population – doctors, lawyers, miners, railwaymen, city gentlemen, housewives, merchants, teachers, shop assistants, nurses, etc. We have a great heritage to preserve. We belong to a country which is still great. Why in God's name are we not proud of our heritage? Why don't we all strive our damnedest to keep this country great? Why don't we stand up and be counted?

I can't say that I believe that things have changed for the better in this country in the last twenty or so years. The churches are no longer full and people have become more avaricious. In fact I think we are not as respectable as we were once. I include the City in this criticism. I am shocked for instance, when a bank that has done business with a client for a hundred years involves itself in supporting a hostile takeover bid against the same client, as happened recently. Many people want to get there too quickly.

From a very early age I have been interested in sport: I am an enthusiastic trout and salmon fisherman; I shoot regularly; I play golf; and in the summer months we always go sailing. In case this sounds as if I have adopted the pleasures of the rich, I must point out that all these pursuits developed naturally. I learnt to shoot in my holidays in Monforte (the surrounding Apennines provide some good rough shooting); the first time I caught a fish was in Scotland in a reservoir above Alloa; and my interest in sailing started with a dinghy in Weymouth in the twenties. When the children were growing up after the Second World War, I bought my first motor cruiser and am now on to my fourth one.

In 1965, a 1,200-acre estate at Ripley, near Guildford, Surrey, with some excellent farmland and some decent shooting on it, came on to the market. I bought it from the Bowater Corporation.

The farm manager lived uncomfortably in a large seventeenth-century cottage. At first we used part of the cottage at the weekends but soon found ourselves rather cramped. So I built a comfortable modern house for the farm manager, helped him to furnish it, and with my wife moved into the other house which we extended and modernized. I still have the estate, and when I was elevated to the House of Lords, I suggested to the College of Arms that I could take the title of Clackmannan, Alloa or Ripley. The recommendation was Ripley, so the territorial part of my title is Ripley.

I have always had a lively interest in the arts even though I do not have the comprehensive knowledge that comes from a university degree in the humanities. My studies stopped at the age of seventeen, but four years in Italy provided me with a good foundation in literature and the arts, which has stood me in good stead. Homer, Virgil, Dante and Shakespeare came into my life at an early stage, not to mention Gibbon, with whom I was force-fed by my Uncle Dominic in Weston-super-Mare.

I have always enjoyed reading, particularly history. I suppose I have also acquired a very passable general knowledge of literature and can claim to have read most of the best authors. However hard I was working, I developed the habit of reading for half an hour or an hour, usually in bed. This always relaxed me and when I put the book down and the light out I dropped off to sleep immediately.

Music came more naturally to me. It was a passion of my father's, as I have said. He was always talking about opera and had a good collection of old-fashioned gramophone records, played with a steel needle. He insisted that I learn to play the cello, which, to my regret, I gave up at nineteen, but at least it gave me an idea of the principles of music. I grew up with good music in my ears and I first heard Verdi's *Requiem* at the Augusteo in Rome when I was fourteen or fifteen. During the post-war years, when I was building up the business, I would go to the theatre or the opera or a concert whenever I could, and then pay a late-night visit to whichever of our branches was nearby, to make sure that everything was in order.

I enjoy *La Traviata* and *Tosca*, and I like Beethoven's symphonies above all, but I have not studied them. I listen spellbound to people who are really knowledgeable about music. I can occasionally contribute an observation or an experience. 'Ah,' people say to me, 'you know a lot about music.' This is not true; I simply enjoy it.

In the visual arts I have a better foundation. The teachers at the Mamiani School in Rome used to take us round the churches and museums, with the object of explaining many of the artistic marvels of Rome. Indeed, many of the churches in Rome are museums in themselves. We were also taken on trips to Florence. Occasionally I became bored with this rigorous pursuit of artistic education, though now I wish I could do it all over again, step by step, church by church, gallery by gallery.

During the pre-war years, I would visit the London galleries and museums and it was then that I developed my preferences. After the war, when things became easier for me financially, I started buying prints, mostly of Old Masters. I bought a Phil May drawing and a Max Beerbohm caricature and had them hanging in my office in the Café Royal building. Max Beerbohm had been a habitué of the Café Royal, so it seemed appropriate.

My most serious early purchases, some time in the mid-fifties, were two Lowrys. I went to an exhibition of his work and was captivated. I was struck most by his original style. As I recall, I paid £250 for each of the paintings but Irene was not very encouraging – she thought they were awful. 'I think they are damned good,' I said and I believe I can say that my judgement has been vindicated.

One of my main regrets is not having availed myself of opportunities to buy other paintings, particularly certain French Impressionists, which I suppose I could just have afforded. I also remember one occasion when I met Isaac Woolfson, the then wealthy head of Great Universal Stores, at his flat in Portland Square. Isaac was a man I liked immensely, for his Scottish accent and Jewish sense of humour, as well as his exceptional judgement and flair in business.

Lying on the carpet was a Modigliani.

'Oh you know the artist,' said Isaac.

'Yes I do.'

'Have you got one of his?'

'I wish I had.'

'You know that they want £16,000 for this picture?'

'Well buy it, Isaac. One day it will be worth half a million.'

I don't know if Isaac did buy it but I hope he did.

Isaac Woolfson could easily have afforded it. I certainly could not, or at least I thought I could not. With that £16,000 I could have opened another milk bar. Perhaps I should have bought a few more paintings and opened fewer milk bars! Or should I?

Let me digress a little on the subject of Isaac: I found him one of the most extraordinary people I have ever met in business. One of his favourite stories about himself has, I think, been told with variations about other successful businessmen. He claimed that he was having lunch one day in a restaurant when he was approached by a young Jewish businessman who told him that he was attempting to make his way in the world and would appreciate a bit of help. All he wanted Isaac to do was to come to his table on his way out and say a few words to him. The man thought this would impress his colleagues and do a great deal for his credit rating. Isaac did as he was requested. But his protégé acted unpredictably – though shrewdly. 'Go away, Woolfson,' he said, 'can't you see I'm busy?'

The last time I saw Isaac was in the South of France. He approached me with a great grin. 'Forte, would you like to buy a bank?'

'Not if *you* are selling it, Isaac,' I replied.

During the fifties I was able to act as an art patron in a small way. A friend of mine, Leonard Boden, is a distinguished artist. He had painted the Queen, Prince Philip and other members of the royal family, and had acquired quite a reputation. Boden asked me if I knew whether a portrait of Pope Pius XII, formerly Cardinal Pacelli, had ever been painted. I said I had no idea.

'I would love to paint him,' said Boden. 'Do you think it could be arranged?'

'I don't know,' I replied, 'but we'll try.'

I went to the parish priests of the Italian Church of St Peter in Clerkenwell, London, and said that if they could persuade Pope Pius to sit for Boden, I would donate the picture to the church. The priests thought that it was a splendid idea and the arrangements were made without too much difficulty. What none of us expected was that the Pope liked the portrait so much he made it known that he would like to keep it. I held a hurried discussion with the London priests and we decided that they should offer the painting to him. His Holiness accepted and so St Peter's in London had to do without it.

Irene and I went to Rome with Leonard Boden for the presentation, which was to take place at a private audience. Irene was quite overcome. She wore a black dress, with a black veil over her head. From the time we left the hotel until we got to the Vatican she spoke not a word. In fact throughout the whole proceedings she said nothing, much as I tried to make her talk.

In the Vatican we were duly received with the traditional panoply. We went into the ante-chamber and waited for the Pope to come in. He was a tall, slim, very impressive figure, dressed in white. He spoke to Irene first, but she could not get a word out. I was less abashed.

'You are looking very well, Your Holiness,' I said to him. He had not in fact been very well for a while.

He looked at me rather humorously and said: 'Well, one does what one can, my son.' (I was expecting him to have thanked God.) He then produced a large gold medallion, which I understand was one of the Vatican's most valued gifts, and gave it to me. But I was rather startled when he said: '*E oro sa.*' ('It's gold, you know.') He also told me that the only other person in England to have his medallion was the Queen.

I am fortunate in having been born in Italy of Italian parents, because it has given me a wider view of life. It gave me an Italian heritage which goes back two or three thousand years. When he was in his twenties, my father thought of his family's future and came to Britain. My future lay here and nowhere else. If my father had left me in Monforte I could possibly have been looking after a few goats, although I like to think I would have found something better to do there as well.

I believe I have contributed to this country by creating an international business and giving employment. In turn, this country has made me well-off, well-known, generally respected and a peer of the realm.

I was playing a round of golf with Peter Alliss one day when he asked me one of his surprise questions.

'Do you feel Italian?'

'What do you mean – do I feel Italian? Of course I am Italian.'

'Do you feel British?' he asked me tentatively.

'Of course I feel British – I am one of the greatest Britishers!' I replied.

But this is a difficult question to answer. I like the idea of being accepted in this country. Some time ago I was walking down Jermyn Street, and eight or nine people whom I knew all said 'Good morning' to me. It seemed all London was a village, and people knew who Charles Forte was.

I want to be liked. If I am in a room with twenty people and I feel that one person dislikes me, I feel awkward and uncomfortable. My innate ambition has always been that when I sit down at a table with people, I should feel equal to them.

In Italy I am English but here I am Italian. My thoughts are not English; my movements are not English; my reactions are not English. But when I am in Italy I get homesick for London.

If you have two parents you love and someone asks you which one you love more, it presents the same dilemma, but it also provides a useful parallel. Britain for me represents the strength and the maleness of my father. I have made it clear how devoted I was to him. Not one day passes even now, when I do not think of him. Italy perhaps represents the love and affection of my mother. I hope this is not too extravagant or romantic a comparison, but to me it is the perfect combination.

If I had to be born again I would not want to be born differently. If someone said to me, you can be reborn tomorrow and you can be born English, I would say no. If they said to me you can be reborn tomorrow as an Italian, I would also say no. I like the way I am. I have the privilege of being able to enjoy an evening with Scottish and English people, uplifted by their sense of fun and humour and their way of looking at life, and I also have the privilege of being able to do exactly the same thing in my home village of Monforte, talking dialect with the locals.

If I was in Rome to watch the English football team playing Italy, I would desperately want the English team to win. I would feel like one Englishman in a crowd of 80,000 Italians and I would pray for my team to score. When Italy plays England at Wembley, I cannot help taking the part of the under-dog, with 100,000 Britons in the stadium. I am delighted with my background. It has always given me a larger perspective of life. I am no less happy than anyone else and I like to think I am a greater patriot than most.

I sometimes wonder if my way would have been made smoother if my name had been Fortescue rather than Forte, I don't think so. ('How naïve can you be,' said one critic when the book first came out!)

I have never stinted myself in anything I wanted to do. I have travelled everywhere. I have been to the best theatres and restaurants. I have stayed in the finest hotels. I have never asked for a penny from the State until now when, like it or not, I get an old-age pension. I have enjoyed the major part of every day, which has been spent working and the work I have done has been my pleasure.

I feel no moral qualms about having become rich. In my case my wealth comes from the business I have created, the employment that it has given, the services it has performed for society. I have not robbed anybody to achieve this. I went into business to create a business, to do something of which I was proud. That was more important to me than the financial rewards.

And the next world? I believe, as most people, I think, do, in an after-life and the existence of a supreme beneficent being. But when I think of it deeply, I have no concept of what that after-life can be like, or can't be like – none at all. Facing us is eternity, immortality, an experience which lies beyond the human capacity to imagine. I am more intrigued than afraid.

CHAPTER SIXTEEN

Granada

THE FINAL CHAPTER is one I would rather not have written. It mainly concerns the take-over of Forte by Granada, the result of which is that Rocco is no longer chairman and chief executive and I no longer have any connection with the company.

I can now lead a life of complete leisure – and luxury – if I want to. Through the take-over I am better off by the many millions which was my share of the money the family received for its shares. A lot of money certainly, but I would much, much rather still be involved in the business that has my name and which I built with my close colleagues.

Maybe I am wrong to be too depressed by these events, and I can certainly look at them from a different perspective. Rocco and Olga distinguished and proved themselves in the battle for our firm. They lost, but what a marvellous fight they put up. They are now making new and challenging careers for themselves.

As for me I must count my blessings. I have the best wife possible, a loving and united family, a clear conscience and, for someone of eighty-nine, I think I can say I have exceptionally good health – I still do fifty press-ups a day and walk for an hour. I am completely certain that these benefits are worth more than millions in the bank.

But to continue the narrative. In 1992 Rocco became chairman as well as chief executive. Stepping down as Chairman is more than a symbolic step. I suppose it was something that we were moving naturally towards but it is always difficult for someone who has founded and developed a business to say that he is finally stepping down and not going to be involved in executive or detailed decisions or actually in any effective capacity again. It was made easier because I could hand over to Rocco and, in fact, it was the only way that I would have ever contemplated stepping down. If Rocco had not wanted it I think I would have wished to continue as chairman, Cadbury or no Cadbury.

On the fundamentals of business Rocco and I agree completely. I remember being very moved when I walked into a party for twenty or thirty people and Rocco said to me out of the blue 'Dad thank you for teaching me how to work like you did.'

But there were details on which we differed. Rocco was keen to rid us of anything that was not part of our hard-core business of hotels and restaurants. I hated to see the businesses which I had acquired going – even for good money. We sold Harvester, Puritan Maid, Grierson Blumenthal, Travelodge USA; the sale of Lilly-white's, the sports store, was finalized during the Granada take-over battle. The total realized was approximately £1.3 billion. And there were other bits of the empire which went. I can't say I liked it, but Rocco was now in the driving seat and commercial logic was on his side, as well as the need for synergy that really added value to our business.

Rocco believed that central management had lost touch with the grass roots and wished to instil the entrepreneurial spirit of earlier days. Maybe so. He believed that after the Trust Houses merger we had become too bureaucratized and complicated. He changed the company name from Trusthouse Forte to Forte (which I was very pleased about). He tried to make sense of our enormous hotel empire by re-branding the hotels into Exclusive, Grand, Post House, Crest, etc., so that each customer would know what to expect in each hotel and, most important, rely on it. He believed that while we had a number of good hotels abroad we were not in a true sense an international hotel business with the ability to expand and develop anywhere in the world. He thus bought the Meridien chain from Air France, fifty-five four-star hotels for £250 million. And there was a lot more.

I don't think I would have seen it all as he did but Rocco was probably right and the results certainly justified his vision. He had to pull the firm through one of the worst market situations we had encountered. The recession bit hard and because of this and the

Gulf War, occupancy rates plummeted. And the situation was further exacerbated by the increased room capacity generated by the speculative property boom of the late 1980s. A lot of hotel companies went bust. Some are still shaky. All UK companies were badly hit. Stakis and Queen's Moat had to restructure and even Ladbroke's Hilton Hotels, with a much broader international spread, suffered dramatically. But Forte recovered the quickest. By the end of 1994 we had trebled the profits in three years. In 1994 the profit was £150 million, £192 million in 1995, and in 1996 we would have been touching £270 million.

Despite these profits, the share price had not yet caught up with performance. Forte shares were a bargain. All credit to Granada that they saw this, and on 22 November 1995 they struck.

Granada is a large conglomerate. Its businesses include: TV, motorway service stations, contract catering, computer services, rental of TV sets, video recorders, personal computers and much more – even nightclubs. It is run by Gerry Robinson.

The Granada bid in cash or shares initially valued the company at £3.3 billion. Forte responded by announcing that it was demerging the restaurant business and its stake in the Savoy. Splitting up a business can add value to its component parts.

On 30 December (it was all moving very fast) Forte agreed to sell the restaurants to Whitbread provided our defence was successful. The price was £1.05 billion. We then announced we were going to spend £800 million to buy back our own shares, increase our dividend by 20 per cent, and distribute the Savoy stake to our shareholders. Things seemed to be going our way. Then on 9 January, Granada increased their offer by £500 million. This enormous extra sum was enough to tip the balance. It was certainly an excellent price for shareholders and you cannot blame them for accepting, though they would have done better by playing it slightly longer and sticking with us for another year or two. But the City institutions, who called the shots, could not resist. And it was thus that a business which I had started with a few thousand pounds was sold for £3.9 billion. Rocco's defence was universally admired.

Actually, I have no feeling of bitterness towards Granada. Once you run a publicly quoted company which you don't control you must accept the market can enrich you and/or take your business from you. Conglomerates are usually in the business of buying and selling businesses without any long-term commitment. I have always been emotionally committed to the business I have worked in – hotels and catering – not only aiming to add value to our shares, but to give employment, develop people's careers and provide a valuable and valued service to the public.

This is a brief and oversimplified account of the battle. But I want now to dwell on certain aspects of it. Rocco was running the defence and I have used his words and detailed knowledge in the pages that follow.

Rocco: I wasn't expecting an offer at all. Obviously the question of whether the company might be bid for was always at the back of my mind. We had discussed it with our bankers and amongst ourselves, but no one thought we were a likely target or that anybody would be prepared to make the financial leap because they would have had to pay a substantial premium to get us. Certainly we felt no one in the hotel industry at the time would be likely to make a bid. On the face of it Granada were a very unlikely purchaser. They were not in the hotel business in any way, and I believe they looked at three or four targets before deciding on us because they thought it might be easier. But they needed to grow, and the only way to keep their momentum was to acquire another business. Actually they got a harder battle than they bargained for.

Gerry Robinson is a perfectly pleasant individual to meet and he handled my father's and my departure from the company in a civilized way. But I do not believe in his approach to business or in his business philosophy.

His approach is very different from mine. I believe that to develop a business of quality the people at the head of it have to care about it, care about the products and the quality of delivery to the customer. Thus they must be closely involved with the customer and with the staff who are responsible for dealing with the customer.

The business has to have an ethos: people who work in it

must believe in what they are doing and again this is reflected in the service the customer receives. At Forte this existed; it had initially been developed by my father and it continued under my guidance. The staff and the customers related to me as they had done to my father, not because I was the boss but because I cared about what we were doing and demonstrated it very clearly.

Of course profit is vital: it is the ultimate measure of business and without a cash flow a business will die. But the long-term health of a business is dependent on how it delivers that profit. If you take too short-term a view you may make a profit initially but at the expense of your reputation and customer base.

Gerry Robinson is a very good salesman and a very good presenter. He has built up a following in the City on the basis of that and there is no doubt that with his previous acquisitions he has delivered. But they were mostly businesses in which you can easily raise prices. It will not be so easy for him in Forte. He has never actually bought a business the size of Forte, so the stretch will be greater. Granada has the benefit of a rising hotel market which will carry them in the short term. But the prices they get for the hotels they are selling off is vital and that will be a major factor in deciding whether their bid was worthwhile, for these disposals have to reduce their immense borrowings incurred as a result of the take-over.

The up-turn in the hotel market which Rocco talks about has been greatly aided by increased tourism. I still remember in the late 1950s when I was instrumental in setting up the London Tourist Board to develop this then underdeveloped market. I was nearly laughed to scorn: 'What about our dreadful weather and awful food?' Anyway, it was suggested I lead the way so I took charge of the tourist campaign. The results speak for themselves.

Rocco: It was my brother-in-law, Michael Alen-Buckley, who rang to tell me there had been a bid made and my first reaction was that they must be bloody mad. It did not make any sense: what did they want with a hotel business? We would see them off!

We had to get busy defending ourselves immediately. It was unfortunate that I was in Yorkshire where I had arrived the night before. Our share price had shown some unusual movement in the afternoon and there were rumours of a potential bid by Granada. I made enquiries through our brokers UBS who said there was nothing untoward. I nevertheless discussed the situation with some of my more immediate colleagues including Keith Hamill, the finance director. We concluded that Granada could have no interest in us and it was all the usual market speculation. So I decided to leave for Yorkshire.

The fact that Granada seemed to know that I was in Yorkshire might smack of special intelligence. In fact what happened was that Gerry Robinson rang me at home first thing in the morning to tell me he was bidding. When he was informed I was not there he asked where I was. Fabrizio, our cook and general factotum, unfortunately told him I was shooting in Kepwick in Yorkshire where I have a pheasant shoot. When Robinson spoke to the media he was asked if he had spoken to me: 'No, he is shooting at Gatwick,' a curious misunderstanding as the only people likely to be shooting at Gatwick are terrorists. The image of me blithely shooting pheasants while my business was under attack did, however, help Granada in the initial stages of the PR war.

It took me quite a long time to get back to London: annoyingly I missed the train because I was on the phone in the station when it drew out, so I had to wait for the next one. When I got back I plunged immediately into discussions with our advisers. Then I went home and spent the whole night awake thinking about the way we would defend ourselves. It was then, in the small hours of the morning, I decided on the strategy of demerging the restaurant business and giving the Savoy back to the shareholders.

There is a sort of dead period immediately after a bid is announced and until the bidding company tables its offer document. Granada got their document out in three or four days which was fast work. They could have had two weeks to do it but that set the timetable for the rest of the bid. Forte had to respond quickly and there followed a series of challenges and responses over the next two months.

> **Rocco:** I received many calls from people wanting to help. One of these was from Roberto Mendoza, an old friend from Downside whom my father has already mentioned. Roberto was the head of mergers and acquisitions and deputy chairman at JP Morgan. He said he was prepared to come over straight away. I enthusiastically accepted this proposition. My view was: that we needed some American expertise; that bid defence is much more developed in the States than here; and that Americans are more innovative and less constrained by form and by what is the norm. I also wanted someone with an aggressive approach.
>
> We already had a long-term relationship with Warburgs where I dealt with John Walker Howarth who was at Pembroke College Oxford with me and was also a friend. I had introduced him to Roberto many years before when he left university, and they had ended up by sharing a flat together. John is more conservative in approach than Roberto, knows his way around the Takeover Panel, having been its chairman and, at the same time, understands the UK market extremely well. Morgan Stanley had also been our advisers and we were glad to add their expertise to the team. UBS were our brokers and had given us excellent support, but I wanted a bit extra so I called in David Mayhew of Cazenove. He asked me what our ultimate objective was. I told him that we wanted to defeat the bid, but the ultimate objective must be to achieve the best possible value for the shareholders. He liked that and on that basis agreed to join. We went into top gear immediately.

Within four or five days Rocco announced the plan to demerge the restaurants. He knew that this would flush out any potential bidders for this side of the business. It also won over much of the press who saw we were not merely sitting back and putting out a normal defence document: we were reacting in an original and dynamic way. While the press had at first tried to write us off, they now recognized we had made a dramatic countermove and had a real chance of winning. Rocco also believed that because Granada said they were primarily interested in the Post Houses and the restaurants they might then decide only to bid for the restaurant businesses and drop the overall bid. But they never showed any sign of being interested in doing that.

Immediately a lot of approaches were received for the restaurant business from all sorts of different firms, but because of the constraints of time, it was essential to deal with the major corporations who could deliver quickly. The two companies we talked to were Whitbread and McDonalds. The latter were interested in Little Chef for the large number of important roadside locations (in many of which they would have introduced McDonalds to operate side by side with the current operation). In the end it was decided that Forte were better off with Whitbread; it was an all cash deal for a sizeable amount which would give us more flexibility for the next stage of our defence.

The figure agreed with Whitbread was £1.05 billion, the deal of course contingent on our defence being successful. It may not have been the best price which could have eventually been achieved, but it was a very good one.

Rocco: When we agreed to do the deal with Whitbread our hope was that they would go into the market and buy our shares to make sure we won. While there had been some discussion on this, it was very difficult to arrange for it on a contractual basis, even if either of us had wanted that.

Whitbread did not go out into the market to buy those shares, and that was one of the reasons we lost. If they had acted immediately they could have bought the shares relatively cheaply and then, even if the shares dropped in value following a successful defence, it would have been a small amount in relation to the total value of the deal they would have secured. Instead, they hummed and hawed and said they probably would come in at the end but they had to have a board meeting to finally decide. Granada got wind of this meeting and while the Whitbread Board was in session carried out a dawn raid on the stock market and bought 10 per cent of the Forte shares to pre-empt Whitbread. They paid a considerable premium for these shares over their cash offer which surprised everyone. This stopped Whitbread in their tracks and afterwards it was impossible to bring them back into the market to buy the shares.

So we had lost that opportunity. Whitbread was typical of a very conservative organization. Peter Jarvis, their Chief Executive, is an excellent operator but his board was not interested. If Whitbread had managed to secure the restaurant business it would have given them a completely dominant position in the UK Lodge and roadside restaurant sector.

Another major factor in Granada's success was the recovery in their share price. At the beginning of the bid, the price had been under considerable pressure and had dropped down from £7.00 to £6.40 (the Granada share price was important because their offer was in cash, or cash and Granada shares). Later, when Granada increased their bid, their share price plummeted. Rocco remembers standing in front of the screen and seeing it drop 23p. He thought at that moment – well this is it, we've won, the market doesn't like this bid and it's not going to support it. But in the next couple of weeks Granada's share price started to recover. This was concerted buying which steadily pushed the price up to £7.00 just before the end of the bid and as a result brought the value of the Forte shares up to £4 (£2.50 pre-bid), a much more attractive proposition.

> **Rocco:** There was a Granada fan club in the institutions: involved were Scottish Widows, Morgan Grenfell and Barings. They had supported Granada in the past and were doing so now with heavy buying. Interestingly, since the take-over the Granada price shot up. It reached £9.79. It has dropped back since and has indeed underperformed in the market subsequently.

A third factor in the Granada victory was the role of Mercury Asset Management, the enormous fund manager handling about £70 million of pension fund money.

They owned 15 per cent of Granada and also 15 per cent of Forte. They were in a very powerful position. Our family owned

8.4 per cent of the shares and the small shareholders about 10 per
cent. Small shareholders are usually ignored in a battle like this,
but they had always been supportive of our business and family – I
usually felt like I was walking on air after I had addressed them.
My daughter Olga consolidated and delivered their support by a
brilliant series of road shows. Another 10 per cent of our shares
were in the hands of City institutions also loyal to us, so we had
effectively support of nearly 30 per cent of the shares. Mercury's
15 per cent could possibly tip the balance either way – though
things might have been different if Whitbread had acquired 10
per cent.

Rocco: I believe it was unlikely that Granada would have
launched their bid in the first place before talking to Mercury.
It would have been imprudent of them not to have done so
bearing in mind Mercury's holdings in the respective companies. It is more than likely that Mercury gave its blessing. But
there was a strong suggestion that Mercury had gone further
than this and instigated the bid. Carol Galley (Vice-Chairman of
Mercury) was clearly a fan of Robinson and from the first day of
the bid every journalist I talked to said that Mercury were
behind Granada. Much as I protested and much as Mercury
protested, the articles written about the bid continually referred
to this. While I believe that Mercury were clearly instrumental
in making the bid possible in the first place, I also think they
were influential in the eventual outcome over and above the
value of their shares, because a lot of the institutions waited
until Mercury had played their hand before actually accepting
the Granada bid.

When my colleagues and I went to see Mercury in the final
week of the bid it seemed clear to me that they had already
made up their minds. After answering a number of their
questions, I concluded by saying to Carol Galley: 'Look, I had a
meeting with you two years ago when we discussed everything
that needed to be done. I have delivered all that and more. You
followed me through the hard times. The good times are coming
now and it is not the time to jump off.'

I noticed that a member of the Mercury team, John Richards,

the man who directed the funds which controlled most of the
Forte shares in Mercury's holdings, had tears in his eyes. The
decision had been made; it was not his decision. Clearly there
had been a discussion within Mercury – but the side of the
angels had not won!

There was an amusing interlude during all this when an
assistant came in with a message. Carol Galley looked at it and
the corner of her mouth went down half an inch. It was not a
smile but it could have been a sort of wry smile. She passed it to
the person next to her and then she saw me looking at it
wondering what the hell it was – had the stock market collapsed?
So she passed it across the table to me. It said there were a
number of photographers outside the front door asking whether
Sir Rocco Forte was there, so would he prefer to leave by the
back door? I shared the note with my colleagues and everyone
on both sides of the table had a good laugh. The cars were in
the garage at the back so we left by the back.

We met again in our offices on the last day of the bid. Carol
Galley and Stephen Zimmerman came to tell me their decision.
They had, as I had anticipated, decided to vote their shares in
favour of Granada. The excuse Carol Galley gave me was a lame
one. She said that they had to make the choice between two
heavily indebted companies and they preferred the cash gener-
ative abilities of Granada. I pointed out that Forte's £1.2 billion
debt was small compared with the extra £3.2 billion Granada
would saddle itself with because of the bid. Anthony Tennant,
my deputy chairman, interrupted me and suggested at this
juncture that there was no point in prolonging things. I then
said, 'Well you can't expect me to be happy about this decision.'
So the meeting broke up.

We walked out to the lobby to the lift and then I could not
contain myself: 'You know from the very beginning everybody
has been saying to me that you have been behind this whole
deal.' They both jumped as if I'd let off a banger: 'Oh no, we
are a very honourable institution and we wouldn't do a thing
like this etc. etc.' All the way down in the lift they carried on in
this vein and this was the first time that Zimmerman had actually
said anything. So I still think there was more to this than met

the eye. I know that a number of the pension funds who had their money managed by Mercury had indicated they did not want their shares voted in favour of the bid and, since the bid, a number of them have said they will only keep their money with Mercury as managers if they have the right to take the decision on how their shares are voted in a bid situation. So to some degree this episode could stop this sort of thing happening again.

We clearly made the institutions think very hard during the process of the defence. It wasn't an easy decision for any institution at the end of the day. I have heard that Granada were very worried up to the last minute because with their previous bid, for LWT, they had a lot of acceptances quite early and with us they received very few until the last two days. They weren't sure which way this one was going to go until the very last minute.

I can sympathize with Rocco's account of a bid situation.

Rocco: If you have not been involved in a bid it is difficult to understand the pressure which the target company is under and what little time there is. People involved on the defence work inhumanly long hours, get little sleep, and are therefore very tired, very tetchy and prone to make mistakes.

There are large numbers of people from the advisory teams who come into your office and effectively try to take over. It is very difficult for the head of the company to keep control and abreast of the situation. But you only drive things forward if you do keep abreast of the situation. Morale is all important. Every member of the team, both internal and external, must believe in winning and in this context the PR battle is extremely important. Nevertheless the business still has to be run and this can be difficult for the managers not directly involved in the defence, but whose personal futures may be at stake. Communicating with them on a regular basis is vital. We had three meetings with our 200 top executives to keep them informed of progress and issued weekly updates to all other staff. I'm told that this was an unusual thing to do in these situations.

During the course of the bid there were many emotional outbursts but at the end of the day the team combined well: we believed in what we were doing and as a result put up an effective defence. It is difficult to single out individual members of the team, but both Keith Hamill, the finance director, and Richard Power, communications director, and their teams, played sterling roles. Anthony Tennant gave a great deal of support and stuck his neck out on occasions, when there was no need for him to do so. Roberto Mendoza added American perspective and aggression. As well as the strong strategic input, Roberto did much to keep everyone's morale high. Almost every evening at about ten o'clock my wife Aliai prepared dinner at home; Roberto was usually there and quite often other members of the advisory team. We would chew over the events of the day and formulate the next steps. Aliai had to contend with a lot. She was clearly very concerned, and not always as up to date with the situation as she would have liked. Unfortunately I hardly had time to speak to her and she had to elicit scraps of information from whomever would give them to her. The emotional strain was thus all the harder for her to bear, and I am sorry for it.

In the final analysis the battle was not won or lost in the pages of the newspapers or in the hearts and minds of the private shareholders. We won those battles. Alan Parker and his team at Brunswick PR played an important role in this, but also important was the relationships which my father, Olga and I had built up over the years with the media and opinion formers. In fact, I understand that at one stage we were doing so well that Granada tried to recruit Tim Bell. Amongst other people who helped was John Hoerner, chief executive of The Burton Group plc. He was introduced to me by Alan Parker as a possible addition to the Forte board to replace Charles Hardie, a valuable and long standing director of over twenty years who was resigning. John disliked the whole concept of the bid, admired what we were doing and wanted to be part of it. It was announced that he would be joining the Board of Forte if the bid was defeated. He had nothing to gain himself from his agreement to join the board, but it was helpful to me and the company for a businessman of his standing and success to show his support in this way.

In effect, five or six major institutions decided things.

Rocco: I had two sets of meetings with most of them. Looking back the one thing I regret not to have done in the eighteen months before the bid was see enough of the institutions – I had been concentrating principally on running the business and securing the Meridien management contracts. I had left the institutions to Richard Power and Keith Hamill, to a certain extent because they were new to our business and I wanted them exposed. It is not that they did not do a good job, which they did, but it distanced me from the institutions. It's always important for them to look the ultimate decision maker in the eye and draw confidence from this. So after the bid was announced I spent two weeks visiting all the major institutions to put myself back on the map and tell them what we were about. We did this again in the last two weeks of the bid. It was a particularly exhausting and time-consuming business, particularly when I wasn't sleeping well and had to be on the ball at 6 a.m. I remember one institution, Friends Provident: I went to see them with Richard the first time and they really gave us a drumming. They attacked us from all sides and from all fronts. There were about six of them. I went out shell shocked. Next time I went around with Keith Hamill; they were all there again, all young people. I rather liked them. After a few introductory remarks, I said to them 'Well, I hope you are not going to pull your punches this time because last time it was rather a soft option.' They saw the humour of this and we got on much better the second time round.

One of the peculiar aspects of the take-over was the role of the Forte Council. It was an anachronism, but potentially a powerful one. It could prevent any bid and was thus a deterrent to any unsuitable bidder.

The Council effectively controlled the company through its ownership of some special shares that gave it the equivalent votes to those of the ordinary shareholders. This trust had been in existence for many years and was in fact the basis of the founding of the Trust Houses Company. When Forte merged with Trust Houses in 1970, it had to be by way of a take-over of Forte by Trust Houses so that the Council would retain its position. At the time of the Allied Breweries bid, the Council had stood on the sidelines and let the ordinary shareholders decide. This was effectively its position with the Granada bid, but it did actually enter into negotiations with Granada, establishing a price for the Council's shares of £50 million *if* the ordinary shareholders accepted the bid.

Rocco: The Council was made up of a number of venerable gentlemen some of whom had held high public office. They were advised that if they went against the wishes of the ordinary shareholders they were liable to be held personally responsible as individuals and that their liabilities could be huge. This frightened them. Those who had held high public office were extremely sensitive to public opinion and the odium they could have brought on themselves if they acted against what could be construed to be the interests of the main body of shareholders. Sir Hugh Rossi, the Duke of Marlborough and Lord Gainsborough took a more robust view, but they were in the minority.

I would have been happier if the Council had made Granada's life more difficult by not entering into discussions and by indicating they were not in favour of the bid (which I knew very well they were not). But at the same time, I was aware that it could have been counter-productive if the Council had shown itself to be supporting management by trying to stop the bid: this could have angered the institutional shareholders and made them all the more determined to accept the Granada offer. Granada went into battle without squaring the Council who exacted a very good price and as a result now have considerable sums to give to charity every year.

But the fact is we lost. At that stage I was so tired I had gone past showing emotion. I really knew by Friday it was unlikely we'd win. We knew definitely on the Tuesday morning we had lost, after the Mercury visit. Many on the team broke down. They had put so much passion into the defence and worked tirelessly for a solid two months without rest. I had to be strong.

The tragedy for me, Rocco and, I think, the public was the loss of the opportunity at Forte to develop a quality hotel business of an international scale and standing which could have stood alongside other quality businesses like the Marks & Spencers and Tescos of this world. And this will never happen now.

Rocco: It is ironic that following the take-over the parts of the old Forte business which traded particularly well were the hotels, particularly the up-market hotels (which are now for sale). The results of the restaurant side of the business have been disappointing, even though it was the restaurant side and Little Chef in particular which Granada made great play of during the bid, trumpeting the improvements it could bring about there. Robinson went round the City brandishing a Little Chef menu pointing out the changes he would make. Since the take-over, Little Chef has traded badly and this has been exacerbated by the action Granada took to reduce quality and raise prices. I cannot drink the coffee in Little Chef any more. I think the logic of our plan to sell the restaurant business and become a pure hotel company has been justified by these developments. Very little additional hotel capacity will come into being before the year 2000. Pannell Kerr Foster estimated in a report publicized in December 1995 that hotel room stock would increase by only 1.6 per cent over the following four years. A pure hotel company would have benefited from this quite significantly with its results undiluted by other parts of the business performing less strongly.

If our defence had succeeded, Forte would have become a pure hotel company. It would have enabled us to cut out a considerable amount of overhead and shorten still further the lines of communication in the business. The top management team could have concentrated solely on the development of the hotel business and continued the process of improvement and expansion which had already been started.

We had already put a huge amount of effort and money into

improving the physical standards of the hotels with a major refurbishment programme of between £100 million and £150 million per year over three years. There was still some catching up work to do, but we had broken the back of the programme and could have developed a refurbishment cycle in the future which would never have let the properties fall behind again.

The physical characteristics of a hotel are only a small part of what the customer gets for his or her money. The level of service offered and the way it is offered are all-important. We had been looking hard at ways of improving the quality and overall sophistication of what we were doing at all levels in the market place. This was the result of careful customer research. Hotel businesses are notoriously adept at ignoring the customers by giving them what they think they want, not necessarily what they actually want. The hotel industry is very behind other industries in this respect. Forte had a well-developed system of controlling a manager's performance in respect of financial results. But we had also developed a system of measuring service on a regular basis, so that managers could see that they were being monitored on this and would react accordingly.

The most important customers are the ones you have *today*. If you look after them in the right way they will come back of their own accord. Every new customer costs time, effort and money to bring in, the existing customer costs you nothing.

Charles Allen, Chief Executive of Granada, was quoted as follows in the *Sunday Times*: 'To increase profits, there are basically only three things you can do: adjust the price, change the volume and change the cost structure.' But where is the customer in this glorious formula? This simplistic message may appeal to the City, but suffering at the sharp end of this kind of thinking are customers, staff and the quality of service. This approach may be a recipe for disaster in the long term.

The acquisition of Forte cost Granada £5.5 billion, made up of the £3.9 billion it paid for the ordinary shares, the £1.3 billion of Forte debt it took over, the £50 million paid to the Council and the £250 million of costs related to the acquisition. The Forte business made £300 million before interest in the year to

January 1996 and even if Granada achieves the much vaunted £100 million cost savings and also adds a further £100 million to the profit, the investment is showing less than a 10 per cent return – hardly the deal of the century.

In the results Granada published for the year ended 30 September 1996 which included eight months of Forte, their profits showed earnings per share growth of 8 per cent before allowing for reorganization costs of £77 million. The businesses Granada held before buying Forte showed profit growth of 30 per cent so the company suffered huge earnings dilution as a result of the acquisition.

Granada is selling the Exclusive portfolio of hotels which were re-valued during the bid at £910 million plus the Westbury in London which was valued at £40 million. The total asset value of the Forte Group was £4 billion. Granada paid £5.3 billion, a premium of over 25 per cent of these asset values. That would indicate that it should sell the Exclusive hotels and Westbury for £1.187 billion to break even. They are unlikely to achieve even the re-valued amount. The Hyde Park, which they have sold for £86 million, was re-valued at £90 million.

One of the main planks of Granada's criticism of Forte during the take-over bid was of its insistence to hold on to the expensive real estate assets in the shape of the Exclusive hotels and the Savoy stake. Our response was that these assets were not easily disposable and that it was the wrong time to sell, as profits had a considerable way to climb following the work and investment we had put into them.

Despite the fact that Gerry Robinson was telling the institutions that Granada would sell the Exclusive hotels, Meridien and the Savoy stake within five weeks of the bid being finalized, eleven months later these assets had not yet been sold (with the exception of the Hyde Park Hotel on 22 November to coincide with Granada's results announcement). The improvement in profitability, which the work previously carried out at Forte and the booming economy has delivered, has been greatest in the Exclusive hotels where some 60 per cent improvement in profit has been achieved. The commentators declare how clever Granada is to delay selling as profitability is improving and values must therefore increase. What was a sin for Forte is now a virtue for Granada.

The reality is that Granada has had extreme difficulty in selling these hotels at prices which will justify the purchase price it paid for Forte as a whole. This is after a highly intensive and well publicized sales campaign. It tried to sell the hotels as a group and entered discussions with Sheraton, Marriott and Prince Al Walheed. When this proved unsuccessful, Granada resorted to selling the properties piecemeal.

Granada has made little inroad into the vast £3.2 billion of debt it accumulated through the acquisition of Forte. The only Forte assets it has sold are the White Hart Group of hotels (which sale had already been agreed by Forte during the course of the bid) and also the remaining 25 per cent stake in Alpha (the airport business). The Alpha stake was sold to Mohammed Al Fayed well below the price at which Alpha was floated two years previously. Under the Sale Agreement, it was stipulated that Mohammed Al Fayed could not make a bid for the rest of Alpha for six months because 'if he paid a higher price for the rest it would not make the price received by Granada for the stake look so low.'

On the Savoy stake, Granada has made no progress at all. The shares Granada holds represent 69 per cent of the economic value of the Savoy but only 42 per cent of the votes: as a result, it is powerless. Granada's stated intention is to move out of the luxury hotel market and therefore its ability to reach a sensible accommodation with the Savoy board is much more limited than it was for me at Forte.

Any buyer of Granada's stake in the Savoy would be forced to make a general offer to the rest of the Savoy shareholders. No buyer would wish to take over Granada's position as it is: and even if they did, the take-over rules would force them to bid for the rest. For a bid to be successful, the Wontner family and the charitable trusts which control most of the high voting 'B' shares would have to be in agreement.

Following Granada's statement that it was a seller of the Savoy stake the Savoy shares have increased in price quite dramatically, valuing the group at an unrealistically high level. Unless it is

extremely lucky, or prepared to sell at a very low price, Granada
will be saddled with the Savoy stake for a considerable period of
time.

It is not easy to see what progress Granada has made with the
business it acquired from Forte other than what it said at its
results presentation. £77 million of reorganization costs gives
scope for presenting figures both for the first year and the
second year in their best light. The figures would indicate that
Granada has delivered no more than the initial budget prepared
by Forte prior to the bid (which we thought we could improve
upon). A strong performance in London Hotels offset a 25 per
cent drop in profits at Little Chef. Granada has no doubt
benefited from the strong improvement in the economy and the
strengthening of the hotel market: every hotel company in the
UK has seen a dramatic improvement to its results. Granada
makes much of its claims to have improved Forte's hotel profits.
But their management can have had no impact because it was
too late for the policies set for 1996 by the previous Forte
management to be dramatically altered by Granada. Welcome
Break, the motorway service area business, has had its margins
severely pressured to fatten it up for sale early in 1997. It has
since been sold at a very good price.

Granada has clearly been able to remove the costs of Forte
top management which were only required for Forte as an
independent company. By integrating the Forte restaurant operations with its own, it has been able to reduce the overhead
structure there. On the buying side, Granada has merged the
Forte and Granada buying teams and in the process cut out all
the quality control staff Forte employed. Granada has a policy of
buying at the best possible price irrespective of the quality.

On the hotel side, it has reduced the operation divisions,
which were five: Post House, Heritage, Meridien, Exclusive and
London, to three by merging Post House with Heritage and
Exclusive with Meridien. Since they were selling Exclusive and
were only a short-term holder in it, this may make sense. In
merging Post House (a modern-style chain aimed principally at
the business market with a very clear brand image) with Heritage
(which includes most of the Country Inns and has a very

different image, approach and market), Granada has made some short-term savings but in the long term this will blur the very different brand values to the detriment of both.

Granada's initial changes meant a significant reduction in supervision and support to hotel managers. Subsequent reductions have included the elimination of hotel mangers. There is now one manager for every three or four hotels. Maybe a short term saving, but a disaster in the long run. Competitors are taking advantage of this by recruiting the dismissed managers and stealing local business. Significant reductions have been made in the hotel sales force, both in the UK and internationally, and the development department has been completely disbanded which brings into question Granada's intention to remain long-term holders of Meridien. A number of Meridien management contracts are under pressure, and two in Portugal, and one in Edinburgh have been lost.

Many of the high-quality executives that Granada tried to keep following the acquisition have left. Of the Forte executives who have stayed to run the hotel division, it is unlikely that most will survive. They will either leave because they do not like the environment they are working in or will be asked to leave because they are incapable of delivering what Granada requires.

The management heritage in the Forte hotel business which is actually delivering today's results will be dissipated quite quickly. The ill-effects of this will be felt once the present boom conditions in the UK hotel industry subsides.

It is extraordinary that less than eighteen months after the acquisition of Forte, before that company has been fully digested and with little inroad made into the debt mountain, Granada was already putting up the idea of a de-merger and a splitting of the Leisure and Media interests of the Group.

Rocco has to put all this behind him, but he still sees his future in hotels. He raised £1 billion in the City to make a substantial offer to Granada for the Meridien and the Exclusive hotels.

Rocco: The re-valued book value of the hotels I was bidding for (they excluded the Grosvenor House, the George V and the

Westbury in New York) was £1.080 billion. My offer was at a small discount to this and therefore a very good one. The difficulty Granada has had in selling the Exclusives underlines this even more.

But Rocco's offer wasn't to their liking. So he will be starting a new hotel business, in the four or five star field, from scratch. He will probably start with only one hotel and then build the business up, and definitely have a lot of fun doing it.

Rocco: Up to now I have been in a big company environment. My new departure will make a stimulating change. I am lucky to have some very good colleagues working with me who will be shareholders in the new venture and my sister Olga who will play an important part. There are a number of others waiting in the wings − managers, waiters, chefs − for when the right opportunity occurs.

I will be able to build a quality business with high levels of service to the customer. I will be able to be in touch with all levels of staff and directly influence the business in a way which it was difficult to do before.

My family has bought the first hotel, the Balmoral in Edinburgh, and my management company had the satisfaction of replacing Granada in the process.

For sons that follow in their father's footsteps in business, there are always comparisons made with the father. It is a great challenge, but it never bothers me too much as I always believed results would speak for themselves.

The whole Granada episode has been much sadder for my father than for me. Forte was a monument to his life's work which could have gone on after he left this world and now is not there anymore. But no one can take from him that he is a man who has achieved a huge amount. Everyone recognizes that. Everyone respects him for it. If I am able to re-establish a successful hotel business it will keep the name alive and be part of his legacy.

INDEX